Pagan Monotheism in Late Antiquity

EDITED BY

Polymnia Athanassiadi

AND

Michael Frede

CLARENDON PRESS · OXFORD

1999

OXFORD

UNIVERSITY PRESS

Great Clarendon Street, Oxford, OX2 6DP

Oxford University Press is a department of the University of Oxford.
It furthers the University's objective of excellence in research, scholarship,
and education by publishing worldwide in

Oxford New York

Auckland Bangkok Buenos Aires Cape Town Chennai
Dar es Salaam Delhi Hong Kong Istanbul Karachi Kolkata
Kuala Lumpur Madrid Melbourne Mexico City Mumbai Nairobi
São Paulo Shanghai Taipei Tokyo Toronto

Oxford is a registered trade mark of Oxford University Press
in the UK and certain other countries

Published in the United States
by Oxford University Press Inc., New York

British Library Cataloguing in Publication Data

Data available

Library of Congress Cataloging in Publication Data

Pagan monotheism in late antiquity
edited by P. Athanassiadi and M. Frede.
Includes bibliographical references and index.
1. Monotheism—History.   2. Rome—Religion.   I. Athanassiadi,
Polymnia.   II. Frede, Michael.
BL221.P34   1999   291.2'11'0937—dc21   98-37019

ISBN 0-19-924801-x

10 9 8 7 6 5 4 3

Typeset in Minion
by Regent Typesetting, London
Printed in Great Britain on acid-free paper by
Biddles Ltd., King's Lynn, Norfolk

Contents

List of Contributors

POLYMNIA ATHANASSIADI is professor of late antique history at the University of Athens; her most recent publication is Damascius, *The Philosophical History: Text with Translation and Notes* (Athens, 1999).

JOHN DILLON is regius professor of Greek at Trinity College, Dublin, and a member of the Royal Irish Academy. His most recent book is *Alcinous: The Handbook of Platonism* (Oxford, 1993).

MICHAEL FREDE is professor of the history of philosophy at the University of Oxford. He is, with G. Patzig, author of a commentary on Aristotle's *Metaphysics Zeta.*

WOLF LIEBESCHUETZ is professor emeritus of Nottingham University and a Fellow of the British Academy. His most recent book is *Barbarians and Bishops* (Oxford, 1990; repr. 1998).

STEPHEN MITCHELL is professor in the Department of Classics and Ancient History at the University of Wales, Swansea. He is author of *Anatolia: Land, Men, and Gods in Asia Minor* (Oxford, 1993) and of *Pisidian Antioch: The Site and its Monuments* (London, 1998).

M. L. WEST is a senior research fellow at All Souls College, Oxford, and the author of many critical editions of Greek poets, and books and articles about Greek literature. His most recent work is *The East Face of Helicon* (Oxford, 1997).

Introduction

POLYMNIA ATHANASSIADI and MICHAEL FREDE

The six chapters in this volume owe their origin to a seminar on 'pagan forms of monotheism in late antiquity', held at Oxford in Hilary Term 1996. The interest shown in the subject matter of the seminar by colleagues from a variety of disciplines and the lively discussions which ensued confirmed us in the idea that we were pursuing an important topic which gave rise to questions of more general significance. Hence we decided to publish revised versions of the papers in the hope of involving a larger audience in a discussion of the issues raised.

The seminar itself arose out of our dissatisfaction with what we take to be a misconception found not only among laymen but even among scholars: that in the Graeco-Roman world—to speak only of what is of direct relevance to this volume—Christianity, in the tradition of Jewish monotheism, succeeded in replacing invariably polytheistic systems of religious belief with a monotheistic creed.[1] By contrast it is our view that monotheism, for the most part quite independently of Judaism and Christianity, was increasingly widespread by the time of late antiquity, certainly among the educated and in particular in the Greek east. And we are inclined to attribute much of the success of Christianity in that world to its advocacy of a way of seeing things, of thinking and acting, which it shared with a growing number of pagans.

Another even more important cause of our dissatisfaction is a general attitude associated with the above, reflecting the simple unqualified belief that, in being converted to Christianity, pagans were induced to reject their polytheism in favour of a monotheistic religion. This approach, which ultimately derives from the Christian Apologists of late

---

[1] The unquestioned acceptance of the axiom that the Middle East has produced three monotheistic religions—Judaism, Christianity, and Islam—has recently led to a reaffirmation of the term 'polytheism' to describe religious belief and practice in the area outside the territory of these three religions. A useful book questioning this convenient terminology and discussing the crucial role of angelology in monotheistic religions is H. Corbin's *Le Paradoxe du monothéisme* (Paris, 1981).

antiquity, emphasizes the differences between Christianity and paganism in a stark and simplistic way which makes one overlook the very substantial similarities between the two, and even the indebtedness of Christian thought and practice to the pagan tradition. It is our belief that nothing is gained, and much is lost, in ignoring these aspects, which form the wider background against which we wish to examine pagan forms of monotheism in late antiquity.

What is at issue here is partly a matter of terminology. It appears to be widely held that pagans by definition believe in and worship many gods, and are therefore polytheists, whereas Christians believe in and worship one God, and hence are monotheists. Some people may indeed feel that this is so obvious that they will wonder why anyone would want to question the validity of this simple and straightforward contrast. Yet if it is correct, how can we account for the fact that there were, at least among philosophers, pagans who did not believe in gods, or who did not consider that gods were appropriate objects of worship, like Epicurus, or who believed in one God alone, like Antisthenes? And quite apart from the consideration of these isolated individuals and groups, we find that a less simplistic concept of monotheism is needed in order to avoid having to think of Jews and Christians as polytheists, and also, by using this concept, that there are significant classes of pagans who turn out to be monotheists.

In approaching late antique religious belief we have therefore chosen not to start with a predetermined notion of monotheism and polytheism, but rather to consider the relevant material in order to decide what it was that ancient Christians meant when they said that they only believed in one God, and indeed what the many pagans meant who by the time of late antiquity would have professed the same. To describe such pagans as monotheists needs a serious qualification of the term, since they believed in many divine beings and perhaps even worshipped them, or at least condoned and perhaps encouraged their worship. But they would have found this perfectly compatible with their belief in one God, since they thought that these gods, though called 'divine' because they enjoy a life of eternal bliss, owed their being to God and were intended to play a certain role in the divine hierarchy. Hence they might have thought that to worship them was just a matter of acknowledging God's ordering of the world and hence a way of worshipping God himself. It is difficult to see that calling such a position 'polytheistic' does justice to it.

When we turn to ancient Christianity we find that the same clarity of approach is needed. We too easily forget that Jewish Scripture freely uses the plural form of 'god', and that the Christian Fathers have no difficulty in understanding and accepting this use quite literally, since in one form or another they do believe in the deification of Man. We also should not forget the doctrine of the Trinity which makes it very difficult to say in precisely what sense Christians believe in one God, and which some early writers at least, like Origen or Eusebius, took to be perfectly compatible with the notion of a 'first' and a 'second' God. And of course there is also the veneration of the saints. A more imaginative understanding of Christianity will allow us to see that none of this contradicts the Christian claim to believe and venerate only one God. But some explanation is required, and once we provide this explanation, it becomes difficult to see why the same imaginative understanding should not be accorded to the pagan point of view. Thus one may conclude that, in order to do justice to Judaism, Christianity, and various forms of pagan thought and worship, one needs in each case to define the term 'mono-theism' very carefully. It is equally clear that even within the confines of the Roman empire the term 'paganism' refers to a vast variety of systems of belief and practice. These are the reasons why in this volume we attempt to discuss some pagan forms of monotheism. Before dealing however with terminology, we should define our chronological boundaries and what the term 'late antiquity' means in the present context.

To the historian of religion and philosophy in the eastern Mediterranean, the end of the second century BC stands out as a natural watershed: the demise of the traditional Hellenistic schools, the Pythagorean revival, and the impetus which animated the 'oriental cults', shaping them into systematic oecumenical messages, are all phenomena which indicate a break with the Hellenistic past and point to new beginnings. Thus, seen from the vantage point of what is being abandoned and what emerges on the intellectual horizon around 125 BC, the first two centuries of Hellenistic history proper can be described as a period of adaptation, a preparatory stage or even a mere background for the formation of the spiritual climate of late antiquity. The furthest limit, on the other hand, of this spiritually fertile period that we call late antiquity can be said to coincide with the rise of Islam, which should be seen as the ultimate consequence of Hellenistic fermentation. Within this long stretch of time, which despite its affluent diversity presents a qualitative homogeneity, it would be possible to allocate subdivisions, but we feel that these might confuse rather than clarify our task. The bulk of the evidence discussed in the present volume comes from the first four centuries AD, with the first and, partly, the second chapter fulfilling an introductory role and therefore covering the whole of antiquity.

Having defined the chronological framework, we should perhaps say a few words about our methodological concerns. In approaching the subject our main consideration was not to do so retrospectively, armed either with the cultural criteria and moral bias of the Christian believer or with the hindsight at our disposal.[2] It is in this spirit that we have systematically avoided the use of the patterns and models of modern disciplines when seeking to understand spiritual belief in another age. Instead we have tried to the best of our ability to approach late antiquity in an objective mood, concentrating on the sources; inherent, however, in this concern was the awareness of the opposite danger: that involvement with the evidence could become so intimate that it might turn one into an apologist of pagan monotheism seen as a cause in need of defence.

For a long time the study of 'paganism' in late antiquity has been treated as an appendix to the study of Judaeo-Christian monotheism, though in this respect modern scholarship can be said to have perpetuated a bias inherent in the sources. Thus, when attempting to approach our subject from a fresh perspective, we found that the terminology at our disposal was that invented by late antique Christians. The Latin *paganus*, whose original meaning is 'peasant', 'rustic', 'unlearned', eventually becomes the opposite of 'Jewish' and especially 'Christian', as for example in legal language, where it is allied with words like *superstitio, error, crimen,* or *insania*.[3] With its additional connotations of idolatry and backwardness,[4] the term 'pagan' is hardly appropriate to describe those highly articulate thinkers like Plotinus or Proclus, who systematically defended their cultural patrimony against the enemy

---

[2] An excellent book like H. I. Bell's *Cults and Creeds in Graeco-Roman Egypt* (Liverpool, 1953) may conclude on the irrelevant note that 'later paganism (. . .) had been conquered by the truer and finer religion which at last brought the solution of problems which paganism had posed but to which it had found no answer' (p. 105). More inauspicious is R. Macmullen in his *Paganism in the Roman Empire* (New Haven, 1981) who, while paying lip-service to methodological orthodoxy (see e.g. p. 134), allows himself value judgements like the following: 'Christianity (. . .) prevailed because it was intrinsically better. It was freely espoused by people who could see its superiority' (p. 136).

[3] Cf. C. Th. 16. 10. 2, 3, 13, 16, 20 (for 'pagana superstitio' when Christianity is a 'religio', 21: 'qui profano pagani ritus errore seu crimine polluuntur, hoc est gentiles'; 25: 'sceleratae mentis paganae'; cf. C. Th. 16. 7. 2.

[4] A definition like Tertullian's (*Cor. Mil.* 11): 'deorum falsorum multorumque cultores paganos vocamus' seems standard.

within and without the empire. Moreover those who were grouped together as pagans by the Christian Apologists, partly for reasons of convenience and partly for reasons of propaganda, would certainly not originally at least have seen themselves as forming one religious entity. What is interesting, though not surprising, in this connection is that certain 'pagans' within the Roman empire eventually came to view themselves as a group with a common cultural past and a common interest, and began to behave accordingly. But this was not a natural development; it came as a reaction to Christian polemic.[5]

If the term 'pagan' perpetuates a historical aberration and a theological inaccuracy, it also reminds us that historically successful groups can, if not obliterate, at least distort a situation by the imposition of simplifying slogans. Yet, despite its strong pejorative connotations, the word appears as the least unsatisfactory term to describe the adepts of non-Judaeo-Christian religions in the Greater Mediterranean in antiquity, as a brief consideration of its alternatives will show.

'Heathen', the normal translation into English of the terms ἐθνικός/ *gentilis*, seems even less appropriate for our purposes, as it represents an even stronger evaluative point of view. Ἔθνος and ἐθνικός correspond to Hebrew terms in the Old Testament which refer to nations or tribes other than God's chosen people. By taking over this term and using it to describe all the others except for the Jews, the Christians imply that they have also taken over from the Jews the role of the chosen people. Moreover in the case of Christianity there is the additional assumption that its new law should be binding on the pagans who nevertheless persist in their own unreformed ways. Here indeed lies the crucial difference between the Jewish and the Christian attitude to outsiders: the Jews saw outsiders as 'different' and, whether they despised them or not, they did not attempt to proselytize them to their own way of life; the Christians by contrast felt right from the beginning that they had a missionary role to fulfil and therefore tried to convert those 'outside the door'.[6] Occurring both in the New Testament (Matt. 5: 47) and in the Apologists, the term ἐθνικός can have, next to its basic meaning of 'outsider', the pejorative connotations of 'rustic', 'uneducated', and 'ordinary',[7] and in that use it appears as an exact synonym of 'paganus'. To a late antique Greek or Roman, this language would have seemed preposterous at the

[5] Thus, on a smaller scale, the term 'Hypsistarian' is a labelling by outsiders of several religious groups: cf. pp. 96–7.
[6] The widely used term θύραθεν to describe the intellectual production of the Greeks is characteristic of this elitist way of thinking.
[7] Cf. Clement, *Paed.* 2. 6 ἐθνικὸν καὶ ἀπαίδευτον.

very least, especially if we pause for a moment to consider the criteria on which the Greeks had divided mankind since late classical times: on one side those of Greek culture and on the other the remainder, the *barbaroi*. What the Christian language suggested was that the Greeks could now be lumped together with any nation or tribe however barbarous, while their customs, when viewed from the Christian perspective, were in reality as peculiar as the customs of the Scythians might appear to a Greek.

If the terms 'paganus' and ἐθνικός are pregnant with the associations of simplicity and foreignness, the term 'Hellene' at least sounds neutral (and, depending on context, does not even exclude all Jews and Christians, since it denotes not only those who were ethnic Greeks, but all the participants in Greek culture in the towns and cities of the Eastern empire). Moreover the term has the authority of the New Testament, being used in the Acts and especially by Paul, who systematically set out to convert non-Jewish Greek speakers. When Paul (Rom. 1: 16) or Luke (Acts 14: 1) speak of 'Jews and Greeks', it is clear that by 'Greeks' they mean all those within the reach of their discourse who are neither Jewish nor Christian. The Apologists, partly defending their faith and partly attacking the 'Hellenes' (whose cultural patrimony nevertheless they wanted to appropriate for themselves), standardized the use of the term in the sense of 'pagan'. Men like Justin the Martyr and Clement of Alexandria even saw Hellenism as a stage in history which prepared mankind for the reception of the Christian message, while others rejected it as something truly evil and incompatible with the Christian spirit. The most famous of these is Tatian who in his treatise *Ad Graecos* uses the term 'Hellene' with strong negative connotations. And it would appear that there was a whole genre 'Ad Graecos', of which little survives besides Tatian's impassioned attack.[8]

Yet both through those who admired Greek culture and tried to dissociate it from its religious content, and through those who repudiated it, 'Hellenism' and 'Hellene' became in Greek at least the standard terms for 'paganism' and 'pagan', a use which remained canonical throughout late antique and Byzantine times. Moreover the term was endorsed early in the day by those whom it described and, through the efforts of the emperor Julian and the Neoplatonists who came after him, it was endowed with the same metaphysical oecumenicity that Christianity claimed for itself. It would therefore have been the best

---

[8] Tatian's master, Justin, is said by Eusebius (*HE* 4. 18. 3–4) to have composed such a treatise; surviving in fragments, the treatise is spurious. Others of whose works nothing survives, were Apollinarius, and Miltiades (ibid. 4. 27. 1 and 5. 17. 5 respectively).

expression to describe the monotheism with which the chapters in this volume deal, if it were not for the strongly technical connotations that the term carries; for this reason we have preferred the commonly used 'pagan', though with the reservations expressed above.

A technical term then in legal and theological language rather than a mere slander, the word 'Hellenism' was used by the Christian elites in the Greek East alongside the universal derogatory terms 'polytheism' (πολυθεΐα) and 'idolatry' (εἰδωλολατρία) to describe Graeco-Roman religion. Before embarking at this point on a discussion of the third crucial word in our title and the central issue of this volume—monotheism—a few additional remarks are needed. The Christian Apologists, followed by the Fathers and chroniclers of the Byzantine world, established a disarmingly simple model according to which mankind—or at least those living in the lands which had formed part of the Roman *Orbis Terrarum*—had progressed from polytheism to monotheism under the catalytic action of Christianity. As we have pointed out above, this proposition forms one of the basic orthodoxies not only of the modern world at large but of modern scholarship as well. The idea of linear, straightforward progress, which constitutes so important a tenet of the Christian *Weltanschauung*, is embedded in the modern consciousness to the extent that attempts have been made to apply it retrospectively to classical antiquity.[9]

The issue of polytheism had constituted a subject of concern for intellectuals long before the slogan 'From polytheism to monotheism' was launched by the Christians, with Greek philosophy being presented as a mere παιδαγωγὸς εἰς Χριστόν.[10] From an early date philosophers had viewed traditional religion with a critical eye, yet at the same time they condoned it either on the ground that it constituted the nearest form in which the uneducated could understand the truth or because it was socially useful or for both reasons. Respect for the customs and beliefs of one's forefathers—the πάτρια or *mos maiorum*—strongly characterizes ancient culture, in which innovation (καινοτομία) was invariably castigated as a negative tendency.[11] Thus the philosophers participated in public cult—often as priests themselves, as in the case of

---

[9] Cf. E. R. Dodds's *The Ancient Concept of Progress and Other Essays on Greek Literature and Belief* (Oxford, 1973), 1–25.

[10] Justin the Martyr's *Dialogue with Trypho* is the classic text propagating this view: it pictures in disarmingly simple terms the ladder of Greek philosophy towards the spiritual life. The depiction of Greek philosophy in purely functional terms as a παιδαγωγὸς εἰς Χριστὸν culminates with Eusebius' *Praeparatio Evangelica*.

[11] An extreme formulation of this position is to be found in Iamblichus *DM* 7. 5. 258–9.

Plutarch—while at the same time feeling the need to qualify their acts of traditional piety.

One way of justifying to themselves and to others their attachment to specific gods was to proclaim that what was really being worshipped under various names and historically sanctioned forms of cult was the one ineffable principle of all things. Unambiguously professed in a sentence like the following: 'God being one, has many names',[12] this belief permeates Greek religious theory. The Stoic Cleanthes can thus address a fervent hymn to Zeus as a god with a definite historical personality, in which we encounter a monistic view of divinity.[13] Indeed this may be the reason why this pagan prayer was selected by Stobaeus, along with a similar Orphic hymn to Zeus, for the anthology that he compiled for his son's use and education. But the most famous passage in ancient literature where the principle of *polyonymy* is enunciated is Lucius' hymn to Isis in Apuleius' *Metamorphoses*. There the goddess Isis is invoked as 'the uniform face of all gods and goddesses (. . .), whose unique divinity (*numen unicum*) is venerated by the entire world under many forms, with various rites, by manifold names' (*Met.* 11. 5). Apuleius' contemporary, the second-century Platonist Celsus, attempted to explain this to the Christians, whom he accused of compromising their belief in the one God by worshipping Jesus as a god (*CC* 8. 12): 'it makes no difference', he said, 'whether we call Zeus the Most High or Zeus or Adonai or Sabaoth or Amoun like the Egyptians, or Papaeus like the Scythians' (*CC* 5. 41). Indeed it is a widely accepted view by this time, at least among the educated, that 'the gods have one nature but many names'.[14]

Another way of saying that monotheism was perfectly compatible with belief in the existence of a plurality of divine beings consisted in the Platonic teaching that these beings formed a strict hierarchy subordinated to the supreme God; they were executors or manifestations of the divine will rather than independent principles of reality. Whether they are called gods, demons, angels, or *numina*, these immortal beings are emanations of the One, and their degree of reality depends on their proximity to the apex of the theological pyramid. Formulated with strength and clarity by the 'anti-ritualist' Plotinus, this view, which accommodated traditional worship with belief in one God only (5. 8. 9–10), was also articulated in straightforward historical terms. Thus

---

[12] Ps.-Aristotle *De mund.* 401ᵃ 12.
[13] *SVF* I (1905), no. 537.
[14] Maximus of Tyre 39. 5; cf. 2. 5.

Aelius Aristides (43. 18 ff.) and Celsus (*CC* 8. 35), among others, drew a parallel between human administration and the divine order, and justified the existence of many partial gods by likening them to the governors or satraps of the Roman and Persian empires, who were themselves subject to the Emperor and the Great King respectively.[15]

This theory of 'ethnic' or 'national' gods ruling their allotted provinces under the jurisdiction of the one and only God was put forward in strong didactic terms by the emperor Julian in his polemical work against the Christians (*CG* 143ab). At the same time, in a dogmatic hymn addressed to the Mother of the gods Cybele, Julian interpreted the myth which forms the backbone of the popular cult of Magna Mater in such a way as to leave no room for the accusations of obscenity and polytheism imputed by the Apologists and the Fathers to pagan religion. Finally, as the *pontifex maximus* of what he called 'Hellenism', Julian instructed the gifted administrator Salutius Secundus to write a short handbook *On the Gods and the Universe* which articulates pagan monotheism as belief and practice in brief catechetical terms.[16]

While the grading of celestial powers allowed the traditional gods of Graeco-Roman paganism to form part of an essentially monotheistic structure, the technique of interpretation—whether this was the *interpretatio romana* or the *interpretatio Platonica*—meant that the so-called 'Oriental' mystery cults, which began to be articulated into full religious systems around the second century BC, could also be seen as organic parts of the same meaningful and consistent whole. This conciliatory spirit, which allowed many gods and cults to coexist peacefully as complementary rather than alternative paths towards metaphysical illumination,[17] was alien to a religion which had an exclusive and at the same time proselytizing mentality. And, while a few pagans saw Christianity under the impact of their own way of thinking as yet another cult in the empire and were intrigued by its personal god and its logos theology,[18] the great

[15] On this theme, which reconciles monotheism with polytheism, in Greek philosophical literature, see H. Chadwick, *Origen: Contra Celsum*, (Cambridge, 1951; repr. with corrections, 1965), pp. xvii ff.

[16] For explicit belief in one God or a first cause, *de diis* 5. 1, 3; 13. 5.

[17] A famous formulation of this principle together with a historical and emotional justification of why it should be applied occurs in Symmachus' *Relatio* 3. 9.

[18] It is reported that Alexander Severus kept in his private lararium statues of certain 'holy souls' which included Apollonius of Tyana, Christ, Abraham, and Orpheus (Historia Augusta Sev. Alex. 29. 2). It had also been his intention to build a temple to Christ in the Capitolium, a plan which may also have been envisaged by Hadrian who was however prevented by the *hieroscopi* from putting it into effect (ibid. 43. 6–7); judging from several anecdotes, Alexander Severus' attitude towards Jews and Christians went beyond toleration (22. 4–5, 45. 7, 49. 6, 51. 7). The Platonist philosopher Amelius on the other hand seems

majority realized that, not only could no syncretistic process be applied to a religion which claimed a monopoly of the truth, but also that this religion had to be extirpated from the empire for reasons of their own survival. It was thus argued in this connection by pagan intellectuals that, unlike Judaism from which it arose, Christianity was not the traditional cult of a particular nation within the empire. The Christians claimed that they had replaced the Jews as the chosen people on earth, yet they also claimed that their kingdom was in heaven; and as the supranational agents of an oecumenical message they naturally aspired to convert the entire world, let alone the empire.[19]

Once it became a *religio licita*, it was to be expected that Christianity would not tolerate any other version of the truth apart from its own, or indeed any other way of reaching that truth. Slowly and very painfully a consensus of orthodoxy, based on Paul's teaching, was established and the main article of this 'true faith' was belief in one God, in other words monotheism, which one was hesitant to share with those 'outside the door', whose beliefs and practices were rapidly becoming illegal.

At this point it might not be out of place to recall that the monotheistic theology of the Apologists and the Church Fathers was formulated in the dominant theological idiom of late antiquity. From Origen to Gregory of Nyssa and Ps.-Dionysius, Christian monotheism was articulated in Platonic terms. Thus, when accused of being polytheistic and idolatrous by people who held the same theological views as themselves, the pagans were rather surprised. Olympiodorus for example, who wrote at the time of Justinian, felt sufficiently indignant at the language of contemporary legislation to insert in a formal commentary on the Platonic *Gorgias* remarks like the following: 'we too are aware that the first cause is one, namely God; for there cannot be many first causes. Indeed that first does not even have a name.[20] (. . .) Thus somebody, addressing a hymn to God, says: "Oh you, beyond all things! What more can I say when singing your praises?" '[21] This hymn, which is to be found in the writings of Gregory of Nazianzus (*PG* 37. 507–8), Proclus, and

to have written a paraphrase on the fourth gospel, or at least to have used John's theology in support of his own thesis; cf. Eusebius *PE* 11. 18. 26; 19. 1.

[19] See in this respect Eusebius' classic statement (*Praep. Ev.* 1. 5. 10): ὅτι μὲν οὖν τὸ γένος Ἕλληνες ὄντες καὶ τὰ Ἑλλήνων φρονοῦντες ἐκ παντοίων τε ἐθνῶν ὡς ἂν νεολέκτου στρατιᾶς λογάδες συνειλεγμένοι τῆς πατρίου δεισιδαιμονίας ἀποστάται καθεστήκαμεν, οὐδ' ἂν αὐτοί ποτε ἀρνηθείημεν.

[20] A literal reminiscence of Plato, *Parm.* 142a2. In even more poetic terms, Proclus will define the first principle as 'more ineffable than all silence and more unknowable than all existence' (*Th. P.* II, 11).

[21] *In Gorg.* (Westerink) 32.

Ps.-Dionysius,[22] is an eloquent comment on the theological unity of the late antique world illustrating as it does the so-called 'negative' theological thinking of the period, which conceives of the first cause as transcending both being and understanding. Later in his Commentary, Olympiodorus quotes more lines from the same hymn which he introduces by the remark: 'The philosophers believe that the principle of all there is is one, and that the cause which is first of all causes and supracelestial is one. From it derives everything. But they did not even call it by a name.' To the accusation of idolatry Olympiodorus retorts: 'and don't go on to think that the philosophers honour stones and idols as divine. It is only because, living as we do according to the senses, we cannot reach the incorporeal and immaterial power, that the idols have been invented as a reminder of things beyond, so that by seeing and worshipping them, we may think of the incorporeal and immaterial powers'.[23]

If the definition of monotheism offered by Olympiodorus does not differ from that of contemporary Christian theologians, his defence of cult anticipates the very formulation reached by the participants of the VIIth Oecumenical Council which restored the icons. Olympiodorus however speaks on behalf of the philosophers, restricting his defence of paganism to his own circle, so that the question of how widespread were such views among those late antique people who did not share in the formal education of the elites springs immediately to mind. In order to answer it we felt that we had to move away from the philosophers (whose monotheistic views are analysed in the second chapter in our volume) towards those areas of anonymous or pseudepigraphic late antique literature which reflect the loyalties of a wide range of social and educational nomenclature. Moving into the region that John Dillon has called 'the Platonic Underworld', we began our search by considering Gnosticism, a wide and variable spiritual movement which in most of its historically attested forms is dualistic. Yet, contrary to what is generally assumed, there existed in late antiquity a monistic variety of Gnosticism which postulated one ultimate principle of good, from which are derived in complicated ways man and the world as we know it. This monistic Gnosticism, corresponding to a monotheistic religious view, was widespread, as the article in this volume argues.

[22] It has recently been argued by M. Sicherl, 'Ein neuplatonischer Hymnus unter den Gedichten Gregors von Nazianz', in J. Duffy and J. Peradotto (eds.), *Gonimos: Neoplatonic and Byzantine Studies presented to L. G. Westerink* (Buffalo, NY, 1988), 61–83, that the original form of this very popular—to judge from the manuscript tradition—hymn should be sought in Ps.-Dionysius.　　　　[23] *In Gorg.* 246.

In contrast to Gnosticism, Hermeticism as a spiritual way in late antiquity is not treated as a separate contribution, and this is why a discussion of its main tenets might not be inappropriate here. It is customary to divide the body of surviving Hermetic literature into a technical and a theoretical part. Yet the latter category, which comprises texts from the late first to the fourth century AD, is far from being homogeneous, and no cogent philosophical-theological system can be extracted from it. On the other hand, the contradictions between the various tractates or even within the same tractate are not such that they preclude us from feeling that the collection of tractates which has come down to us forms an organic whole. Its contradictions are those of a living and evolving body and they surely stem from the fact that in different parts of the Roman world different teachers interpreted in their own way a common doctrine, which they believed to have been divinely revealed. This was the revelation of Hermes Trismegistos, but also that of Isis and of other Egyptian gods and holy men. For the Hermeticists had the vivid awareness that they belonged to a cogent tradition which stretched back to Hermes-Thoth through a continuous chain of divinely inspired teachers.[24]

Some of the tractates are characterized by Gnostic tendencies of a dualistic character, but in their majority the theological Hermetica preach a monistic view of the world (16. 19). Indeed from the Renaissance onwards the basic collection (first edited and translated by Marsilio Ficino) was considered a typical work of Neoplatonic mysticism, and it was not until the publication of Reitzenstein's influential work on the *Poimandres* in 1904 that the view that the Hermetica are permeated by Gnostic pessimism—a view already enunciated by Zeller—became widespread. The range of Hermetic belief is wide and in this Hermeticism can be compared with Sufism or any other mystical theory and practice.

A definition of God such as 'He himself is what there is and what there is not' (5. 9) unambiguously proclaims the Platonic dogma in the existence of one principle only, that of good, from which everything proceeds. According to this belief evil is, as implied in the passage just quoted, but a lessening of existence, until what we might call absolute evil becomes tantamount to mere absence. For those Hermeticists who understood the teaching of Trismegistos in strictly monistic terms this world is the visible manifestation of God; it is eternal, without beginning or end, and the very quintessence of goodness and beauty (11. 3; 16. 19; 11.

[24] Cf. *Kore Kosmou* fr. 23. 32.

6, 22). Thus the man who chooses evil instead of the good, the man who goes out of his way to seek what in theological terms does not exist, is himself responsible for his ill-fortune, and God 'the one and only' is blameless (4. 8).[25] By contrast the man who realizes his true nature, the ὄντως ἄνθρωπος who is led by the νοῦς (10. 24), becomes 'a mortal god, just as God in heaven is an immortal man. It is through these two—cosmos and man—that all things exist through the action of the One' (10. 25). To this absolutely transcendent One, whose name is unknown, Hermes sings his 'mystic hymn': 'Let every nature in the cosmos attend the hearing of the hymn. Open, o earth; let every lock that bars the torrent open to me; trees, be not shaken, I am about to sing a hymn to the lord of creation, to the universe, to the One' (13. 17). The one and only God should be worshipped by noetic means. Indeed burning as much as a grain of incense when praying is a sacrilegious act (*Asclepius* 41). So far from being idolatrous, the adepts of the wisdom of Hermes Trismegistos addressed thanksgivings to God for three things: *sensus, ratio, intelligentia*, as the Latin translation of the *Perfect Discourse* has it: the mind, reason, and understanding with which God has endowed us.[26]

How widespread a road to salvation the Hermetic Way was in late antiquity is now gradually beginning to emerge thanks to prosopographic studies in the field.[27] It is also becoming clear that its adherents were not confined to the 'Platonic Underworld'. Indeed through a thinker like Iamblichus, about whom it has been recently argued that he spent many years in Egypt teaching Hermetic wisdom,[28] 'the mysteries of the Egyptians' found their way into Neoplatonism, as did that other late antique revelation, the Chaldaean Oracles.

Not delivered by a public oracle, but by the use of a medium, the Chaldaean Oracles, as their title suggests, claimed to provide wisdom in the Chaldaean or Babylonian tradition or were obtained through the invocation of Chaldaean gods. Their content reveals the influence of philosophy, as there are clear connections with Numenius, a somewhat older contemporary of the two Julians who are responsible for this collection of oracular sayings and for its circulation.

The details of the theology of the Chaldaean Oracles are controversial. Yet there is no room for doubting that here too we have a monotheistic

---

[25] The word ἀναίτιος which we translate as blameless seems to constitute a conscious reminiscence in this context of Plato, *Rep.* 617de.

[26] Anti-ritualism was a conscious choice of many pagans. For Plotinus' attitude to formal worship, Porphyry, *V. Plot.* 9.

[27] See G. Fowden's *The Egyptian Hermes* (Cambridge, 1986).

[28] Cf. P. Athanassiadi, *JRS* 85 (1995), 246.

theology, though there is some dispute about the nature of the one God: is it trinitarian, and if so, are we dealing with a subordinationist or a co-ordinationist trinitarianism? This ambiguity results from the way in which the fragments of the Chaldaean revelation have been interpreted by the authors who have handed them down to us. Thus it is not clear whether in the original revelation the divine first principle was a monad or a triad, and, if it was a triad, whether its second and third persons proceeded from the first or whether the triad as a whole constituted the first principle, from which then further triads proceeded.[29]

Unlike the Gnostic and the Hermetic wisdom, however, the Chaldaean revelation never broke the narrow philosophical circle in which it made its first appearance to reach the wider world as a message of salvation. Espoused by the Neoplatonists as the way to God *par excellence* and allied by them with the Orphic–Pythagorean and the Platonic theology, it remained their exclusive preserve, and this is why its doctrines have reached us in so enigmatic a form, entangled as they are in several layers of exegesis. What the relevant chapter in the present volume attempts to do is to show that if any sense is to be made of the surviving fragments, the two main exegetes of the Oracles, Proclus and Damascius, ought to be considered separately as expounding often conflicting views on the same basic doctrine.

More straightforward than the Chaldaean oracles, and certainly more public, were the utterances of the prophets in the sanctuaries of the late Roman world, who now spoke a language which has been described by A. D. Nock as 'theological'. Thus in the early second century of our era the priest of Apollo at Delphi declared: 'the god is no less a philosopher than a prophet',[30] a claim that was to be fully justified by Apollo's subsequent activity. When Plotinus died, Amelius journeyed to Delphi to ask where the philosopher's soul had gone. The god had no difficulty in producing for the occasion a reply in fifty lines of verse, partly based on an allegorical interpretation of an episode in the *Odyssey*, which satisfied Porphyry enough to quote it in full in his *Life of Plotinus* (23. 14–63). No less philosophical than the reply of the god at Delphi was his utterance at Didyma when he was asked by a certain Polites what happens to the soul after death:

[29] Basing his own Collection of the oracles on that compiled by Psellos, the 15th-cent. pagan philosopher Pletho interprets them in an unambiguously monistic spirit: see now, Μαγικὰ λόγια τῶν ἀπὸ Ζωροάστρου μάγων. Γεωργίου Γεμιστοῦ Πλήθωνος Ἐξήγησις εἰς τὰ αὐτὰ λόγια. Text, translation, commentary by B. Tambrun-Krasker, with a section by M. Tardieu on the Arab version (Athens, 1995).
[30] Plutarch, *Mor.* 385b.

So long as the soul is imprisoned in the perishable body,
though impassible, she still yields to its pangs.
But once released from its faded mortal frame,
she quickly finds her way to the aether where she dwells in her entirety
youthful for all eternity, altogether indestructible.
Such is the decree of divine first-born providence.[31]

The answers given to Polites and Amelius are characteristic of the new concerns of the enquirers. Traditionally the questions posed to an oracle had been of a practical nature with either a personal or a wider political relevance. Cities and individuals had been exclusively interested in their terrestrial fortunes, but as from the second century AD an increasing curiosity about theological matters brings enquirers to the sites—old and brand new—where revelation is dispensed. The nature of the divine now preoccupies the average man who sets out from his home town to seek 'the unknown god'. In the mid-second century a man from Tios journeyed to the newly founded oracle of Glycon at Abonoteichos to engage in an existential dialogue with the god:

—Who are you?
—A new Asclepius!
—Different from the old one?
—You are not allowed to hear that.
(. . .) —What about the other oracles? the one at Didyma, the one at Claros, and the one at Delphi? Do they still have with them your father, Apollo, or are the prophecies given out by them false?
—This you should not wish to know either. It is not permitted![32]

Another enquirer with a similar question to that of the man from Tios arrived at the temple of the Nubian Mandulis in Talmis (Kalabsha) some time in the third century. The god graced him with a vision, and accordingly the pilgrim dedicated to him his revelation: 'Then I knew you Mandulis to be the Sun, the all-seeing master, the king of All, omnipotent eternity.'[33] At about the same time Apollo at Claros was asked 'who is the supreme God?' His reply was consistent with the tenets of transcendental monotheism propagated by contemporary philosophers,[34] and this was not an isolated instance. On several occasions

---

[31] Porphyry, *Phil. ex. Or.* (Wolff), p. 178; Lactantius, *Div. Inst.* 7. 13. 5; *Theos. Tub.* 37. Cf. L. Robert, *CRAI* 1968, 590.

[32] Lucian, *Alex.* 43.

[33] E. Bernand, *Inscriptions métriques de l'Egypte gréco-romaine* (Paris, 1969), no. 166; cf. A. D. Nock, 'A Vision of Mandulis Aion', in Z. Stewart (ed.), *Essays on Religion and the Ancient World* (Oxford, 1972), 357–400.

[34] Cornelius Labeo *ap.* Macrobius, *Sat.* i. 18. 20.

Apollo declared that the supreme God was superior to him, ineffable and unknown even to him:

> Alas, you have not come to enquire about small matters.
> You want to know who is the king of heaven
> Whom even I do not know, yet revere according to tradition.[35]

The epigraphic and literary evidence on late antique oracles shows that the theological interest of the enquirers was dominated by the twin issue of monotheism and cult, two subjects which occupied contemporary philosophers. At the same time, however, this same evidence gives insight into the two-way process which made these philosophers use the oracular replies to the layman's enquiry as evidence of the truth of their own theoretical assumptions. Porphyry could thus write a whole treatise using oracular sayings in support of his theological views. More significantly however, the monotheistic theology propagated by the official oracles of the pagan world suggested in due course to the Christians the ingenious idea that these oracles could be used to support their argument of the gradual passage of humanity from polytheism to monotheism, with the pagan gods foretelling the triumph of the Christian god. Judging from the surviving evidence, several such collections preserving 'monotheistic oracles' were compiled in late antiquity,[36] one of the most interesting being the so-called *Theosophia Tubingensis*. An anonymous work, the *Theosophia*,[37] which was composed between 474 and 491, comprised eleven books of which the first seven, now lost, expounded 'the right doctrine' (Περὶ τῆς ὀρθῆς πίστεως), while books eight to ten, of which we have substantial fragments, showed that 'the oracles of the Greek gods and the so-called theologies of the Greek and Egyptian sages as well as the Sibylline oracles agree with the objective (σκοπός) of the divine scriptures' (§1). Probably the most famous oracle in this collection, discussed on several instances in the present volume, is an answer to the irreverent enquiry of a certain Theophilus to Apollo at Claros: 'are *you*, or another, God?' Apollo's answer, which was widely publicized by his priests, ran as follows:

---

[35] *Theos. Tub.* 12. Cf. 34, 38, 39.

[36] See R. van den Broek, 'Four Coptic Fragments of a Greek Theosophy', *Vig. Christ.* 32 (1978), 118–42; S. Brock, 'A Syriac Collection of Prophecies of the Pagan Philosophers', *OLP* 14 (1983), 203–46 (an important article); id. 'Some Syriac Excerpts from Greek Collections of Pagan Prophecies', *Vig. Christ.* 38 (1984), 77–90. For an overview, G. Dagron, *Constantinople imaginaire: Étude sur le recueil des Patria* (Paris, 1984), 127–59.

[37] According to the author (§ 5), the title was chosen to indicate τὸ ὑπὸ τοῦ Θεοῦ καὶ τοὺς Ἕλληνας σοφισθῆναι.

Born of Himself, untaught, motherless, immovable,
Not contained in a name, many-named, dwelling in fire,
This is God. We angels are but a particle of God.

This is clearly the one supreme God whom, as Celsus claimed, all nations worship though calling him by different names (*CC* 5. 45); the one God whom, as Maximus of Madaura wrote to Augustine, we call by many names, since we do not know his real name.[38] To the mind of the priests of Apollo at Claros, the traditional gods of paganism were not God, but his angels; monotheists themselves, they encouraged Theophilus in what he was already prepared to believe while seeking Apollo's authority.

The angels of the one and only God belong, as two chapters in this volume point out, to the theological *koine* of the period.[39] But nothing better exemplifies the common monotheistic culture shared by so many late antique men and women than the cult of *Theos Hypsistos* which, on the basis of the archaeological evidence available, was particularly widespread in Asia Minor. The father of Gregory of Nazianzus for one was a Hypsistarian before converting to Christianity and becoming a bishop,[40] while Gregory of Nyssa is sufficiently angered by the spiritual tenets of this group, which was neither Jewish nor Christian but clearly hovered on a religious frontier, to expose in a polemical work their stark monotheism which rejected belief in the Son.[41] And the heresiologist Epiphanius felt obliged to castigate what he saw as an influential movement which, as is argued in this volume, allied monotheistic theory with cultic practice.

The epigraphic evidence presented in this volume suggests that the Hypsistarians were ordinary people. Such were some at least of the 'magicians' whose liturgical formulas are preserved on papyri from late antique Egypt. Our collection of magical papyri, which assembles texts from the second century BC to the fifth century AD,[42] certainly portrays a great variety in the social, intellectual, and spiritual level of the users, some of whom had purely practical everyday concerns, while others

---

[38] *Ap.* Augustine, *ep.* 16. 1: 'nam Deus omnibus religionibus commune nomen est'. Even more daringly Saturninus of Thugga had said in a Council held in Carthage in the 3rd cent.: 'Gentiles, quamvis idola colant, tamen summum deum patrem creatorem cognoscunt et confitentur' (*PL* 3, col. 1197).

[39] In the 6th cent. John Lydus could still refer to a temple near the sacred city of Cybele, Pessinus, which was dedicated τῇ ἀχράντῳ στρατιᾷ τῶν ἱερῶν ἀγγέλων τοῦ ἀρρήτου Θεοῦ (*Mag.* 3. 74).

[40] *PG* 35, col. 990.

[41] *In Eunomium* 38 (Jaeger), 2, 327.

[42] H. D. Betz, *The Greek Magical Papyri in Translation* (Chicago, 1986), pp. xlii–xliii.

turned to magic as a discipline capable of providing them with the union
with the divine. Yet despite the diversity of purposes and levels represented, the collection forms an organic unity which is based on the ultimate monotheism, implicit or explicit in all its texts. The conciliatory
spirit, which often goes so far as to embrace the Jewish god and his
angels, is not different from that shown by the Clarian Apollo in the
oracle quoted above. Indeed Pap. II contains a long invocation to Apollo
of Claros, who is addressed as ἀστυφέλικτος (90) and πολυώνυμος (109).
Yet as 'the first angel of Zeus' (Pap. I 300),[43] Apollo is different from the
παντοκράτωρ θεός (Pap. III 219), who is characterized by the familiar
epithets αὐτομαθής and ἀδίδακτος (III 221–4). Papyrus III is of especial
interest for our purposes. The text is uncertain and partly corrupt; but in
591 ff. we clearly read the following: 'We owe you thanks, with all our
soul and our heart outstretched towards you, ineffable name, honoured
by the address "God".' Whatever the uncertainties of the text, it proceeds
to refer to a god who is the source of all knowledge, understanding, and
reason, indeed a god reminiscent of the one to whom the final prayer of
the Hermetic Asclepius is addressed.[44] PGM IV and V in particular seem
to refer to a god to whom all other gods are subordinate, or conceived as
his manifestations. The recipe in IV 930 ff. for obtaining a vision of the
highest god (989), the God of gods, ruler of gods, angels, and demons
(999), also addressed as 'Pre-father' (949), is of especial interest in the
present context. Indeed it is tempting to see in the term 'Pre-father' an
attempt to appeal to a being higher than the father of all there is, which
brings immediately to the mind Numenius' term πάππος, describing the
principle above the Creator.[45]

A major theme of the literature that we have been surveying is that of
light and of its material source, fire. Both Hypsistarian worship and
magical practice involve the lighting of lamps, while the Magical Papyri,
the Chaldaean Revelation, and the prophecies delivered by late antique
oracles often suggest that the first principle is fiery, or they identify it
with the sun.[46] Admittedly this is a supra-mundane sun, as in Julian's

---

[43] On the legions of angels and archangels under the command of a πρωτοφυὴς θεός,
Pap. II 197 ff.
[44] Passage quoted above, p. 13. The similarity in the language between the two texts has
already been noticed: cf. Nock–Festugière, *Hermès Trismégiste* II, 353 ff. For a specific
reference to the wisdom of Hermes Trismegistus in the Magical Papyri, IV 885 ff.
[45] A term Proclus mocks: *In Tim.* I, 303, 27 ff. On προπάτωρ, a Hermetic term which also
occurs in Iamblichus *DM* VIII, 4 (267. 3), cf. PGM IV 1988, XII 236.
[46] Cf. e.g. PGM IV, 649 ff.

Hymn to King Helios, whose material manifestation is the ruling planet
of the universe, which formed the object of important worship in the late
empire. Yet in order to understand how solar worship could be conceived as an expression of monotheistic belief, a short digression on the
two fundamental and antithetical ways of conceiving God in ancient
philosophy might not be out of place: Platonists and Aristotelians
defined God as absolutely immaterial and therefore transcending the
world of the senses, while the Stoics taught that, though incorporeal,
God displays a form of materiality, but of a very subtle and literally
ethereal nature, and likened him to intelligible light or fire.[47] Yet, as is
argued in the second chapter of this volume, both had a monotheistic
view, and the Christians, who drew on Greek philosophy for the formulation of their own theology, recognized this. Of the two views on offer
orthodox Christianity opted for the first, without however being able to
reject the Stoic position altogether, as Tertullian's rhetorical question
testifies: 'for who will deny that God is a body, though he is a spirit?'[48]
This ambiguity is even more clearly present in pagan theological literature, which combines belief in a transcendental God with the worship of
the Sun seen as the representation of God in this world. An attempt at
articulating this duality was made by the emperor Julian who integrated
it in the system of Iamblichan Neoplatonism, postulating between the
transcendental fiery first principle, whom he qualifies as the intelligible
($\nu o\eta\tau\acute{o}s$) Helios, and its material counterpart (the $a\grave{\iota}\sigma\theta\eta\tau\grave{o}s$ $\mathring{\eta}\lambda\iota os$), a
Helios accessible to the human intellect ($\nu o\epsilon\rho\acute{o}s$), that Julian identifies
with the intellectual god Apollo, but also with the Mithra of the popular
Roman mystery cult.

An ardent pagan who served under Julian as proconsul of Achaea was
Vettius Agorius Praetextatus, who is presented by Macrobius in his
Saturnalia as the exponent of a philosophical position very similar to
that of Julian. Relying among other things on Stoic treatises, Macrobius'
Praetextatus identifies the Roman gods with those of other nations, and
views them as aspects of the one God who governs the universe. Thus
when worshipping these encosmic gods (1, 17, 2) who form the intellectual manifestations of the One, as Praetextatus argues, we worship the
one and only God.

The analysis of the speech of Praetextatus in Macrobius concludes
this volume in which we have attempted to survey some of the most

---

[47] The conception that the angels are made out of a subtle, spiritual form of matter also
dominates mystical Islam, cf. Corbin, *Le Paradoxe du monothéisme*, 117.
[48] *Adv. Praxean* 7.

significant forms of pagan monotheism in late antiquity.[49] We will be content if a preliminary case has been made for the thesis that not only philosophers, but a very substantial portion of late antique pagans was consciously monotheistic. And though in the course of this discussion certain important issues, such as the distinction between belief and worship, have not been addressed, we hope that it emerges clearly enough from what has been argued in this volume that being a pagan in the period under discussion did not necessarily mean that one was not a monotheist. Moreover the first two chapters show that, far from arising as a reaction to Christianity, pagan monotheism was a deeply rooted trend in ancient philosophy which developed under its own momentum, broadening sufficiently to embrace a good part of the population. Indeed we are inclined to believe that Christian monotheism is, historically speaking, part of this broader development. Christianity did not convince because it was monotheistic; rather it would appear that in order to convince, it had to be monotheistic in a society which was fast moving in that direction.

Yet, living as we do in at least nominally Christian societies, we seem to have inherited and unquestioningly absorbed, as part of the culture in which we were raised, the Christian point of view on our historical past, which often results in a distorted perspective. To rectify this we should question our acquired assumptions concerning the antithesis *paganism—Christianity* in the light of a strict analysis of such issues as faith, grace, salvation, prayer, icons or idols, and sacred places. We should emerge from such delving with a better understanding not only of Christianity and its roots in antiquity, but also of antiquity itself, which gave Christianity its original historical shape. In this volume we have attempted in a small but crucial area to identify the *comparanda*. And it seems to us that it is highly unlikely that those pagans who converted to Christianity did so because they felt that the Christians had a monopoly on monotheism.

[49] So crucial an area of pagan monotheism as the theology of the mystery cults has not even been touched upon in this volume; it is our intention to examine this important theme in a future seminar.

1

Towards Monotheism

M. L. WEST

A standard dictionary definition of 'monotheism' is 'the belief in only one God'. That seems simple and straightforward, except for the problem of what is meant by a god. There are probably many different definitions of the term 'god' to be found in theological and anthropological literature, and different ones may be suitable for different purposes and in different contexts. For the purposes of the present essay, I will define a god (and gods, of course, embrace goddesses) as an entity identified or postulated, by one or more members of the species *homo sapiens*, as a wilful agent possessing or exercising power over events that appear to be beyond human control or not governed by other intelligible agencies.

The difference between polytheism and monotheism, then, comes down to this: do we postulate different gods to account for different kinds of event, or do we adopt a reductionist approach and postulate one highly versatile God, responsible for every kind of divine intervention, from the Big Bang to the school chaplain's deliverance from temptation?

In the modern world monotheistic religions have the highest profile: Christianity, Judaism, Islam. But we know enough about the history of these religions to see that they are not survivals from a primitive monotheism. Christianity and Islam are descended from Judaism, and Judaism developed fitfully and recidivistically from a polytheistic background. Among the ancient civilizations polytheism was the norm. You had many gods and goddesses—hundreds, in some cases—with differing functions, worshipped accordingly on different occasions, in different circumstances, by different groups of people. You prayed to one deity for victory or survival in battle, to another for recovery from illness, to another for redress of injustice, to another for a safe sea crossing, to another for success in love, to another for success in fishing. Or you revered a certain god because you were a potter, or a metalworker, or a seer, or a singer, or a burglar, and he was the patron god of your particular craft. Or you worshipped a certain god because he was the god of your clan or your tribe, while accepting that it was perfectly natural and proper for other tribes to worship their own gods.

The point of polytheism is that the gods are independent individuals with different interests and different constituencies. In real life, that is, in the worshipper's mind, they remain dormant most of the time and come alive when the appropriate need arises or when the cult calendar says it is their day. Normally they come alive singly and not collectively, because they are significant as individual, autonomous powers, not as part of a collective body of gods.

In poetry, however, a different picture is presented. In the Homeric epics, from which many people get their first and strongest impression of Greek polytheism, we see the gods indeed often acting as individuals, and sometimes at cross purposes. Some of them support the Achaeans and some the Trojans; some have a specific relation to certain individual heroes; now and then they are seen to exercise specialized powers, as when Apollo sends and later dispels a plague, or when Poseidon stirs up a storm at sea. On the other hand we find the gods from time to time meeting in assembly in the house of Zeus on Olympus and debating earthly affairs there. Zeus is represented as their chief (in Hesiod and later he is called their king). He is stronger than the rest of them, and if they fail to agree with his plan he can impose it on them. Hesiod calls the gods' assembly a βουλή; the Homeric poet speaks of their ἀγορή or ὁμήγυρις, and of their being ὁμηγερέες. The gathering is thus described in terminology parallel to that for a civic assembly. But it is not a democratic body; it is monarchic. Sometimes the chief god simply issues his orders, and there is little or no discussion. Sometimes he invites proposals on what should be done in a particular situation; sometimes other gods initiate things by expressing discontent or making representations about some matter; but it is for the chief to decide on or approve any action that is taken as a result. A god may go away in rebellious mood and take action behind Zeus' back. But the idea implicit in the assembly procedure is that the gods act in concert and promote a single plan.

This motif of the assembly of the gods is equally at home in the literatures of the Near East, in Sumerian, Akkadian, Hittite, Ugaritic, Phoenician, and Hebrew.[1] The Akkadian texts refer to the *puḫur ilāni*, 'assembly of the gods'; the Ugaritic texts refer to the 'congregation of the

---

[1] E. T. Mullen, *The Divine Council in Canaanite and Early Hebrew Literature* (Cambridge, Mass., 1980).

gods', 'the assembly of El, or of the sons of El, or of the gods, or the sons of the gods', or to the 'assembly congregate'. Like the expressions used in Homer, these are terms appropriate to a political assembly. So are two of the terms used in the Old Testament for the Lord's heavenly entourage, עֲדַת-אֵל 'congregation of El' and קְהַל קְדֹשִׁים 'assembly of the holy ones', whereas another term, סוֹד (complemented by קְדֹשִׁים or יהוה or אֱלוֹהַ) suggests a private circle or company.[2]

In the Near East mention of this divine assembly is not confined to literature, as it is in Greece. It appears in Old Babylonian and Ugaritic ritual texts, not in a functional role but appended to lists of individual deities to cover all who may not have been mentioned, as in Greek cult inscriptions lists of deities are often rounded off by 'and all gods and all goddesses'. Similarly in Phoenician inscriptions, such as the temple rebuilding inscription of King Yeḥimilk of Byblos, dated c.940 BC, which contains the prayer, 'May Ba'alšamēm and the Lady of Byblos and the assembly (מפחרת) of the holy gods of Byblos lengthen Yeḥimilk's days and his years over Byblos.'[3]

Where the workings of these divine assemblies are portrayed in poetry, they are similar to what we see in Homer, in that the chief god is the convener, the chairman, and the essential taker or ratifier of decisions. The effect is, at intervals in the narrative, to unite the potentially divergent wills of the sundry gods and goddesses into a single collective will. This is advantageous in literature, or in officially scripted cultic settings, when the poet or theologian has a whole college of gods present to his consciousness and wants them to authorize a particular situation. But this collectivization of the gods really negates the principle of polytheism. These gods were meant to function separately in different situations as individuals; not contradicting each other, but simply not running into each other. In this Near Eastern poetic tradition, then, which goes back at least to the early part of the second millennium BC, we see the emergence of a tendency to imagine the gods as a body of councillors who fall in with the will of their chief executive—a mirror of the earthly king in council. This means in effect that just as the king's will prevails on earth, so in heaven, in the end, there is only one god who counts. Oriental monarchy is at least one historical factor predisposing towards a monotheistic theology.

The idea of a unified divine purpose finds a more pointed expression

---

[2] Ps. 82; 89: 6(5)–8(7); 1 Ki. 22: 19–22; Job 1: 6–12; 2: 1–7; 15: 8; Jer. 23: 18, 22.

[3] J. C. L. Gibson, *Textbook of Syrian Semitic Inscriptions*, 3 (Oxford, 1982), 18 no. 6 (*KAI* 4).

in Homer in the phrase Διὸς νόος or Διὸς βουλή, the mind or will of Zeus, which is represented as prevailing over all oppositions and temporary setbacks and governing the final outcome. Mortals cannot apprehend it, and the lesser gods sometimes misconstrue it, so that the final outcome cannot be predicted in advance; but when it comes to pass, people realize that that was what Zeus planned all along. Zeus, then, is not merely an autocrat but a Master Mind. In some circumstances, at any rate, he operates according to a long-term plan. The events of much of the *Iliad* are governed by the plan which he adopts in book 1 in order that Achilles may be restored to the honour which is his due. In the *Cypria* (fr. 1) the whole Trojan War was represented as having been designed by Zeus in order to relieve the earth of her burden of excess population. Divine plans on such a scale are essentially a feature of monotheistic thinking. In the Hebrew prophets we find national victories or defeats interpreted as reflecting a divine plan or purpose: for example, Isaiah 14: 24–7,

> The Lord of Hosts has sworn, saying
> 'As I have planned, so shall it be,
> and as I have purposed, so shall it stand forth—
> to smash Assyria in my land, and on my mountains trample her . . .
> This is the purpose that is purposed over all the earth,
> and this is the hand stretched out over all the nations.'

Monotheism may seem a stark antithesis to polytheism, but there was no abrupt leap from the one to the other. No one, so far as we know, suddenly had the revolutionary idea that it would be economical to assume a single god responsible for everything rather than a plurality of gods. Where we see a god emerging as plenipotentiary, the existence of other gods is not denied, but they are reduced in importance or status, and he is praised as the greatest among them. This is what is sometimes called 'henotheism'. Let me quote a couple of sentences that Miriam Lichtheim has written about Egyptian religion:[4]

As early as the Old Kingdom [third millennium], Egyptian religion had tended to attribute supreme power to one god, and to subordinate the other gods to him. But while increasingly heaping attributes of universal power on the sun-god Re, the religion remained essentially polytheistic.

In the fourteenth century Amenophis IV, otherwise known as Akhenaten, took this sun-worship to an extreme which has often been

---

[4] *Ancient Egyptian Literature: A Book of Readings*, vol. 2: *The New Kingdom* (Berkeley and Los Angeles, 1976), 89.

interpreted as a monotheism. In his Great Hymn to the Aten (the sun-disc) no other gods are mentioned, and the Aten is even addressed with the words 'O unique god, beside whom there is none!'—or as others translate, 'with whom there is none to compare'.[5] Whether this amounts to a denial of the existence of other gods, as is sometimes maintained, I am doubtful. We find a parallel situation in the Gathas of Zoroaster. In general we have the impression of a monotheistic exaltation of Ahura Mazda, but in two passages Zoroaster uses the expression *Mazdåsčā ahuråŋhō* 'Mazda and (you other) lords', showing that he did not after all deny the existence of the other gods.[6]

There had always been a tendency, in hymning a deity, to dwell on those aspects and accomplishments in which he or she surpassed the rest. It was not a big step from this to awarding the deity in question absolute supremacy. In Mesopotamia, for instance, 'king of the gods' was a standard title, applied at different times to the gods Anu, Narru, Shamash, Marduk, and Aššur.

In the case of Marduk we have a detailed narrative about his acquisition of the kingship in the Babylonian Creation Epic, *Enūma eliš*, which dates from the latter part of the second millennium BC. It is a particularly interesting case because the concentration of the gods' powers into Marduk's hands is dealt with rather explicitly. He has come forward as the saviour of the gods from the oppression of Tiamat and her followers, and he demands the supreme power as his fee. The gods (after becoming extremely merry at a feast) agree to this, and confer power on him. They tell him that he is honoured among the great gods, and that from this day forth his command shall be irrevocable, his utterance shall be law, none of the gods shall transgress the limits he lays down; his word shall be pre-eminent in the assembly. After he returns from defeating Tiamat, they all kiss his feet, hail him as king, and undertake to obey his every command. He assigns to them their various stations and functions. From this point on, the picture is of a completely harmonious company of gods with Marduk as sovereign. But although nominally they are all just as divine as before, in effect they have downgraded themselves and become mere functionaries of Marduk.

We find rather a similar picture in Hesiod, whose *Theogony* certainly owes much to Near Eastern mythology. The disputes and conflicts among the gods all belong to a time now long past. Zeus led the Olympians to victory over the Titans; they then urged him to assume

---

[5] Ibid. 96–100.   [6] *Yasna* 30. 9, 31. 4.

kingship over them, and he allotted them their functions and privileges.[7]
Now he rules benignly over them, and the impression is given that they
are all in perfect accord.

The Old Testament, despite its reputation as a monotheistic publication, preserves many relics of the polytheism that prevailed widely in
Palestine, at least down to the seventh century. Yahweh introduces himself to Moses as 'the god of your fathers, the god of Abraham, the god of
Isaac, the god of Jacob'. He says 'You shall have no other gods besides
me'; not 'there are no other gods but me'. He is the god of the Hebrews,
the god of Israel; the Hebrews call him *our* god, the Egyptians call him
your god, or, when speaking among themselves, *their* god. It is acknowledged that other nations have other gods. Jephthah says to the king of
the Ammonites, 'Why will you not be content with what Kemosh your
god has given you, and we will keep what Yahweh our god has requisi-
tioned for us?'[8] In one of the oldest Hebrew poems, the Song of Moses,
it is explained that

> When the Most High gave the nations their inheritance,
>   when he divided the sons of Adam,
> he fixed the bounds of the peoples
>   according to the number of the sons of God.[9]

The 'sons of God', as we shall see in a moment, represent the gods of the
old polytheism. The sense of the verse, therefore, is that there was an
original allocation of one god per nation.

Hebrew poets took over the old Canaanite motif of the assembly of
the gods, presided over by El, which we find in the Ugaritic poems, and
they made Yahweh the central figure, identifying him with El and sometimes giving him this name. We read of his assembly in several passages.
In the 82nd Psalm, for example, he speaks fiercely to the other gods:

> God (אֱלֹהִים) was standing in the congregation of El;
>   amid the gods (אֱלֹהִים) he was holding judgment.
> 'How long will you give unjust judgments
>   and show favour to the wicked?'

And a few verses later he threatens them with demotion:

> 'I say: you are gods (אֱלֹהִים) and sons of the Most High (בְּנֵי עֶלְיוֹן), all of you,
> yet truly like man you will die, and like some chieftain you will fall.'

---

[7] Hes. *Th.* 624–720, 881–5.

[8] Jdg. 11: 24.

[9] Deut. 32: 8. 'Sons of God' is restored from LXX ἀγγέλων θεοῦ; the Hebrew text has 'the
sons of Israel', i.e. אל has been expanded to יִשְׂרָאֵל.

Those who attend these gatherings are elsewhere referred to as 'the holy ones', קְדֹשִׁים, or 'the sons of gods', בְּנֵי אֵלִים or בְּנֵי אֱלֹהִים; according to normal Semitic idiom 'sons of gods' means 'members of the class "god", not individually distinguished', just as 'sons of craftsmen' means 'craftsmen'. In the 29th Psalm these lesser deities are actually addressed directly:

> Render to Yahweh, O sons of gods, render to Yahweh glory and strength; render to Yahweh the glory of his name, worship Yahweh in the splendour of holiness.

In more orthodox parts of the Old Testament the lesser divinities surrounding Yahweh are reduced to emissaries and agents of his will, his 'messengers' (מַלְאָכִים), correctly translated into Greek as ἄγγελοι, from which we have made them into 'angels'; but this shift does not always succeed in concealing their originally independent status. The later myth of the Fallen Angels formalizes the elimination from the world of all those divinities who persisted in showing independent spirit: only the lackeys are left.

This polarization is parallel to what we have seen in the Babylonian and Hesiodic myths. Those who oppose the chief god, such as Tiamat or the Titans and Typhon, are killed or consigned to the underworld, while those who remain around him subordinate themselves completely to his will. Prometheus in the pseudo-Aeschylean play is another who defies Zeus and is sent down; much is made of his αὐθαδία, his independence of spirit, while he for his part mocks Zeus as a tyrant and Hermes, the messenger of Zeus, as a lackey. All these myths, then, convey the notion of a great shakeout, in which plurality and diversity of divine agents, with the potential for conflict between them, are reduced to a totalitarian unity.

Aeschylus in the plays of his last years (especially the *Supplices* and *Agamemnon*) glorifies Zeus in such exalted terms that many older critics saw him, not exactly as a monotheist, but as a noble heathen straining towards the enlightenment that would culminate in monotheism, in Christianity. He is in fact continuing and developing the Hesiodic theology of a Zeus who has vanquished the opposition and imposed his law on the world. We have only to think of the roles of Apollo, Athena, and the Erinyes in the *Eumenides* to realize that there is no question of monotheism in any real sense. But Aeschylus has devoted that play to the subject of the reconciliation of these gods' past differences and their harmonization in one cosmic system. The last words of the play,

chanted as the Eumenides take up residence in their new lodgings at
Athens, are

> Παλλάδος ἀστοῖς Ζεὺς παντόπτας
> οὖτω Μοῖρά τε συγκατέβα.

> With the citizens of Pallas Zeus the all-seeing
> and Fate have thus come to terms.

We have seen Athena and the Erinyes come to terms on stage, but the
final message is that this new dispensation is a dispensation of Zeus and
Fate—a Zeus and Fate so closely linked that they govern a singular verb.
In general it is a feature of Aeschylean tragedy that the poet interprets the
myths, much more consistently and insistently than epic poets had done,
in religious terms, as case histories of the workings of divine forces.
These forces have various identities, but they operate in a principled way
as parts of a unified system governed by Zeus.

Aeschylus considerably develops the idea of Zeus as Master Mind, lay-
ing a novel emphasis on the depth and profundity of Zeus' thinking. The
Danaids observe that Zeus' wishes are not easy to track down,

> δαῦλοι γὰρ πραπίδων
> δάσκιοί τε τείνου-
> σιν πόροι, κατιδεῖν ἄφραστοι.

> For the paths of his mind
> stretch thick-grown and deep in shadow,
> and cannot be pointed out to the view.[10]

His intellect is vast, insuperable, 'a bottomless vista' (ὄψιν ἄβυσσον).[11]
Mysterious in his designs, but mighty, he is a unique being whose nature
cannot be apprehended but who commands faith.

> Zeus, whoever he may be . . .
> I cannot find a likeness (for him)—
>   though I try everything in the scales—
> save Zeus (himself), if the vain burden of thought
> is truly to be shed.[12]

He alone controls the outcome of events and the fulfilment of human
expectations:

> What of these things is not brought forth by the mind of Zeus?

---

[10] *Supp.* 93–5.   [11] *Supp.* 1049, 1057 f.   [12] *Ag.* 160–6.

What is fulfilled for mortals without Zeus?
What of these things is not divinely ordained?[13]

These and some other features of Aeschylus' Zeus are clearly taken over from Near Eastern theology. Very similar predications can be quoted from the Hebrew poets:

> How great are thy works, Yahweh: very deep are thy thoughts/designs.
>
> He does not tire and he does not grow weary:
> there is no searching out his cleverness.
>
> To whom will you liken El, or what likeness will you set against him?
>
> For who is God apart from Yahweh, or who is a rock except our God?[14]

The Sumerian poet of a hymn to Enlil already describes the complexity of the god's mind in imagery that Aeschylus would not have disdained:

> Enlil, by your skilful planning in intricate designs—
> their inner workings a blur of threads not to be unravelled,
> thread entwined in thread, not to be traced by the eye—
> you excel in your task of divine providence.[15]

In other Sumerian and Akkadian works a god is said to have a heart 'unfathomable as inmost heaven', or an extensive wisdom and a heart so profound (*rūqu*, lit. 'remote') that none of the other gods can grasp it. As Aeschylus' chorus asks 'What is fulfilled for mortals without Zeus?', so in Assyrian and Babylonian hymns we find the formula 'Without him who can do what?' Such parallels confirm that the Greek poets' development from a pantheon of independently minded divine agents towards a quasi-monotheistic régime, in which Zeus is the only real source of divine initiative and the other gods are supporters and executants of his will, is the reflection of a similar but earlier development in the Near Eastern traditions.

It is time to turn to the so-called philosophers, those Greeks of the sixth and fifth centuries who thought critically and constructively about the physical world, the place of gods and souls in it, the relationship between reality and appearance, and the origins and nature of human society.[16] It might be thought that, inasmuch as they were trying to explain the world in terms of intelligible physical principles and laws, it must have

---

[13] *Supp.* 599, *Ag.* 1487–8, cf. *Supp.* 823.
[14] Ps. 92: 6; Isa. 40: 28; 40: 18; Ps. 18: 32 = 2 Sam. 22: 32.
[15] T. Jacobsen, *The Harps that Once . . .* (New Haven, 1987), 109, lines 131–4.
[16] Cf. W. Jaeger, *The Theology of the Early Greek Philosophers* (Oxford, 1947).

been their ambition to eliminate the realm of the unintelligible and capricious, which is the realm of God. To invoke God as an explanation of phenomena is to confess that you do not know how to explain them rationally—unless, that is, you are prepared to supply a rational explanation of God. The Presocratics, however, did try to explain God. What they sought to eliminate from the world was not divinity as such but caprice and the arbitrary events which had formerly been ascribed to divine initiative.

Given this aim, they were bound to discard some aspects of the traditional gods. They had to depersonalize them; they could no longer treat them as beings with humanoid emotions, reactions, and impulses. But instead of rejecting divinity altogether, they sought to locate and identify it in new ways, making a selective use of the traditional names and predicates. Find the unchanging forces and agencies which govern the working of the universe, and there (they considered) you will have the immortal and ageless powers that truly deserve the title of gods.

Among the principles that informed these men's theorizing were economy and coherence. They preferred single causes to multiple ones, and to account for as many of the phenomena as possible with the fewest hypotheses. In theological terms, this meant that the number of gods, at any rate of top-rank gods, should be kept to the minimum, and for a really unified universe there would be much attraction in having one god as the supreme guiding force. I say top-rank gods, because some of these thinkers operate with several different orders of divine being.

As regards Thales' theology, we have only the intriguing report that he said 'everything is full of gods', or 'there are gods everywhere'. This is usually associated with the statement that he held the magnet to have a soul, because it moves iron. Would he have classed this 'soul' as a god? We cannot say; but if these reports are reliable, they at least give an indication that Thales had started on the road of emancipating such terms as 'soul' and 'god' from the limitations of their conventional applications, and making them stand for forces intrinsic to the natural world. On the other hand, they suggest an unlimited plurality of such forces, with no hint of anything pointing towards monotheism. If Thales attributed divinity to the water from which everything came, or to the $\delta i \nu \eta$ by which it must have been possessed, Aristotle has heard nothing of it.

He and we know much more about Anaximander. Anaximander wrote that everything came out of the Infinite. He described this Infinite as encompassing and 'steering' everything ($\pi \acute{\alpha} \nu \tau \alpha \ \kappa \upsilon \beta \epsilon \rho \nu \hat{\alpha} \nu$), and as being 'eternal and unageing' ($\acute{\alpha} \acute{\iota} \delta \iota o \nu \ \kappa \alpha \grave{\iota} \ \acute{\alpha} \gamma \acute{\eta} \rho \omega \nu$). From this last predication Aristotle inferred that Anaximander identified his Infinite as τὸ θεῖον, the divine element in the universe. We do not know whether Anaximander said this explicitly, but he did hold that the Infinite is in ceaseless motion, which leads to the formation of worlds in it. This intrinsic property of perpetual motion, which has no ulterior cause but functions as the driving force of the universe, would seem to make the Infinite a prime candidate for divine status, even though there is no question of its having consciousness or intelligence. Alcmeon of Croton (24 A 12) said that the soul was immortal because it was always in motion and so like immortal and divine things which are in constant motion, such as the sun, moon, stars, and the whole heaven. We might conclude, then, that Anaximander was not only a monist but a monotheist, in that he derived everything from a single divine principle.

However, it is not quite so straightforward as that, because we are also told[17] that he identified as gods the numberless worlds that form and pass away within the Infinite in the course of time, each world being a globular system enclosed by a heaven and with a solid earth at the centre. These gods would not be immortal and ageless, only very long-lived. If the Infinite was the supreme God, we might say that the worlds were the sons of God, born from him and manifesting his powers at the material and local level. In this way we could find a surprising (though perhaps fanciful) structural analogy with the contemporary Hebrew conception of an unfathomable supreme God who communicates with us through Messengers who are perishable divine beings of an inferior order.

There is yet a further candidate for high godhead in Anaximander's system, namely Time. He wrote that all things perish back into what they came out of, by necessity (κατὰ τὸ χρεών), 'for they pay the penalty to each other for their unrighteousness according to Time's ordinance/ assessment' (κατὰ τὴν Χρόνου τάξιν, 12 B 1). Basically this means that the formation of a world or of the things inside it is an imbalance in the Infinite, an 'injustice' which must in due course be corrected. But Anaximander has chosen to express the idea in personalized, theological language. The world-gods, like rebellious Angels, are out of order and will have to pay the penalty. Time is the deity who lays down the law. Is Time the same as the eternal Infinite? It seems clear that Anaximander did not say so, or the doxographers would have told us. He might have found it an interesting suggestion. But as it is, we must allow that he was not overly concerned to concentrate the attributes of divinity on one object.

17 *Placita* and Cicero, A 17.

Anaximander's younger fellow-citizen Anaximenes replaced the
mysterious Infinite by infinite Aer, giving it the same qualities of immortality and perpetual motion leading to the formation of worlds. He
derives everything from a particular material substance, but it is a live
substance, akin to the soul that is in us. That Anaximenes identified it as
divine is stated by one branch of the tradition[18] and is entirely credible.
But some sources[19] say that he spoke of gods who were born from the
Aer. Who or what these were is not recorded, but clearly there is a
parallel with Anaximander's long-life cosmic gods born from the
Infinite. Hippolytus also refers to 'descendants' (ἀπόγονοι) of these
second-order deities, suggesting that the cosmogony was to some extent
cast in the form of a theogony. No monotheism here, then, but again a
unified system in which one supreme divine principle is ultimately
responsible for everything, while lesser divinities have a dependent,
mediating status and a less permanent existence.

If Anaximander's Infinite and Anaximenes' Aer qualify as gods, it is
because they have immortality and unfailing vitality and because they
make things happen; but they are mindless gods. There is no suggestion
that they conceive intelligent designs, or indeed take any thought for
what is happening, what is going to happen, or what should happen.
Other philosophers soon supply this element, taking us back closer to
the poetic concept of the Master Mind who plans ahead. The philosopher's god, though, could not be anthropomorphic.

The first we know of who made this explicit was Xenophanes. He
ridiculed Homer and Hesiod for their accounts of gods who practised
thieving, adultery, and mutual deception, and he exposed the folly of
men's conceiving the gods in their own image, arguing that if horses and
cows were capable of producing paintings and sculptures, they would
represent the gods as horses and cows.[20]

It is in Xenophanes that we first encounter what was later to become
a significant religious slogan: εἷς θεός, One God. This sounds like a

18 Placita and Cicero, 13 A 10.
19 Hippolytus, A 7 § 1; Augustine, A 10.
20 DK 21 B 11–16. On the last point I think Xenophanes was wrong. I feel sure that the
domestic cat, for instance, does not conceive of a feline deity but identifies his or her owner
as the supreme power in the world, providing each day his daily bread, capable of project-
ing articles through the air, of opening or closing the most massive and unyielding doors,
of turning a room in an instant from light to dark or from dark to light, a controller of
heat sources, no doubt also responsible for day and night, sunshine and rain. It is by no
means self-evident that it was natural for man from the beginning to conceive his gods in
human form. Many peoples ascribe divinity to animals, which, after all, are often more
mysterious, unpredictable, and terrible than other humans.

declaration of monotheism; only the line goes on ἕν τε θεοῖσι καὶ ἀνθρώποισι μέγιστος. 'One god, the greatest among gods and men.' So this god is not the only god that exists, but a god who towers above the rest. This is a pattern we are becoming accustomed to. Xenophanes goes on to say that this supreme god is not like mortals either physically or mentally, οὔ τι δέμας θνητοῖσιν ὁμοίιος οὐδὲ νόημα. According to three further hexameter fragments which are likely to come from the same context (21 B 24–26), the god sees and hears with his whole being; by means of his mind, without effort, he shakes everything; he stays always in the same place, motionless, for it does not befit him to travel about. Here, all of a sudden, is the Unmoved Mover, a mighty Mind with no moving parts that controls matter. Yet there is mention of other gods, not only in the line I have just quoted, but in others too. Xenophanes says that 'the gods have not revealed everything to mortals from the beginning', and that 'no man has ever known or ever will know for sure about the gods and all the things I speak about' (B 18, 34).

Heraclitus thought Xenophanes a fool; but he had his own version of the brainy supreme god. Here for the first time we find intellect without sex: not a male θεός but a neuter σοφόν, a Wisdom or Skill which is unitary (ἕν) and exists independently of everything else, πάντων κεχωρισμένον (B 108). It does and does not want to be called by the name of Zeus (B 32); in other words, it has certain attributes which might justify its equation with the traditional Zeus, but not others. In two further fragments, both unfortunately corrupt, Heraclitus seems to be saying that this ἕν σοφόν knows everything, or knows that knowledge which steers everything through everything (B 41, 50). Elsewhere (B 64) he said that everything is steered by the thunderbolt, κεραυνός, or (according to Philodemus' version of the fragment) by the thunderbolt and Zeus. The thunderbolt was the traditional instrument of Zeus' will, and at the same time it is presumably to be associated with Heraclitus' concept of the world as an ever-living fire (B 30). The combination suggests that the disembodied intelligence, the ἕν σοφόν, manages and directs the world by directing a fiery pulse through the universe, and this is assimilated to Zeus sending his thunderbolt.

Again we seem to be close to monotheism; but again the picture is confused by references to other gods. We hear of Erinyes who monitor the movements of the sun. They are the agents of Dike, who is the embodiment of cosmic balance (B 94). Dike is identified with Eris, Conflict, which Heraclitus regarded as essential to the maintenance of the cosmos (B 80). He speaks of Polemos in the same sense, as king and father of all, a power which makes some into gods and others into men, some slaves and others free (B 53). He mentions Dionysus and Hades, stating that they are really the same (B 15). He says that gods and men honour those slain in battle (B 24). He criticizes people who pray to statues, 'as if one were to hold conversation with a house, not recognizing what gods or heroes are' (B 5). 'Immortals are mortals, mortals are immortals, these living out the death of those and being dead for the duration of their life' (B 62). I have not the time or the stomach to discuss the question of how many of these statements are genuinely theological, or how they are all to be fitted into one system. But it is clear that we cannot call Heraclitus a monotheist without qualification.

In both Heraclitus and Anaximander we have met the notion that the world is 'steered' (κυβερνᾶν) by a divine power. 'Steer' must not be understood too literally; it was not a matter of turning the universe to port or starboard, but of guiding cosmic events in chosen directions. Parmenides, in his account of the phenomenal world, the δόξαι βρότειαι, refers to a goddess who steers everything, a δαίμων ἣ πάντα κυβερνᾷ (B 12). She is located in the middle of a system of circles of fire and darkness, and she rules over all birth and mixture by bringing male and female together. The *Placita* tradition identifies her as Dike or Ananke, figures whom Parmenides names elsewhere, but in view of her matchmaking activities it is plausible to equate her with Aphrodite, as Plutarch seems to have done. Another fragment (B 13) is quoted from a cosmogonic context, in which 'first of all the gods she contrived Eros'. 'Contrived' translates μητίσατο, which implies creation by the exercise of mental power or ingenuity. Once again we have to reckon with a hierarchy of gods. There is a first-order deity who is credited with steering everything; for Parmenides it is love that makes the world go round, not lightning. But there is also a category of lesser deities created by the goddess of love. And there are the figures of Dike and Ananke, who exercise cosmic power on a wide scale but whose relationship to Aphrodite we cannot define and Parmenides may well have left undefined.

Parmenides' poem has a number of points of contact with the oldest of the Orphic theogonies, the one which in my study of the Orphica I have called the Protogonos Theogony. I have argued that, whether or not Parmenides knew it, it was composed at the same period as his poem and in a related area of tradition.[21] Now, a theogony by definition relates the births of a whole series of gods; one cannot have a monotheistic theogony. But in this Orphic one a remarkable thing happened. On

---

[21] *The Orphic Poems* (Oxford, 1983), 8–92, 109 f.

succeeding Cronus as king of heaven, Zeus swallowed Protogonos or Phanes, the bisexual god who first appeared from the cosmic egg with the seed of the gods inside him or her. By swallowing him, Zeus swallowed the universe. At once

> all the immortals became one with him, the blessed gods and goddesses
> and rivers and lovely springs and everything else
> that then existed: he became the only one.

There followed a hymnic passage about Zeus in which stood the verses:

> Zeus was born first, Zeus last, god of the bright bolt:
> Zeus is the head, Zeus the middle, from Zeus are all things made . . .
> Zeus is the king, Zeus the ruler of all, god of the bright bolt.

Zeus then re-created the gods and the world out of himself. He 'brought them up from his holy heart'; the poet's phrase suggests the execution of an intelligent design.[22] In this poem, then, there is still a full pantheon of gods, but they have all become creatures and emanations of Zeus, after an episode in which he was temporarily the only god.

This extraordinary story of a god who absorbs the universe into himself and then regenerates it from out of himself is evidently one of the models that inspired Empedocles. In Empedocles' system the four divine elements which represent the totality of matter are periodically absorbed under the influence of Love into one uniform mass, becoming a single god called Sphairos, the Sphere. This rotund divinity 'rejoices in his circular solitude', until the return of Dissension sends tremors through his body and the separating elements begin to take the shapes of all the beings that are now in the world (B 27–31).

Empedocles has taken over something of the pattern of the Orphic story, but his theology is differently balanced. The Sphere that takes the gods into himself is a bigger god, but not a controlling agent. He is not Zeus, for Zeus is identified with one of the four elements. He is a poor, passive figure and a short-lived one, his self-satisfaction rudely shaken as the seismic waves of Strife course through him and he starts to crack up. A monotheism based on him would soon leave us in the lurch.

Empedocles is not, after all, a monist in the way that Anaximenes is. For Empedocles four elements, earth, air, fire, and water, represent the irreducible minimum stock of ingredients for the cosmic cake. Each of them is identified with a different god; so there is an irreducible minimum of four gods. In fact there are others besides these. There are Love

---

[22] *P. Derveni* xvi [formerly xii] 3–6, xvii–xix + fr. 21a Kern.

and Strife, who govern the relations of Zeus, Hera, and the other
elemental gods, not by sporadic assaults as in Homer but in regular alter-
nation according to the terms of a treaty. There is also a general class of
θεοὶ δολιχαίωνες, long-life gods, included among the things produced by
the mixture of the elements, together with trees, men and women,
animals, birds, and fishes (B 21. 9 ff.). These are the gods whose mis-
behaviour can condemn them to 30,000 years of incarnation in animal
and vegetable bodies (B 115). In one fragment (B 134) Empedocles
describes a god who does not have human form—no head, no arms, no
feet, no knees, no hairy genitals—but consists simply of a marvellous
holy mind, darting across the whole universe with its swift thoughts.
This may remind us of Xenophanes' and Heraclitus' accounts of a
disembodied intelligence; but they were speaking of a unique being,
whereas Empedocles' description may have been applicable to any of
the long-life gods. Ammonius, who quotes the fragment, says it refers
primarily to Apollo, but likewise to divinity in general.

The philosopher who first gives us a clear statement of the role of the
controlling Mind in the material universe is Anaxagoras, who was a
little older than Empedocles. Like Heraclitus, he emphasizes that Mind
or Intellect is something separate from everything else. He says it is
unlimited, unalloyed, homogeneous, eternal, autonomous, the finest
and purest of all substances, with knowledge of everything and the
greatest power, governing all living beings, and responsible for initiating
the rotation of the cosmos, which led to the separation of all things from
the original mixture and continues to be productive in the same way.
Every combination or separation has been decided by Mind (πάντα ἔγνω
νοῦς); whatever kinds of thing were to be, or were and are no longer, or
are now, or will be in the future, all have been organized by Mind (πάντα
διεκόσμησε νοῦς) (59 B 12).

Here we have a single power, uniquely responsible for shaping
the world we know. There is no mention of other gods. We might
say that here at last is a clear case of a monotheistic system, except
that it is difficult to justify treating Anaxagoras' Nous as divine. He does
give it some godlike attributes: it is everlasting, powerful, and subject to
no higher power; it intervenes in the world according to its own judgement. On the other hand he makes it quite clear that it is a material
substance, differing from other substances in being λεπτότατόν τε
πάντων χρημάτων καὶ καθαρώτατον, the most rarefied and the purest of
all things. It is unique in not combining with other substances, though it
is *in* some things, namely living creatures. We may say that it is fulfilling

the role of a god, being invoked by Anaxagoras to account for what he cannot explain by means of physical mechanisms; only he is doing his best to portray its activity *as* a physical mechanism, and he avoids calling it 'divine' or applying predicates strongly associated with divinity such as 'immortal and ageless'. He did, after all, attain notoriety as a thorough-going scientific rationalist who went about reducing the supernatural to the natural and whose doctrines made him vulnerable to the charge of impiety or actual atheism (cf. A 17 etc.). Nevertheless, theistic or not, his system interestingly illustrates the tendency to look for a single, intelligent governing power in the world.

The cosmology of Diogenes of Apollonia, which formed the prologue to his treatise on human physiology, stands very much in the tradition of Anaximenes, with air as the primary element from which everything else is constituted. We saw that Anaximenes regarded his Aer as divine, but that he also accorded divine status to the products of Aer, and indeed to more than one generation of them. In Diogenes' case the identification of Aer with God is more absolute, and we are fortunate enough to have his reasoning on the point. It is by breathing air that human and other animals live: this is their soul and consciousness ($\psi\upsilon\chi\grave{\eta}$ $\kappa\alpha\grave{\iota}$ $\nu\acute{o}\eta\sigma\iota\varsigma$).

> And it seems to me that the carrier of consciousness is what people call air, and that all are steered by this element and it has power over all. For this is precisely what seems to me to be God, and to extend everywhere and dispose everything and be in everything; there is nothing at all that does not have a share of it, though nothing has a share in it in the same way as anything else, there being many forms both of air itself and of consciousness. (64 B 5)

Diogenes considers that the world shows evidence of intelligent design; for without $\nu\acute{o}\eta\sigma\iota\varsigma$, he says, 'it would not have been possible for things to be so distributed as to preserve the balance in everything, winter and summer, night and day, rains and winds and fine spells. And for the rest, if one cares to consider, one will find that they are arranged in the finest possible way.'[23] These meteorological phenomena are of course conditions of the air, and it is Aer itself that is responsible for their orderly planning.

Like Anaxagoras, Diogenes connects mind or consciousness with a material element, but he differs from him in identifying this element as one of which we have direct perception, namely air, and in calling it God. Is this the only god? We are told that Diogenes commended Homer

---

[23] DK 64 B 3. On the Argument from Design in the 5th cent. see R. C. T. Parker, 'The Origins of Pronoia: A Mystery', in *Apodosis: Essays Presented to Dr W. W. Cruickshank to Mark his Eightieth Birthday* (London, 1992), 84–94.

for speaking of the divine not just in mythical but in real terms, for he held that when Homer spoke of Zeus and of Zeus' omniscience he meant the air. Now, allegorical interpreters of Homer usually had explanations for all the Homeric gods, not just one. So we wonder whether Diogenes had other equivalences for other gods. That would imply that on one level, at least, he was prepared to acquiesce in a polytheistic construct. On the other hand we may be sure that in his interpretation of Homer the dominance of Aer was absolute and all other powers subordinate.

The idea of a divine agency which has organized the world with intelligent forethought appears also in Herodotus. He tells of the flying snakes of Arabia, which would overrun the world if it were not that the female has the salutary habit of biting through the male's throat at the climax of mating, and that the unborn young avenge their father by eating their way out of the mother and destroying her in the process. Herodotus here digresses with the observation that divine Providence (τοῦ θείου ἡ προνοίη, literally 'the forethought of the divine'), being σοφή, has seen to it that all those species which are timorous and edible are also prolific, so that they do not die out from being eaten, while those which are tough and disagreeable have few offspring (3. 108 f.).

This theory might be thought to imply belief in a single God; but it does not. The Greeks were quite capable of combining the Argument from Design with polytheistic language, as we see from two well-known passages in Xenophon's *Memorabilia* (1. 4; 4. 3). Socrates argues for theism from the usefulness of each part of the human body, the existence of life-preserving instincts, the order of the heavens, and so on, but he says things like 'the gods have made man, alone of all creatures, to stand upright . . . they have given other creatures legs, but to man they have given arms too . . . they give us light to see by'. He does not stick to the plural consistently but moves easily between οἱ θεοί and ὁ θεός, as well as using the less specific term τὸ θεῖον, which means something like 'the divine element in the world' without commitment as between a singularity or plurality of powers. Herodotus too, in different contexts, uses οἱ θεοί, ὁ θεός, or τὸ θεῖον, without a significant doctrinal difference.

These terms are typical of the fifth century, and can be paralleled in the Hippocratic corpus and in tragedy. Whenever some theological truth is formulated, some statement about the régime under which mankind lives, the writer typically does not name one of the traditional gods but says οἱ θεοί or ὁ θεός (in tragedy commonly without the article). The indifference as between singular and plural is possible because when someone says 'the gods', the assumption is that these gods act as a unanimous body. Because of the force of tradition there was no hurry to discard polytheistic language, and yet there was a general disposition to see the divine regimen as unified and purposeful. This was a situation in which monotheism could develop without causing upset.

It is time to recapitulate. All the ancient cultures were polytheistic from the earliest times for which there is evidence, and there is no reason to imagine that at some earlier stage of human history monotheism had prevailed. When people started postulating unseen agencies to explain phenomena, they naturally attributed one kind of phenomenon to one agency and other kinds to others.

So long as different gods act at different times and in different contexts, there need be no conflict among them. But once people imagine them living together in one divine society, the question arises whether their individual wills and interests clash, or whether they all agree on what is to be done. In Near Eastern literature from at least the early second millennium, and in Homeric poetry in the first, we find the *fable convenue* of the assembly of the gods at which courses of action are established. In this forum the poet can show that the individual gods do indeed disagree over some matters, and the clash of their wills can be represented dramatically. On the other hand the clash has to be resolved, because the story can only accommodate one sequence of events. There are essentially two ways of achieving this: the monarchic way and the democratic way. Either there is one god powerful enough to impose his will on the rest—in this case the independent status of the rest is compromised, and they become the chief god's agents and representatives— or the gods' debate issues in consensus, and we arrive at the concept of the plural pantheon with a united policy.

Already in the second millennium it was common to exalt one god as supreme and to represent the others as having willingly subordinated themselves to him after he had definitively defeated his and their enemies. This points the way towards the Hesiodic or Aeschylean scenario as opposed to the Homeric: a scenario in which the various deities work together as members of a unified organization enacting the designs of Zeus, the Master Mind.

The philosophers' search for economical explanations of the universe naturally led to economy in the assumption of divine principles, with in some cases a single divine element or entity being identified as responsible for the formation, design, or direction of the world. Yet it is difficult to find a Presocratic who can be counted as a monotheist without qualification. They nearly all admit some sort of hierarchy of 'divine' beings, or they feel the need to accommodate conventional names of gods, even if only with figurative or allegorical value. The non-philosophical writers of the fifth century also continued, under the influence of tradition and habit, to speak of 'the gods', while increasingly thinking in terms of a unitary divine will and even a purposefully designed universe. At the same time they will sometimes speak of ὁ θεός in the singular—avoiding identification with any of the old named gods—or still more non-committally of τὸ θεῖον.

It was a small step from here to dogmatic monotheism; but there was no pressure or haste to take that step. People are slow to adjust their religion to their philosophy.

SELECT BIBLIOGRAPHY

AESCHYLUS, *Tragoediae*, ed. M. L. West (Stuttgart, 1990).

DALLEY, S., *Myths from Mesopotamia* (Oxford, 1989).

DIELS, H., *Die Fragmente der Vorsokratiker*, 5th edn. by W. Kranz (Berlin, 1934–5).

FALKENSTEIN, A., and VON SODEN, W., *Sumerische und akkadische Hymnen und Gebete* (Zurich, 1953).

GIBSON, J. C. L., *Textbook of Syrian Semitic Inscriptions*, 3 vols. (Oxford, 1971–82).

HAAS, H., 'Der Zug zum Monotheismus in den homerischen Epen und in den Dichtungen des Hesiod, Pindar, und Aeschylos', *Archiv für Religionswissenschaft* 3 (1900), 52–78, 153–83.

HESIOD, *Theogony* and *Works and Days*, trans. M. L. West (Oxford, 1988).

JACOBSEN, T., *The Harps that Once . . . Sumerian Poetry in Translation* (New Haven and London, 1987).

JAEGER, W., *The Theology of the Early Greek Philosophers* (Oxford, 1947).

KELLENS, J., and PIRART, E., *Les Textes vieil-avestiques*, 3 vols. (Wiesbaden, 1988–91).

LICHTHEIM, M., *Ancient Egyptian Literature: A Book of Readings*, 3 vols. (Berkeley and Los Angeles, 1973–80).

MULLEN, E. T., *The Divine Council in Canaanite and Early Hebrew Literature* (Cambridge, Mass., 1980).

PARKER, R. C. T., 'The Origins of Pronoia: A Mystery', in *Apodosis: Essays presented to Dr W. W. Cruickshank to Mark his Eightieth Birthday* (London, 1992), 84–94.

SEUX, M.-J., *Hymnes et prières aux dieux de Babylonie et d'Assyrie* (Paris, 1976).

TALLQVIST, K., *Akkadische Götterepitheta* (Helsinki, 1938).

WEST, M. L., *The Orphic Poems* (Oxford, 1983).

—— *The East Face of Helicon* (Oxford, 1997).

ZELLER, E., *Die Entwicklung des Monotheismus bei den Griechen* (Stuttgart, 1862).

2

Monotheism and Pagan Philosophy in Later Antiquity

MICHAEL FREDE

There is a temptation to think that one thing which ultimately distinguished Christians from pagans in antiquity was that the Christians, following the Jews, believed in one God, whereas the pagans believed in many gods. Sometimes this is expressed by saying that the Christians were monotheists, while the pagans were polytheists. Obviously, even in antiquity, Christians were tempted to present matters as if they believed in one God, whereas the pagans believed in many gods. This is the way matters are presented, for instance, by Marius Victorinus.

Marius Victorinus in his short treatise *De homoousio recipiendo*, a few lines into the first paragraph, says: 'The Greeks, whom they call Hellenes or pagans, talk of many gods, the Jews or Hebrews of one, but we, as truth and grace have come later, against the pagans talk of one God, against the Jews of the Father and the Son.'

It seems to me that both the Christian and the pagan positions are a good deal more complex than this simple contrast would suggest. But in what follows I will not discuss the position or the positions of the pagans in late antiquity generally, but focus on the vast majority of philosophers in late antiquity. I will argue that, as far as the question whether there is one God or whether there are many gods is concerned, it is extremely difficult, if not impossible, to distinguish between the Christian position and the position of Plato, Aristotle, Zeno, and their followers in later antiquity and thus the vast majority of philosophers in late antiquity.

However, before we look at the Platonists, the Peripatetics, and the Stoics, let us very briefly consider the other major groups of philosophers in later and late antiquity.

The Epicureans had no difficulty in believing in any number of gods. But it was crucial for them to insist that we and these gods have nothing to do with each other, that these gods have not the slightest inclination to destroy their bliss by meddling in human affairs, even if they could interfere, and that hence it is completely irrational to believe that we have anything to fear from them, in this or a supposed afterlife, or that we could expect any help from them or could gain their benevolence by worshipping them. The existence of the gods is simply irrelevant to our lives. This critical attitude of the Epicureans in religious matters must have contributed significantly to their extinction in late antiquity.

There is little of substance to say about the Cynics, except perhaps that they apparently tended to reject traditional religion. Demonax was accused of impiety for refusing to worship Athena, and Oenomaus criticized the oracles, but also sorcery.

Then there were the Sceptics, first the Academics and then the Pyrrhoneans. It was part of their radical scepticism not only to think that they did not know the truth concerning the gods, but even not to know what to believe about them. So in this sense they certainly did not believe in any gods, let alone in many gods. Some of them, though, like Sextus Empiricus, thought that this was perfectly compatible with worshipping the gods of one's forefathers. Given that one had to do something—either to continue in joining the cult of the traditional gods of one's community or to refuse to do so—and given that reason offered no guidance one way or the other, it seemed most sensible simply to continue to do what everybody in one's community since times immemorial had been doing.

But there were also representatives of a form of mitigated scepticism, introduced into the Academy by Philo of Larissa and Metrodorus, whose most familiar representative is Cicero. Through Cicero's later influence in the Latin world, especially among those in the Latin world who had little or no direct access to Greek thought, this mitigated form of scepticism also continued to find its adherents long after it had been given up by philosophers. Augustine, for instance, was attracted to it for many years. A sceptic of this kind would still insist that we do not know the truth about the gods, but he would think that his scepticism was perfectly compatible with the assumption that one had some rational justification for believing certain things, for instance, for believing that there are certain divine beings.

Minucius Felix in his *Octavius*, a dialogue between a pagan and a Christian in which the pagan is won over to Christianity, represents the pagan Caecilius as holding a position of such mitigated scepticism. Caecilius argues that the truth in matters divine is hidden and impossible to know. But, given that there are cults with an ancient tradition, it seems most reasonable to believe in and worship the gods of these traditional cults. Against this Minucius Felix has Octavius argue that, looking at the world and the way it is organized, it seems much more reasonable to believe in one God who providentially governs the universe.

There are various things which are noteworthy or even puzzling about this dialogue. One thing to note is that, if we set aside Epicureanism, whose adherents did not worship any gods, the position espoused by Caecilius is the only philosophical or at least philosophically inspired position in late antiquity I am aware of which reasonably straightforwardly corresponds to our conception of polytheism. Caecilius does believe in and worship many traditional gods, in part precisely because his scepticism, however mitigated it may be, prevents him from committing himself to a more theoretical, more speculative conception of matters divine. In this he is completely unrepresentative of the attitude of philosophers in late antiquity, but, I suspect, also of the general attitude of the educated elite at least in the East. Platonists, Peripatetics, and Stoics all took the position Octavius tries to persuade Caecilius of, namely that there is one God who providentially governs the universe.

Now the phrase 'belief in one God who governs the universe' hides a certain ambiguity, and one might argue that everything turns on this ambiguity. One might argue that the Platonists, the Peripatetics, and the Stoics believe in one highest god who governs the universe, but that they also believe in many other gods. By contrast, one will say, the Christians believe in one and only one God, namely the being which governs the universe. And one will rightly insist that to believe in one highest god is not the same as to believe in one God, even if this highest god should be conceived of in such a lofty fashion as to be thought of as governing the whole universe.

But the matter, primarily for two reasons, is more complicated than this. In the first place, the Platonists, the Peripatetics, and the Stoics do not just believe in one highest god, they believe in something which they must take to be unique even as a god. For they call it 'God' or even '*the* God', as if in some crucial way it was the only thing which deserved to be called 'god'.[1] If, thus, they also believe that there are further beings which can be called 'divine' or 'god', they must have thought that these further beings could be called 'divine' only in some less strict, diminished, or derived sense. Second, the Christians themselves speak not only of the one true God, but also of a plurality of beings which can

---

[1] e.g. Plotinus, *Enn.* 6. 8. 1, line 19 in conjunction with lines 1 and 6.

be called 'divine' or 'god'; for instance, the un-fallen angels or redeemed and saved human beings.

I will return later to the Christian position and to a comparison between it and the position of our philosophers. We have to consider first the position of these philosophers in more detail. Their theology—even in its, for our purposes, most crucial respects—is a vast and complicated subject, and my discussion will therefore be determined more than I would like by considerations of expediency of exposition, mainly of brevity. As a matter of such expediency I begin by considering Aristotle's position.

As is well known, Aristotle in the *Metaphysics* is concerned to identify the ultimate principles of what there is. *Metaphysics Lambda*, presumably originally an independent treatise, makes a fresh start in this endeavour. It is also well known that Aristotle elsewhere, but in particular in *Metaphysics Lambda*, identifies as one of these first principles (indeed in some sense as *the* first principle) the so-called unmoved mover. On this principle, he claims in *Λ*7, 1072^{b}13–14, the heaven and the whole of nature depend. He goes on to refer to this principle as ὁ θεός, 'the God' (1072^{b}25, 28–9, 30). This is what tradition came to regard as Aristotle's God.

This traditional interpretation, however, has been rejected by Ingemar Düring,[2] and since these objections are highly relevant to our concerns, we should take time to consider them. Düring claims that ὁ θεός here cannot refer to a single and unique god, but must be referring to the whole class of divine beings; Aristotle is supposed to use the phrase 'the god' collectively, just as one might talk about 'the French farmer' or 'the tax-payer', not referring to a single and unique individual, but to any and every number of a group of persons, or to them as a group (p. 214).

To assume otherwise, Düring argues (p. 219), is to fall prey to a grievous anachronism, namely to suppose that Aristotle was concerned with the issue of monotheism versus polytheism. He quotes Eduard Meyer who remarks that the Greeks were interested in the question whether there are gods, but hardly in the question whether there is one or whether there are many gods.[3] He goes on to claim that to assume that Aristotle is talking of one God when he speaks of 'the god' is to follow a

---

[2] I. Düring, *Aristotle* (Heidelberg, 1966).
[3] This, incidentally, is a point often repeated in the literature, e.g. by Guthrie in his comments on Xenophanes (W. K. C. Guthrie, *A History of Greek Philosophy*, i (Cambridge, 1962), 375).

'medieval interpretatio Christiana'. The suggestion is that Aristotle could not be speaking of one God, since the issue of whether god is one or many arises only with Judaism and Christianity.

To begin with a minute point, we find here the romantic association of Christianity with the Middle Ages, as if Christianity were not a thoroughly ancient phenomenon, one without which antiquity would not be fully understood, and one which would not be fully understood, at least historically, without understanding its origins in antiquity. There is a more important point, namely the close association made here between monotheism and Judaism or Christianity, as if one had to be confronted with Judaism or Christianity to think of the possibility, and conceive of a reason, to assume that there is just one god. This is obviously mistaken. Antisthenes for instance, as the Christians were well aware, claimed that in reality there is just one god.

It is also untrue that this is exclusively the medieval Christian interpretation of Aristotle; it is already the ancient pagan learned understanding of Aristotle. And this is not surprising, as it so obviously is the correct interpretation. Aristotle begins his argument in Λ6 with the assumption that, since time does not have a beginning or an end, there must be something which always has been and always will be moving in a circle. He goes on to argue that this never-ending motion can only be explained if we assume that there is something which itself is not subject to motion or change and which causes this motion. But it would be a mistake to assume that this is Aristotle's argument for the so-called unmoved mover. It is just an argument which purports to show that there must be objects which unceasingly are in motion and that such a motion in each case has to be explained in terms of an eternal object which itself is not in motion. In fact, it turns out in chapter 8, as Aristotle hinted in chapter 6, 1071^{b}20–2, that there are quite a number of such eternally moving objects, and hence quite a number of such unmoved movers. What Aristotle primarily is concerned to show is not that such eternally moving objects have a certain kind of principle and explanation, but that there is one unique principle which is a principle of everything there is, and in this sense the principle of everything there is. He does so by showing in the second part of chapter 6 and in chapter 7 that there is one object which eternally moves in a circle on whose motion the motions of all other eternally moving objects—and indeed all other motions and changes—depend, namely the heaven of the fixed stars. It follows, given what he has argued at the beginning of chapter 6, that this motion can only be explained in terms of an unmoved mover. It is this first unmoved mover which he then goes on in chapter 7 to identify as the God.

It should be obvious that it is difficult enough to follow Aristotle in the assumption that the motions of the heavenly spheres each require an unmoved mover. It is impossible to see why Aristotle should compound his difficulties by assuming that there are any number of gods who are involved in moving the one first heaven of the fixed stars. Indeed, Aristotle explains at 8, 1074^{a}36–7 why this first mover has to be numerically one, rather than just one kind of thing, possibly instantiated by any number of things. He also explains (e.g. 10, 1075^{a}11) that the relation between God and the world is rather like that of a general to his army: it is a good general who makes for a good army, rather than the other way round. The simile does not make much sense, unless we assume that Aristotle thinks of the God as an individual. For though there are many armies and perhaps some good armies and hence some good generals, there is just one world which, if we follow Aristotle, needs one God. Nor does the final sentence of *Met. Λ* (1076^{a}3–4) make any sense on Düring's interpretation 'What there is does not want to be governed badly' (οὐκ ἀγαθὸν πολυκοιρανίη· εἷς κοίρανος).

Hence, I conclude that when Aristotle talks about 'the God' he does not use the phrase in that vague sense we sometimes find in classical times in which it might be used interchangeably with τὸ θεῖον and οἱ θεοί to refer to a vaguely conceived divine source of the order of things. On the contrary, Aristotle does mean to talk about one particular being which governs the world. There must be some deep-rooted prejudice at work, if one wants to deny this in the face of all the evidence to the contrary.

But Aristotle's text also allows us to see a crucial point which Düring seems to miss entirely, namely, why, long before the issue of monotheism versus polytheism arose, Greek philosophers had very good reason to assume that there is one unique God who is the, or an, ultimate principle of what there is. Aristotle quite rightly thinks that philosophy from its very beginnings had consisted in an attempt to identify the principles of reality and to explain whatever there is in terms of these. Aristotle in the *Metaphysics* also points out quite rightly that philosophers originally identified these principles with the ultimate material constituents of things, in terms of which they then tried to explain the phenomena. But it is also not surprising that some philosophers should have thought that an explanation just in terms of elementary or basic material constituents was bound to fail: some bits of earth, air, fire, and water do not in themselves suffice to explain the existence of an object, let alone its behaviour. An object which behaves in a certain way must have a certain structure or organization imposed on its material constituents. It is only because the material is thus organized that the object thus constituted can behave in its characteristic way. Moreover, one might think, it takes something or somebody to impose this structure or order on the material. And one might finally think that at least in some cases the behaviour of an object is to be understood in terms of the end it tries or is meant to achieve, or the good it aims at. Against this background we readily understand Socrates' remarks in the methodological section in Plato's *Phaedo*. Socrates complains that natural philosophers talk as if one could understand Socrates' behaviour in terms of his physical constituents. And he reports how delighted he was when he first heard of Anaxagoras' theory of a cosmic intellect, only to be bitterly disappointed when he found out that Anaxagoras, having introduced such an intellect, then continued to explain the world in terms of its material constituents.

For our purposes it suffices to point out that it lies in the very nature of the enterprise in which Thales, Anaximander, and later philosophers were engaged that, sooner or later, somebody would claim, and that many would follow him in claiming, that to explain the world we not only need some ultimate material principle or principles but also an agent who imposes an order on this material. It is in this spirit that Plato in the *Timaeus* introduces a demiurge who, looking at the forms or ideas, imposes the order determined or defined by the ideas on matter, a position later doxography summarizes by saying that according to Plato there are three principles: God, the ideas, and matter. And it is for similar reasons that the Stoics say that there are two ultimate principles, an active and a passive one, God and matter.

It also lies in the very nature of the enterprise that one tries to explain the world in terms of as few principles as possible. The principles themselves, moreover, must be such that they themselves do not stand in need of further explanation. For they are supposed to constitute the final answer to any question. Given this, it would ruin the whole enterprise to assume more than one principle which is divine, unless there turns out to be some special reason for this. A pressure is generated by the very nature of the enterprise to have either no God or a God whose postulation has enough explanatory power for there to be no need to postulate further gods as ultimate active principles. Having a number of them would create immediate pressure to try to reduce them to an ulterior single divine principle. Thus, if one does postulate an intelligent agent as an ultimate principle at all, one will try to postulate a unique, single agent of sufficient power, unless there are overwhelming considerations to the contrary. This will be done for the same reason as one will try to get away with postulating fire as one element, rather than a whole number of irreducibly different kinds of fire. Hence, though it is perfectly true that Aristotle did not have to concern himself with the question of monotheism versus polytheism, he, like Plato before him and philosophers like the Stoics after him, had a precise reason to assume that there was one particular, individual, active principle which governs the world.

We may ask why such an active principle should be regarded as divine. Here it will be relevant that even the first philosophers of nature, when they tried to explain how everything had arisen out of such stuff as their *arche* or their *archai*, used the language appropriate to the divine for their first principles. Presumably this has something to do with the fact that their accounts were meant to replace creation stories. Second, it lies in the nature of a first principle, as the philosophers quickly came to see, that it is not subject to generation and corruption itself and hence in this sense is immortal. Third, an active principle was seen as an intelligent, indeed wise, agent, being not only immortal but also, in his wisdom, not beset by the troubles and confusions we mortals suffer from and thus enjoying a life of never-ending bliss. Tellingly, it is only after Aristotle in *Λ*7 has explained that his first unmoved mover is an intellect enjoying an eternal life of bliss that he identifies him as the God (1072^{b}24–30).

It may be noted in passing that Aristotle seems to go out of his way to characterize this divine principle as a living, thinking being. This should be enough to set aside another prejudice, namely, the view that, though ancient pagan thought may have moved in the direction of postulating one supreme God, this God was conceived of more as an abstract principle than as a concrete person. There is nothing impersonal about Aristotle's God, or the God of the Stoics, or the God of Numenius or Plotinus.

What we have said explains why Aristotle regards the first unmoved mover as a god; it also explains why he regards the first unmoved move as a unique individual. We need numerically only one item in our ontology to fulfil the role of a first principle of this kind, and, in the absence of particular reasons to the contrary, there does not seem any place or justification for more than one item of this kind. And this already in itself goes some way to explain the special status of the first unmoved mover as a divine being. But to the extent that we regard a god not only as a living, intelligent being which is immortal and enjoys eternal bliss, but also as a source of order and goodness, and as of some power, the first unmoved mover also, in this regard, has a not only very elated but a unique status. As the principle of everything it is, according to Aristotle, the ultimate source of all order and goodness in the world. And Aristotle explicitly attributes unlimited power to it. So when Aristotle talks about the God, he means one particular divine being whose status, even as a divine being, is so unique that it can be called 'the God'.

It is perhaps not entirely inappropriate to dwell on this point for a moment. Any theory which postulates one divine being as a first principle automatically puts the status of all other beings one may want to call 'divine' into a perspective in which their divinity appears limited, subordinate, derived. So, for instance, the traditional gods will appear at best as very derivative beings with a highly subordinate role to play in the general order of things. Indeed, given the way philosophers conceive of the order of things and the derivation of subordinate beings from first principles, no philosopher accepts the traditional gods as they are traditionally represented. Aristotle, for instance, at the end of chapter 8 of *Metaphysics Lambda* explains that the traditional stories about the gods are due to the fact that our ancestors grasped that nature is governed by the divine and that there are gods, namely immaterial substances, but that they cast these simple truths into the form of the traditional myths. Otherwise ordinary people would not have accepted these simple truths. Their belief in these traditional stories also serves an important social function, for instance in that it makes people more inclined to abide by the laws. Even if the order of things envisaged leaves room for beings which can be called 'divine', it is clear that they will be so fundamentally derivative and subordinate to the God that, for instance, talk of a 'highest God' is in some ways quite misleading. For the relation between a first principle and those things which depend on the principle involves a much more radical subordination than that involved in a pantheon or hierarchy of gods with one god at the apex. A fortiori, the analogy with Zeus is somewhat misleading. The relation between the first principle and other divine beings is quite unlike the relation between Zeus and, for instance, the other Olympian gods. It would be quite misleading to say that somebody who believes in one divine first principle and five further divine beings believes in six gods. To say this would be to disregard the categorial difference between first principles and the things derived from them. This becomes particularly clear if we consider the Platonist position. The demands Platonists tend to make on first principles are so stringent that most Platonists come to insist that God cannot be regarded as a being, let alone as a further being, as one further item on a list of things which are. Hence, if one talks of a first principle as 'the God', and yet allows for other things to be called 'god', the predicate 'god' here will not be used in the same way or sense. It is for this reason that Aristotle can call the first unmoved mover 'the God' and then go on to talk of other beings as gods, as if there were no conflict. There is no conflict because the way the first principle is a god is unique.

Given that it is clear that there is a substantial sense in which Aristotle believes in one God, though there are many other things he is prepared to call 'divine', let us briefly consider these. Having introduced the first unmoved mover in *Λ*6–7 as a substance which is not subject to any kind of change, but rather is the ultimate source or principle of all change, Aristotle in chapter 8 turns to the question whether there are other substances which also are not subject to any change and, if so, how many they are. He argues that we have to postulate forty-seven spheres to account for the motion of the planets, the divine bodies, as he calls them (1074^{a}30), and that hence there must be forty-seven further substances which are not subject to change to account for the never-ending rotation of these spheres. It is these substances which, in 1074^{b}2–3, he calls 'gods'. So, apart from the first unmoved mover, he also calls the unmoved movers of the planetary spheres, and thus of the planets, 'divine'. It is easy to see why he does so. It is part of the order of the universe which depends on the first unmoved mover that there be immaterial substances, pure unembodied minds who, being immortal, enjoy eternal bliss contemplating the first unmoved mover and the order which depends on him. But it is also part of the order of the universe that there be planets which eternally move in the same way, not to be derailed from their steady path by passion, and which thereby can be seen to be superbly intelligent and wise beings which are equally immortal and enjoy eternal bliss. Obviously there are great difficulties in understanding the details of this, but the main point for us seems rather simple and straightforward. On Aristotle's view of the world it is part of the order of things determined by the God that there be intelligent, living beings which are not subject to generation or corruption and which enjoy a life of eternal bliss. This alone, given ordinary Greek usage, suffices to call them 'divine'.

I have discussed Aristotle in some detail, because he offers us in *Meta-phisics Lambda* a short text on the basis of which we can establish and understand the relevant points with considerable confidence. Once we have understood the crucial points in his case, it is also much easier to see them in the case of Stoicism and Platonism, though the evidence to be taken into account there is much more complex and controversial. Since Platonism raises a further problem relevant to our inquiry, I will begin with the Stoics.

According to the Stoics there are two ultimate principles, an active and a passive one, God (or the God), and matter. There is a controversial problem of interpretation here which I will not try to resolve. Given the way God and matter are contrasted, one might think that God is conceived of as immaterial. But the Stoics not only think that all beings are material or corporeal, they also, more specifically, identify God or Zeus with a certain kind of fire which is supposed to be intelligent, active, and creative. So perhaps we have to assume that the Stoics distinguish two aspects of the fiery substance which is Zeus, two aspects, though, which in reality are never separated, namely its divine, creative character, and its material character. Thus God and Zeus are the same to the extent that Zeus is active, creative, intelligent. Now the Stoics also believe that the world is a rational animal that periodically turns entirely into the fiery substance which is Zeus. What happens is that the reason of this animal is itself constituted by this fiery substance, and that this reason slowly consumes and absorbs into itself the soul and the body of the world. Thus, in this state of conflagration, the world, the reason of the world, and Zeus completely coincide. But as soon as the conflagration has taken place, Zeus, the creative fiery substance, sets out to create the world anew, or, put differently, the reason of the world creates for itself a new soul and a new body. Zeus does so by partially turning himself first into air and then through air into water and ultimately into earth and, again, fire, while at the same time completely pervading these newly created elements, mixing them and mixing with them in such a way as to shape them into the world as we know it. As part of this process the stars arise which consist of this divine fiery substance and human beings which are governed by reason, which also involves a high concentration of the fiery substance. Some Stoics believe that this human reason, if perfected, has enough stability to survive the death of a human being, only to be reabsorbed into Zeus or cosmic reason at the next conflagration.

The details of this are complicated or even controversial, but the points which concern us stand out clearly enough. On this view of the world there is one intelligent being which governs the world and which alone survives all of its changes, including the periodic conflagrations. It alone is eternal. All other beings are the product of its providential creation. So we readily understand that it, being a first principle in this way, should be called *the* God. That this for the Stoics means that, strictly speaking, there is just one God is made clear also by the following detail. Plutarch (*De comm. not.* 1051 E–F) reports that everybody is in agreement that a god is not subject to generation and destruction, and he then specifically quotes Antipater of Tarsus for the Stoic view that the natural notion of a god is one according to which a god is enjoying a life of bliss, is not subject to destruction, and is provident for, or beneficent of, human beings. On the basis of this he accuses Chrysippus of contradicting himself when he claims that fire or Zeus alone among the gods is not subject to destruction (1052a; *De comm. not.* 1077 E), whereas the other gods are consumed by the fire in the general conflagration. But it is also clear how the apparent inconsistency is to be resolved. We also learn from Plutarch (*De comm. not.* 1075 C) that the Stoics distinguish between 'not subject to destruction' and 'not subject to death' or 'immortal'. This allows them to say that Zeus alone is not subject to destruction, but that the other gods are at least immortal in that they last till the conflagration, when they do not die, but are reabsorbed by Zeus. Nevertheless, this clearly means that only Zeus satisfies the criterion for being a god fully, whereas all other gods only satisfy the criterion by not insisting on strict indestructibility, but by accepting a weak form of immortality. It is only in this diminished sense that things other than Zeus can be called 'god'. More importantly, though, these other gods only exist because the God has created them as part of his creation of the best possible world, in which they are meant to play a certain role. The power they thus have is merely the power to do what the God has fated them to do. They act completely in accordance with the divine plan.

Given this radical subordination one may ask why the Stoics are prepared in the first instance to accommodate a plurality of gods by the questionable manœuvre of attributing a rather tenuous form of immortality to them. Here we have to take note of a significant shift in the attitude towards traditional stories about the gods. As we saw, Aristotle was only willing to acknowledge that these stories had a minimal element of truth, which truth was presented in mythical form both to make it acceptable to ordinary people and also because of the social utility of popular belief in the truth of these stories. By Aristotle's time there was also a tradition of reinterpreting these stories allegorically to justify them as true, though perhaps veiled, accounts. This tradition the Stoics take up and carry to an extreme. They see these traditional stories about the gods as veiled accounts of the truth as explicated by Stoic physics. So they will identify each of the traditional gods with some entity in true physics, Zeus with the creative fire, Hera with air, Poseidon with water, etc. They will account for the divinity of the stars in terms of their being constituted by the divine fiery substance. They might, in particular, account for the divinity of the sun as the seat of the divine reason which governs the world, analogous to the heart which, according to the Stoics, is the seat of the *hegemonikon* of a human being, i.e. its reason. They might account for the quasi-divinity of the souls, or rather minds, of the departed who have achieved wisdom and virtue in terms of their high proportion of the fiery substance which gives them the stability to continue to live the life of the mind until the conflagration. The crucial point in all this is that the Stoics see themselves able, by virtue of their theory, to accommodate popular beliefs concerning the gods. That they do so does not mean, though, that they accept these stories and the corresponding religious beliefs at face value, and it does not mean that they are prepared to compromise their belief in one God, the God who providentially governs the universe. It is very clear in their case, even more so than in Aristotle's, that these further divine beings are radically dependent on the God and only exist because they have a place in the divine order of things. Far from governing the universe or having any independent share in its governance, they only share in the execution of the divine plan; they are not even immortal, strictly speaking. Theirs is a rather tenuous divinity.

When we come to the Platonists, matters for a variety of reasons are more complicated, too complicated to do justice here even to all the major details. Let us begin with the view concerning first principles, which later doxography ascribes to Plato. According to Plato the first principles are supposed to be God, the ideas, and matter. The report clearly is based on the *Timaeus*, according to which the world is created by a demiurge who realizes the intelligible order defined by the ideas in an antecedently given matter to the extent that this is possible. This creation not only includes the stars but also the soul of the world and the souls of human beings. Now one crucial element of the account is that the beings which have been created by the demiurge directly, having been created, are not by their very nature eternal, but are granted immortality by the demiurge who promises to see to it that they will not face death and destruction (*Tim.* 41 A). This allows Plato to talk not only of the world (34 A, B), on his view a living intelligent animal, but also of the planets (similarly intelligent beings) and certain beings or powers which reveal themselves in the workings of the world as gods. So there is one God, but there are also other beings which are called 'divine', though they are created, because they are by Divine grace immortal and enjoy a good life. But they only exist as part of God's creation and they are immortal and hence divine only due to the God's benevolence or grace, that is to say they owe their very divinity to God. So far, then, the Platonist account, in its essential features, is very much like that of Aristotle and that of the Stoics.

In late antiquity, though, this account becomes much more complex in the following way. The one God of the *Timaeus*, the demiurge, comes himself increasingly to be seen as something of considerable internal complexity, a complexity according to later Platonists only hinted at in the *Timaeus*, for instance when Plato speaks of the world as an *agalma* of the eternal gods, as if there were a plurality of truly divine beings of which the creation is a reflection.

The reasons for this are easy to see. If we think of the demiurge as being constrained by the ideas as something antecedently given to him, this in itself, combined with the complexity introduced into him by assuming that he tries to realize these ideas in the visible world, seems to be incompatible with his status as an absolutely first principle. Hence we see that Platonists begin to distinguish between God (the first principle) and the divine intellect (mind or reason, which will be identified with the ideas as the thoughts of the divine intellect). Once we come to Numenius and to Plotinus we have a further distinction between the divine intellect which is purely contemplative and a third divine principle which is demiurgic or creative. Thus Numenius can talk of a first and of a second God and, by implication, of a third God. But Platonists after Plotinus think they can articulate this trinity further.

In spite of this vertical articulation of the God into a first God, a second God, and a third God and further subarticulations, the plurality thus introduced is not supposed to obscure the fact that we are just dealing with different hypostases of the one God. The second God, very roughly put, is simply the first God who in himself is beyond being and intelligibility, but reveals himself at the level of being and thinking as the divine intellect. Thus the vertical articulation is supposed to preserve the unity of the one God. What is true of his vertical articulation also is true of a certain horizontal articulation. Consider the divine intellect. It is identified with the Platonic ideas. It is thus a plurality of things, indeed a plurality of intellects. For each idea is a divine thought, and each thought is an intellect. And yet the divine intellect is not supposed to lose its unity as one intellect. So the one God turns out to be many things, without thereby losing his unity. Instead of pursuing this, though, I want to consider one detail concerning the divine intellect. According to the *Timaeus* the rational part of the soul is created by the demiurge himself and is thus immortal by divine grace. But Plotinus and others consider the possibility that there are ideas, not only of kinds of things, but in the case of man also of individual men. So these will be intellects, too. This raises the question whether the individual human intellect may not be part of the divine intellect insofar as the divine intellect contains the idea of the individual human being. In any case, Platonists generally assume that the human intellect is part of the intelligible rather than the sensible world. And this introduces a lack of clarity as to whether there are two creations or just one, whether part of the intelligible world is already created.

However this may be, we see that the God who creates, according to later Platonists, in truth reveals an internal structure and multiplicity which allows us to talk not only of uncreated gods, but also of any number of gods which are created but proceed from the first principle. But this plurality is not supposed to affect the unity of God. After all, the divine intellect is just the intellect of God, the way God presents himself in thought. Hence, though the Platonists can talk of many gods, at the level both of created and of uncreated beings, this is not supposed to undermine the belief that there is one God.

To sum up our discussion so far. There is a clear sense in which Platonists, Peripatetics, and Stoics and thus the vast majority of philosophers in late antiquity believed in one God. They believed in a god who not only enjoys eternal bliss, but in a god who as a god is unique in that he is a first principle which determines and providentially governs reality. There are, as part of the divinely imposed order of things, derivative beings which also enjoy immortality and bliss, and which, hence, following Greek usage, are also called 'divine'. But in the case of Plato's and the Stoics' created gods even this immortality exists only through divine benevolence and, for the Stoics, is not even a genuine immortality. The fact that they assume the existence of such divine beings does not in the least conflict with their belief in one God. This simple picture is complicated in the case of late Platonists by their belief in uncreated gods. Though they are completely subordinated to the first principle they are nevertheless divine in a much more powerful sense than the secondary created gods we have been considering. This reflects the fact that they are so intimately connected with the first principle as to be articulations of what is already contained in it. But for this very reason belief in them would surely threaten the belief in one God as little as the belief in God's justice or God's wisdom would threaten the belief in one God who is absolutely simple.

I want to conclude this part of my argument by referring to at least some of the evidence which indicates not only that the vast majority of philosophers in antiquity believed in one God who providentially governs the universe, but that this is also what they were perceived to believe by the ancients themselves.

In later antiquity there were two basic issues for theology: namely, whether there is a God who governs the universe and whether God is provident. Stoics, Peripatetics, and Platonists, and thus the vast majority of philosophers, answered both questions affirmatively, whereas Epicureans answered them negatively. These also are the only theological issues which Sextus Empiricus at the end of the second century AD addresses in the *Outlines of Pyrrhonism*. He does so in the context of considering the views of the dogmatic philosophers concerning the principles and causes of reality (3. 1 ff.). Dogmatic philosophers, according to Sextus, distinguish between active and passive or material principles. They claim that the active principles are more important, or may be more justly called 'principles', than the material ones. And the majority of philosophers, he says (3. 2), claim that the most important active principle is a God, or, as he also puts it (3. 3, 4, 5, 6), the God. He then attacks this view arguing that it is quite unclear how we are supposed to conceive of a god and that, moreover, it is quite unclear whether there is such a thing as a god. He then goes on to consider the question whether we should think of a god as provident for the things in this world (3. 9 ff.). Here he adduces Epicurean arguments against providence. He concludes his remarks in this way (3. 12):

As a result of this we come to think that perhaps those who insist on claiming that there is a god are forced to be impious. For in claiming that he is provident about all things they will be saying that he is the cause of all evil, but if they claim that he is provident only about some things or nothing, they will be forced to say either that the God lacks good will or is weak; yet obviously only people who are impious will say this.

So Sextus' discussion, to say the very least, strongly suggests that at the end of the second century AD, if you were a philosopher you would usually assume that there is a god, the God, who is the most important cause or principle of reality and who is provident. And this God would not be conceived of as just the highest of a plurality of gods, but as unique in his divinity, as the expression 'the God' shows.

We get the same impression from many other texts, for instance from Justin's *Dialogue with Trypho*. Trypho, a Jewish refugee from the war in Palestine, has been attending the lectures of a philosopher. Questioned by Justin as to whether he really expects to draw the kind of enlightenment from philosophy one gets from Moses and the prophets, Trypho answers, 'Don't the philosophers talk all the time about God and do not their enquiries always concern divine monarchy and providence?' (1. 3). Justin's response (1. 4) is less enthusiastic. He agrees, but complains that the great majority of philosophers have not sufficiently considered the question whether there is one God or whether there are many, and whether divine providence extends down to each individual among us or whether, as some philosophers argue (he has Aristotle in mind), is limited to the general order of things. Yet even Justin's criticism confirms that the vast majority of philosophers in the later second century AD believe in one God who) overns the universe and who is provident to some degree. What Justin's response also shows is that he has some difficulty appreciating the distinction between the sense in which there is one God and the sense in which there are many gods, or at least that he sees some lack of clarity in this distinction. Justin's response may also reflect the fact that the distinction was not always sufficiently clear to the pagans.

Before I turn to the Christians, it must be at least briefly noted that there was a further source of confusion. Both Stoics and Platonists assumed that the world above the earth was filled with demons. Not all of them were divine. Some of them were far from living a life of bliss, because they were far from being wise and virtuous, if not outright malevolent. Nevertheless, they might have extraordinary powers and knowledge, for instance, about the future. If one knew how to do it, one could, because of their weaknesses, manipulate them to exercise these powers for one's own benefit or to reveal their knowledge. This line between good demons and questionable demons, or rather the line between enrolling the help of good demons and manipulating questionable demons, was not so easy to draw.

If we now turn to the Christian view, it should be clear that the position Minucius Felix' *Octavius* converts Caecilius to, namely, the belief in one God who providentially governs the world, does not differ from the belief of most pagan philosophers. But, one might argue, the difference is that the Christians only believe in the one god who providentially governs the world, whereas the pagans also believe in many other gods. I have already tried to explain that this is a prejudicial and misleading way to put the matter: the pagans believe in one God, but also in further beings which, for reasons which are easy to understand, they also are willing to call 'divine', without thereby wanting to deny that there is a strict sense in which there is one and only one God. But we should not overlook that the Christians themselves, in fact, did not differ from the pagans in being willing to acknowledge a sense in which there are further beings which can be called 'gods'.

Though the Christians in general avoided speaking of gods in the plural (in particular the West had difficulties with the plural, both in the case of the Trinity, and in general; cf. Synod of Rome 382, Tomus Damasi, §24, Denzinger 176) there were doctrinal reasons which made it difficult for them to deny that even created beings could be called 'divine' or 'gods'. After all, there was scriptural authority for this. Scripture, Psalms for instance, is full of references to the gods in the plural, for example in such phrases as 'the God of the gods' (Ps. 49: 1). Even the Suida, hardly a source suspect of unorthodoxy, has an entry *theoi*, drawn from Theodoretus (*In Ps.*, PG 80. 1229C), explaining 'those created in the divine image who have managed to preserve the image undefiled' and referring to Psalms 49: 1. Origen (*C. Celsum* 5. 4) refers to this and other passages to show that talk of 'gods' as such must be unobjectionable, and so does Augustine (*De civ. Dei* 9. 23). Origen takes Scripture to refer to the angels. After all, they do enjoy a life of eternal bliss. Augustine in 9. 23 takes Scripture to refer in this way both to angels and to the saints, because they are immortal and blessed. Notoriously, Arnobius in his *Adversus Nationes* repeatedly speaks of 'gods'; as if he believed in a plurality of divine beings (e.g. 6. 3). This has given rise to great puzzlement and been taken to be an indication of Arnobius' lack of proper instruction in Christian doctrine. But presumably Arnobius, too, is just referring to the angels. We also find Boethius in *Contra Eutychen* (1. 29) speaking of 'God and the other divine beings', thinking apparently of the angels (2. 28).

So we understand why the pagan philosopher to whom Macarius Magnes responds in his *Monogenes* (4. 21) can claim that surely it is just a matter of terminology whether one calls these beings 'angels' or 'gods'. This claim presupposes that from the point of view of this pagan philosopher there is really no issue here between Christians and pagans.

It is often assumed that the philosopher in question, in fact, is Porphyry.[4] What speaks in favour of this hypothesis, among many other things, is that Augustine in *De civ. Dei* (9. 23) seems to respond to the same point, and, indeed, to agree that it is just a matter of terminology whether one calls these beings 'gods', provided that they are wise and virtuous. Augustine says:

If the Platonists prefer to call these 'gods' rather than 'daemons' and to count them among those of whom their founder and master Plato writes that they are gods created by the highest God, let them say what they want. For one should not engage with them in a controversy of words. For if they say that they are not blessed by themselves, but by being attached to him who has created them, then they say precisely what we say, whichever word they may use for them. . . . For even as far as the word is concerned, that they call creatures which are immortal and blessed in this way 'gods', this is not really a matter of disagreement between us and them.

What is no longer a matter merely of terminology is the doctrine of the deification of man, that is to say the doctrine that human beings who have been redeemed and saved are divine, which Augustine also alludes to as we saw. As we noted, there are many passages in the Psalms which speak of 'gods' in the plural.[5] Another such passage is Psalms 81: 6: 'I have told you: you are gods.' The commentary attributed to Cyril of Alexandria again takes this to be a reference to human beings who by participation are gods, and so do others. Athanasius in *Contra Arianos* (1. 9) has no difficulty in referring to this text according to which even human beings might be divine. He argues that Arius' mistake does not consist in regarding Jesus as God, but in regarding him as divine only by participation, rather than as divine in himself, as we might become divine by participation, but, of course, are not divine in ourselves. This is a view which we also find in Origen. Thus, for instance, in the *Commentary on John* (2. 16–17) Origen discusses the difficulty some Christians have in acknowledging the divinity of Christ for fear of compromising their belief in one God. Origen thinks that the way to resolve the problem is this: we have to distinguish between 'the God' with the article and a 'god' without the article. There is the Father who is the God, but this does not prevent us from believing that there is a god or even

---

[4] Cf. A. von Harnack, *Porphyrius, 'Gegen die Christen', 15 Bücher Zeugnisse, Fragmente und Referate* (Abh. Berliner Akad. d. Wiss. 1916, no. 1), fr. 76.

[5] One such passage is Psalms 95: 4. Cyril of Alexandria (*PG* 69. 1244D) warns us not to take this to be a reference to the saints, not because the saints cannot be called 'gods', but because the next line, he argues presumably wrongly, makes it clear that the Psalmist is speaking of demons.

that there are many gods by participation in the God. And again he refers to Psalms 49, 'The God of gods, the Lord has spoken', to assure us that there is nothing wrong about speaking about gods in the plural. The fact that later orthodoxy will think that Christ is placed here on the wrong side of the participation relation and that Origen thus reveals himself as a precursor of Arius should not distract us from the fact that Origen distinguishes between the God and a god in the very terms I have ascribed to pagan philosophers, and that there is nothing unorthodox about the distinction as such. So the Christians are willing, and even committed, to talk of a plurality of created beings as 'gods'. For they take it to be understood that these beings are not the God himself, but mere creatures of him.

But what about the uncreated gods of the Platonists? It is also Origen who, following the precedent of Philo of Alexandria, but more importantly of Numenius, can speak of a first and a second God, referring to the persons of the Trinity. In this he is followed by Eusebius (e.g. *PE* 11. 14. 3). It is true that later orthodoxy will avoid this language which reflects Origen's subordinationist view of the persons of the Trinity. But even authors of unquestionable orthodoxy will not deny that there are three uncreated persons each of whom can be called 'God'. Yet neither the language of a first, a second, a third God, nor the language of a plurality of divine persons is supposed to undermine the Christians' claim to believe in just one God. A Platonist does not have any difficulty in accepting this.

Given all this, I do not see any way in which the Christians are in a position to claim that they believe in one God, whereas the pagan philosophers believe in many gods. We have seen that the belief in one highest god, combined with the belief in many gods, might or might not be monotheistic, depending on whether or not the many gods are subordinated to the highest god in the appropriate way. If, as in the case of our philosophers, they are subordinated to the first principle in the way they are taken to be subordinated to it, the fact that these philosophers also talk of many gods does not in the least mean that they do not believe in one God precisely in the way the Christians do.

This seems so obvious as to raise the question how Christians even could have been tempted to present things otherwise. To make this question appear more pressing, I want to consider what might seem to be a more differentiated and more promising attempt to distinguish between pagans and Christians, namely Augustine's in the *De Civitate Dei*. This has the added advantage that Augustine specifically addresses the philosophers. I want to argue that this attempt is not a particularly successful one. But I hope that its discussion brings us somewhat nearer to an answer to the question why the Christians might have been tempted to claim that the Christians believe in one God, whereas the pagans, even their philosophers, believe in many gods.

As Augustine himself tells us towards the end of his life in his *Retractations* (2. 43 *init.*), he wrote the *De Civitate Dei* in response to those who, after the sack of Rome by Alaric in 410, 'tried to put the blame for its fall on Christian religion, being themselves worshippers of false and many gods, those whom we call "pagans", to use an established term' (*quos usitato nomine paganos vocamus*). The definition is based on Tertullian, *Cor. Mil.* 11.

In the *De Civitate Dei* itself he sets out to show that it is true of even the most respectable among pagan philosophers, the Platonists, that they worship many false gods. Following Augustine's actual argument we can analyse this claim into the following three assertions:

1. even pagan philosophers believe in many gods;
2. these gods, some or all of them, are false gods;
3. even if they are not false gods, it would be wrong to worship some or all of them.

We have already seen that Augustine in the course of his argument concedes that, properly understood, there is nothing wrong as such about believing in many gods.

He also concedes that the sense in which the best Platonists believe in many gods is unobjectionable. So, though Augustine still tries to accuse the pagans of polytheism, the emphasis of his attack has shifted. It is now a question of believing in the right god and of worship. So the suggestion now is that the pagans are in the wrong, because they believe in the wrong gods, that is to say either in pure fictions or in things which, though real, are not divine. Augustine is encouraged in this thought by scriptural authority. In 9. 23 he refers to Psalm 95: 4–5 where we are told that, though there are gods, the gods of the Gentiles are mere demons. Already Origen, in *Contra Celsum* 8. 3–4, had not only referred to five passages in the Psalms to show that besides the God of gods there are gods, but also, on the basis of some passages in Paul, distinguished between gods and so-called gods, and then quoted from the Psalms the same passage according to which the gods of the Gentiles are mere daemons. Superficially, both Origen and Augustine have some evidence to support their claim. Origen (*C. Celsum* 8. 67) can point out that

Celsus defends the worship of demons, and Augustine can rely on Apuleius' *De Deo Socratis* to give him an excuse to spend nine chapters criticizing Apuleius' praise of demons (*De Civ. Dei* 8. 14–22). I will just note that both Stoics and Platonists believed in demons, that there was some lack of clarity or even confusion about the boundary-line between gods and demons, but that no Platonist would have taken a demon who was a demon also in the Christian sense to be a god.

Rather than pursuing this, it seems more promising to take up the general claim that the many gods of the pagans are false in the sense that they are not truly gods, a claim constantly repeated in Christian anti-pagan literature right from its beginnings. Given that the philosophers in question believe in one God and many derivative divine beings, one naturally asks oneself whether the Christians want to claim that all these gods are false or whether they accept that these philosophers at least believe in the one true God, though they also believe in many false gods.

The Christian argument tends to rely on a conception of a god which is in essence the conception that the Stoics' claim to be natural or common (cf. Plut. *De Stoic. ref.* 1051 E–F). A god has to be incorruptible and eternal, that is to say he must be without beginning and end, since anything which has a beginning, at least as far as its nature is concerned, also has an end. He must, moreover, enjoy eternal bliss. This is supposed to exclude his being subject to passions, let alone to moral corruption. And he must be benevolent or provident, in particular towards human beings. Given this notion, it is easy to see how the Christians can argue that neither the God of Aristotle, nor the God of the Stoics qualify. The providence of the God of Aristotle does not extend to the sublunar realm and hence to human beings. Moreover, there is some confusion already in the pagan doxography concerning Aristotle's first principles which allows Christians to think that Aristotle regards ether, the quintessence, and hence the stars as divine (cf. Clem. *Recog.* 8. 15, Athen. *Leg.* 6. 3). But if Aristotle's God is corporeal, he is created and hence not eternal, at least by his own nature. Lactantius notes the conflicting evidence about Aristotle (*Div. Inst.* 1. 5), but is inclined to think that on balance Aristotle believes in a divine intellect governing the world. Even in this case, though, Aristotle's God is ruled out by not being sufficiently provident.

Similarly the God of the Stoics sometimes is rejected on account of his corporeality (cf. Tatian *Ad Graecos* 25; Clem. *Strom.* 5. 14). In fact, it is remarkable that some authors like Athenagoras do not avail themselves of this argument. Athenagoras argues (*Leg.* 20. 3) that the created gods of the Stoics cannot be gods, because they perish in the conflagration, but somewhat later (22. 5), in a rather tortuous paragraph in which he makes the same point, he also seems to adduce the Stoic doctrine of the one God as if it were testimony in favour of the Christian belief in one God. He addresses the Stoics: 'if you believe that the highest God is one, has not come into being and is eternal . . .'. So the Christians can argue, as far as the God of the Stoics and the Peripatetics is concerned, that although these philosophers believe in one God, they do not believe in the one true God. But when it comes to the Platonists, Athenagoras, for instance, definitely thinks, as we can see from *Leg.* 6. 2, like most Christians Fathers do, and as Augustine does in *De Civ. Dei* (10. 1), that the God of Plato and the Platonists is the one true God.

So, the picture, as far as the God is concerned, is not entirely clear. Put in terms which are most favourable to the philosophers, Aristotle makes the mistake of not attributing universal providence to God. This need not prevent one, as the attitude of Platonists and some Christians in late antiquity and the Middle Ages shows, from thinking that Aristotle is talking about the God, though his conception of him is limited and inadequate. The Stoics do not make the mistake of denying God universal providence, but think of him as a spiritual, rather than as an incorporeal being. Only the conception of the Platonists seems to be beyond reproach. Nevertheless, all these pagan philosophers believe in the God the Christians believe in, certainly from a time when they are almost invariably Platonists. On the other hand, even at this abstract level, one can see why the Christians might insist that the philosophers in general do not believe in the one true God, since believing in the one God from their point of view would be a matter of believing not only in the one true God, but in 'the God who has revealed himself in the Old Testament and in Christ'.

As far as the created gods are concerned, the Christian argument rarely seems to take into account that they are not meant to be measured by the criteria of what it is, strictly speaking, to be a god. Hence, for instance, Athenagoras' argument against the Stoic secondary gods, which we mentioned earlier, seems to miss the point. He should have argued that they are not even immortal by divine grace, rather than that they are not eternal. He and other Christian authors seem to forget that they themselves want to assume gods by participation. It is easy to see why the Christians are not prepared to regard the elements divine even in the secondary sense. But they can hardly, given their own views, reject Aristotelian immaterial substances, later interpreted as angels, or the

Platonists' secondary gods or good demons or angels. One would also have to discuss under this heading why the Christians reject the divinity of the stars. They are, no doubt, right in this, but one suspects that in this regard the stars fall victim to the Christian's rejection of fatalism and astrology.

This is a very summary discussion of the question of the secondary gods. But even so, it should emerge clearly enough that the Christians are doubtlessly right in rejecting many of these gods as false. But it should be equally clear that, given their own views, they are not in a position to declare all of them as false. Most importantly, given the appropriate kind of Platonism, they are hardly in a position to declare the Platonist gods as false.

It is in part for this reason, I take it, that Augustine finally resorts to the claim that these beings, even if they are gods, should not be worshipped. I say 'in part', because one might argue that to believe in the one God anyway was not just a matter of, as it were intellectually, assuming there to be an entity of a certain kind, but having a sufficient grasp on the fact that it, and it alone, in virtue of being this kind of entity, demanded a certain kind of attitude towards it expressed by worship. One might argue that this attitude was part of what it was to believe in the one God. Hence it is incompatible with this belief to worship other beings, even if they are divine. Augustine argues that, being created, they owe their immortality and their salvation to God. Hence it is absurd to expect salvation from them, when they themselves owe their salvation to divine grace. This again obviously is a complex topic which I can only address very briefly here.

Notoriously in the *De oratione* (15) Origen took the position that only God the Father should be invoked. But obviously there are a number of increasingly wider Christian positions in this regard. One is that God is to be worshipped; another is that God in all of his persons is to be worshipped. Paul (Col. 2: 18) warns the Colossians not to give themselves to the worship of angels, but now the question arises what we mean by 'cult', 'worship', 'invocation'. Even on an orthodox view there is a place for the invocation or even the veneration of the angels and the saints in some sense of these words.

On the pagan side, one crucial text is Plato, *Timaeus* 37 c, according to which the world, itself divine, is itself an image (*agalma*) of the ever-lasting gods. We certainly do not expect Plato or any Platonists to worship the world. What we do expect is that they treat the world with respect, given that it is an image of higher things. It is clear, at least in the case of Platonists, that divine beings form a hierarchy in which the lower beings are images or reflections of the higher beings, and in which each being, however modest its position in this hierarchy, represents the divinely ordained order of things and is a reflection of the God. It is clear even from what Origen quotes from Celsus that Celsus argues that we should pay respect to or even worship demons because in doing so we show respect for God and the divine order. This suggests a line of thought which justifies the worship of lesser gods, as long as they are understood to be mere images, pale reflections of the God. On the other hand, it is also clear from Augustine (*De Civ. Dei* 10. 26) that Porphyry, at least at times, thought that we should not worship or invoke any secondary gods or angels, but only take them as an example, emulate them. This is a position strikingly similar to the one Origen takes in *Contra Celsum* 5. 5. Origen enjoins us to invoke God only through Christ, and not the angels, but to imitate the angels so that they may be well disposed towards us and that in this way we may achieve a clearer understanding of Christ. Augustine himself points out that Porphyry's view in this regard corresponds closely to the Christian position (*De Civ. Dei* 10 26 *init.*). It should also be pointed out that neither Porphyry nor any Platonist will expect salvation from a secondary god. For salvation consists in the vision of the first principle through which one becomes like God. And this vision one can only achieve oneself—if, that is, God reveals himself to one. Hence I also think that Augustine's claim that even the Platonists worship beings which do not deserve to be worshipped in this generality does not stand up too well to closer scrutiny. Either Platonists do not invoke and worship secondary gods, and from what we know about Platonists like Plotinus it would be incongruous to imagine him as, say, sacrificing to the gods or consulting oracles; or, when Platonists so invoke and worship secondary gods, we have to see whether this does not happen in the rather qualified sense in which the Christians venerate and invoke the saints and the angels.

Nevertheless, it also becomes clear from *De Civ. Dei* 10. 26 what part of Augustine's concern is here: he accuses Porphyry of not sufficiently distancing himself from those who engage in magic and theurgy. At this point it may help to note that, though philosophers always remained critical of traditional religious belief and cult, their attitude towards traditional religion from Aristotle's time onwards became more and more positive. Aristotle had been willing to admit that traditional religious belief contained a very small though important element of truth, but was willing to defend it as the only way ordinary people would accept this element of truth and because of its social utility. The Stoics and, following them, the Platonists believed that traditional belief by and large was true in the sense that it had an elaborate hidden meaning which corresponded to the truth in whose knowledge salvation consists. If this truth was only accessible to ordinary people in the disguised form of traditional belief, it nevertheless offered them some kind of access to the truth which saves, an access which can be deepened by reflection and philosophical instruction. And it seems that Porphyry took a similar attitude to traditional worship—that, despite of all its distortions, it does reflect the truth and thus, if only properly understood, is perfectly acceptable. If properly engaged in and reflected on, it does put one in touch with a higher reality, which in turn would be a reflection of a yet higher reality and so forth. Hence Porphyry seems to have thought that worship, engaged in the proper way, might put one on the road to salvation. It might be the only way open to a non-philosopher to come nearer to the truth. Some later Platonists took a much more positive attitude towards cult as a means of attaining the truth which saves. In any case Porphyry clearly defended and encouraged the traditional cults of the gods, perhaps even as a means to salvation of a limited kind. Porphyry, of course, did this on the understanding that there was a true reinterpretation of these gods and their cults. And it was open to the Christians to argue, obviously correctly, that the traditional stories about the gods did not contain a hidden message which made them true, but that they were to be taken at face value, and taken this way were an abomination. If this was the position one took, Porphyry's advocacy of the traditional pagan cults could not but seem an invitation to worship false gods.

Porphyry also defended the use of oracles, indeed the use of oracles to gain philosophical knowledge and understanding. For a Christian like Augustine it seemed clear that this involved, if not the appeal to, then the use of questionable demons. So for Augustine oracular cults amounted to the worship of false gods.[6]

Given Porphyry's aggressive defence of paganism and the impact it had, it is perhaps somewhat easier to understand why a Christian like Augustine might be tempted to say in arguing against them that the pagans, even pagan philosophers, instead of worshipping the one true God worship many false gods. But, however far we go in understanding and accepting this claim, it seems that it will not be quite the truth.

---

[6] Needless to say, this is not how Porphyry looked at the matter: for him revelation was a genuine possibility, a possibility Christians could hardly deny.

What are we to make of all this? One conclusion which suggests itself is that the pagan philosophers we have been considering, in particular the Platonists, were monotheists in precisely the sense the Christians were. Given this, it is tempting to assume that also the Hellenes Marius Victorinus refers to in the passage quoted at the beginning—at least those among them who thought of themselves as representing, maintaining, and defending the tradition of Hellenicity, for the most part under the influence of the philosophers—were monotheists. We have to be cautious here, though, because, as we have seen, the mere belief in a highest god who rules the universe does not in itself qualify one as a monotheist. But even with this qualification it seems likely that a good part of the educated elite was monotheist. It thus seems all the more puzzling why the Christians insisted on their monotheism as a distinguishing mark.

Another puzzle which arises is that the discussion we have been reviewing from a Christian point of view seems to obscure the real issue. The real issue is whether Jesus is God. The pagan response to this claim, as we can see from Celsus, is that it compromises the belief in one God, for, if it were true, the Christians would believe in and worship two gods, God the Father and Jesus. Moreover, there is no way in which Jesus can be God himself, being a man. He, given his life, cannot even claim to be a divine man. This might go some way to explain the Christian emphasis on pagan polytheism as a polemical response. If the pagans are unwilling to countenance even the possibility that Jesus is God, why should the Christians take the claim seriously that idols and the traditional gods, properly understood, are true reflections of God? The Christians could then go on to argue that, even with a reinterpretation of the traditional gods, the pagans were still believing in and worshipping many false gods, instead of the one true God.

The fact that the Christians availed themselves of this sort of argument to maintain their position should not mislead us, though, into believing that pagans in late antiquity almost by definition were polytheists.

SELECT BIBLIOGRAPHY

DENZINGER, H., *Enchiridion Symbolorum* (37th edn., Freiburg, 1991).
DÜRING, I., *Aristotle* (Heidelberg, 1966).
GUTHRIE, W. K. C., *A History of Greek Philosophy*, vol. 1 (Cambridge, 1962).
VON HARNACK, A., *Porphyrius, 'Gegen die Christen', 15 Bücher Zeugnisse, Fragmente und Referate* (Abh. Berliner Akad. d. Wiss. 1916, no. 1).

3

Monotheism in the Gnostic Tradition

JOHN DILLON

It may well be that, when one's thoughts turn to the Gnostics, monotheism is not the first topic that comes to mind. Rather, I should say, it is the reckless multiplication of immaterial and quasi-divine entities for which the various Gnostic systems would generally be noted, as well as their strong dualistic tendencies. However, though certainly salient features, these phenomena are not after all incompatible with monotheism, as I shall proceed to argue.

To begin with an essay at theorizing: I would distinguish, broadly, two types, or levels, of monotheism, which one might term, on the model of many similar distinctions, 'hard' and 'soft'. Hard monotheism is of the type characterized by the statement, 'I am the Lord your God; I shall not have any other gods before me!',[1] and exemplified by such religious traditions as the Jewish and the Islamic, where nothing more formidable than an angel is allowed to compete with the supreme and only God. Soft monotheism, in the ancient Mediterranean context, is exemplified by the intellectualized version of traditional Greek religion to which most educated Greeks seem to have adhered from the fifth century BC on, according to which Zeus represents something like a supreme cosmic intellect, which can also be referred to, more vaguely, as *ho theos* or *to theion*, but which is prepared to recognize also, on a lower level of reality, as it were, the full Olympic pantheon of traditional deities, and a host of little local gods as well, who can all be, if necessary, viewed merely as aspects of the supreme divinity, performing one or another specialized function. The religious philosophies of Stoicism and Platonism may be seen, I think, as further rationalizations of this position, also finding a place for the gods of traditional religion, as aspects or manifestations of the supreme cosmic, or supra-cosmic, intellect.

[1] Chosen, amusingly, as the arrogant slogan of the ignorant cosmic demiurge Ialdabaoth, or Sakla, in the Gnostic tradition (for which he is duly rebuked by his mother, Sophia), cf. e.g. *Apocr. Joh.* 13. 5–12; *Hyp. Arch.* 86. 27–87, 3; *Gosp. Eg.* 3. 58. 23–59, 4.

As for Christianity, in its developed form at least, it seems to me to fall somewhere in the middle between these two extremes. On the one hand, it inherits the jealous and absolutist god of Judaism, but on the other, at least after the first generation or so of its intellectual contact with contemporary Hellenic philosophy (particularly Platonism and Stoicism), in the second century AD, it finds room not only for a secondary divinity, on the model of the Platonic demiurge, in the person of Christ, who acts both as a world-creator and as a mediator between God and man, and, increasingly, for a succession of powerful saints with specialized functions—not to mention the reinstatement of a female divine figure in the person of Mary, who takes on many of the functions of Mediterranean mother-goddesses.[2]

Christianity, then, seems to me to evolve as a masterly combination of monism and pluralism, which is no doubt part of the secret of its success. It is not, however, mainstream Christianity with which we are concerned at present, but rather with the various forms of fringe Christianity, grouped together in modern terminology under the umbrella title of Gnosticism.

Whether or not Gnosticism is basically a Christian phenomenon—an issue on which controversy persists[3]—there is no question that it is based on the premiss of a single first principle of some sort. The Gnostic variety of dualism[4] does not involve two co-ordinate opposed principles of the type manifested in Zoroastrian religion, for example; the evil or negative principle arises, rather, out of the entourage of the supreme positive principle, and is on an inferior plane to it. All that the Gnostic

---

[2] The lack of a female principle at the highest level in Christianity is something that arises, it seems to me, from the grammatical accident that the Spirit of God (*ru'ah*) of later Judaism, which is feminine in Hebrew, becomes neuter when translated into Greek—*pneuma*—(and masculine in Latin—*spiritus*), which makes for various theological problems, until Mary, as Mother of God, is accorded something of this status. I have discussed this question in 'Female Principles in Platonism', *Ithaca*, 1 (1986), 107–23 (repr. in *The Golden Chain*, Aldershot: Variorum, 1990, Essay 4). Gnosticism avoids this excess of male chauvinism by presenting its second principle, the Barbelo, as having at least a female aspect, cf. e.g. *Apocr. Joh.* 5. 5–6, where it is described as a 'mother-father', 'a womb for the pleroma', and a 'thrice-androgynous name'. It is habitually described as the 'male virgin' Barbelo, which is admittedly a rather ambiguous status.

[3] A good discussion of this question may be found in Kurt Rudolph, Gnosis, tr. R. McL. Wilson (Edinburgh, 1983), 275–94. I myself find it difficult to imagine how the full complexity of the Gnostic metaphysical system could have arisen from Christianity alone, but that may not mean that there was ever a pre-Christian system which would be recognizably Gnostic. The complexities could be the result of progressive accretions.

[4] On this see A. H. Armstrong 'Dualism: Platonic, Gnostic, and Christian', in R. T. Wallis and J. Bregman (eds.), *Neoplatonism and Gnosticism* (Albany, NY: SUNI, 1992), 33–54.

systems disagree, or at least show some variation, on is whether or not to take this secondary deity, the cosmic demiurge, as positively malevolent or just ignorant,[5] and whether or not to postulate a female, generative principle as co-ordinate with the supreme principle. Even when this latter move is made, however, such a second principle is generally no more than the 'thought' (*ennoia*) or 'will' of the supreme principle, and thus does not constitute a very serious threat to his uniqueness.[6]

In one respect, indeed, the Gnostic systems can be seen as being even more monistic than either Christianity or Platonism: they do not postulate even an independent material principle, such as appears in the *Timaeus*, which constitutes a refractory element in the universe, resistant to the complete control of the demiurge in his creative activity. In Gnosticism, as in the system presented in the *Chaldaean Oracles*, even matter is generated ultimately from the first principle.[7] Admittedly, the Gnostic demiurge, Ialdabaoth, faces a world which he cannot entirely control, but that is because he is an imperfect and inferior deity. One could argue that the fall of Sophia shows evidence of a flaw or imperfection in the universe, but, if so, the flaw is *internal* to the system; it is not provoked by any outside power, nor even by a refractory substrate of any sort.

So we are left with a single first principle. On the other hand, the first principle in Gnosticism is subject to being characterized by negations to the extent of almost being deprived of, or rather, raised above, divinity proper. Certainly, he or it is a far more impersonal entity than the Judaeo-Christian deity, and much closer to the One or Good of later Platonism. It can relate to the lower reaches of creation only through a series of emanations, creator figures such as Barbelo and the Aeons, and, at a lower level, the Demiurge Ialdabaoth or Sakla, which take over all

---

[5] His ignorance in proclaiming himself the supreme god, and his reproof for that by a higher power, is a recurring theme in the texts (see above, n. 1).

[6] The Valentinians in particular, as we shall see, postulate as co-ordinate with their supreme principle a female entity called 'Silence' (*Sigē*). By contrast, in the *Apocryphon of John* (4. 26 ff.), the first principle exercises Forethought (*Pronoia*), and this emanates as the second principle, the Barbelo, in a way very similar to the production of Nous from the One in Plotinus' system. See on this question the discussion of Elaine Pagels, *The Gnostic Gospels* (New York, 1979), ch. 3: 'God the Father/God the Mother'.

[7] That is to say, immediately from the foolish actions of Sophia, but ultimately, if indirectly, from the first principle. Cf. Rudolph *Gnosis*, 73 ff. A particularly simple and straightforward theology, close both to mainline Christianity and to Platonism (and possibly composed by Valentinus himself), is to be found in the *Gospel of Truth* (18–19), where the Father contains all things, while being himself uncontained—a formulation with deep roots in Greek philosophical thought. Cf. W. R. Schoedel, 'Gnostic Monism and *The Gospel of Truth*', in B. Layton (ed.), *The Rediscovery of Gnosticism* (Leiden, 1980), i. 379–90.

activity concerning creation, both intellectual and physical—though it is
seen as exercising an overall providential care, or *pronoia*.

Rather than generalize any further, however, we would do best to consider a few key passages from central Gnostic documents, and try to
isolate their salient features. Let us turn first, then, to the *Apocryphon of
John*, 2. 33 ff., which is a document that presents perhaps the most comprehensive account of Gnostic metaphysics.[8] Here we find a description
of what is termed the Monad, father of all, 'existing in uncontaminated
light, towards which no vision may gaze'.

It is not fitting to think of it as god[9] or as something of the sort, for it is
superior to deity; nothing is above it, for nothing has mastery over it. It is not
inferior to anything, because it lacks nothing. For it is utter fullness, without
having become defective in anything so that it might be completed by it; rather,
it is always utterly perfect in [. . .]. It is unlimited, because nothing exists prior to
it so as to bestow limit on it; unfathomable, because nothing exists prior to it so
as to fathom it; immeasurable, because nothing else has measured it; invisible,
because nothing else has seen it; eternal, since it exists into eternity; ineffable,
because nothing has been able to reach it so as to speak of it; unnameable, since
there is nothing that exists prior to it so as to give a name to it.

This is by no means the end of this litany, but we may pause here to draw
breath, and consider what we have got so far. What we have got is a
sequence of negative characterizations, most of which, when translated
back into Greek, should be thoroughly familiar to us from contemporary
Greek philosophical texts.[10] If we turn, for instance, to ch. 10 of Alcinous'
Didaskalikos, a notable exposition of Middle Platonic theology, we find
a good many of the same epithets produced, in a context of negative
theology.

First of all, the Gnostic first principle is declared not to be thought of
as god, since it is superior to deity. The Hellenic source will not go so far
as to say this; it will merely declare that it is superior to other divine
entities, such as the world-soul and the mind of the world-soul (10. 164.

---

[8] This was originally composed in Greek, but no Greek text survives (though Irenaeus,
in *Against All Heresies*, 1. 29, appears to preserve a summary of at least something very like
it). The text is known in Coptic translation, attested in four MSS, *NHC* II, pp. 1–32; *NHC*
III, pp. 1–40; *NHC* IV, pp. 1–49; and *PBerol.* 8502, pp. 19–77. There is a long version and
a short version, the former represented by *NHC* II and IV, from which I quote here. I
borrow the translation of Bentley Layton, in *The Gnostic Scriptures* (New York, 1987), 29,
slightly adapted.

[9] The Coptic *noute* presumably translates *theos*.

[10] If Irenaeus is referring to this text, it must date at least from before AD 180.

18 ff.). It is also, however, described a little further on (164. 33) as *theiotēs*, 'divinity', an epithet the significance of which is not explained here, but may have the meaning 'activity' or 'essence' of god, or 'what makes god god', even as its companion epithet *ousiotēs*, essentiality', seems to mean something like 'what makes true being true being', with in either case the connotation of superiority to the entity in question, be it *theos* or *ousia*. However that may be, other epithets find a more exact correspondence in *Did.* 10. There the primal god is described as 'eternal (*aiōnios*), ineffable (*arrhētos*), self-perfect (*autotelēs*)—that is, deficient in no respect—ever-perfect (*aeitelēs*)—that is, always perfect—and all-perfect (*pantelēs*)—that is, perfect in all respects' (164. 30–3). All this is to emphasize his total superiority to, and independence of, all of the rest of creation. Of the epithets appearing in the *Apoc. Joh.*, 'unlimited' (presumably *apeiros*), 'immeasurable' (*ametrētos*),[11] 'invisible' (*aoratos*), 'eternal' (*aidios*), 'ineffable' (*arrhētos*), 'unnameable' (*akatonomastos*), all are thoroughly familar to Hellenic theology, and most appear in this chapter of the *Didaskalikos*.[12]

The idea is also introduced that this god is to be credited with certain characteristics in a *causal* capacity, i.e. not because he possesses these characteristics—he is superior to that—but because he engenders them in others (4. 3 ff.):

He is eternity, as bestowing eternity. He is life, as bestowing life. He is blessed, as bestowing blessedness. He is knowledge (*gnōsis*), as bestowing knowledge. He is good, as bestowing goodness. He is mercy, as bestowing mercy, and ransom. He is grace, as bestowing grace. He is all these things, not as possessing attributes; rather, as bestowing them.

This has its counterpart in *Did.* 10. The author, at the end of the list of epithets listed above, first cautions us that 'I do not speak as though distinguishing these things as aspects of it', indicating by this a concern not

---

[11] I leave aside 'unfathomable', as there seems to be some problem about its exact translation.

[12] *Ametrētos* does not occur here, but it does in a notable passage of Plotinus, *Enn.* 1. 6. 9, where Plotinus is actually talking about how one can be united with the beauty of the supreme principle through contemplation of beauty: 'If you have become this, and see it, and are at home with yourself in purity, with nothing hindering you from becoming in this way one, with no inward mixture of anything else, but wholly yourself, nothing but true light (*phōs alēthinon*), not measured by dimensions, or bounded by shape into littleness, or expanded to size by unboundedness, *but everywhere unmeasured* (*ametrēton*), because greater than all measure and superior to all quantity' (9. 16–22). Note here the same combination of light, unmeasuredness, and superiority to all measure that we find in the *Apocryphon of John*. We should also note the epithet *aperimetros*, found in Apuleius, *De Platone*, 1. 5. 190 (a term that does not occur in any surviving Greek source).

to attribute qualities or other characteristics to his supreme principle; and then continues:

And it is 'good', because it acts beneficently towards all things to the full extent, acting as cause of all goodness; 'beautiful', because by its very nature it is perfect and proportional; 'truth', because it is the source of all truth, just as the sun is the cause of all life; 'parent', in being the cause of all things, because it orients the celestial intellect and the soul of the universe in an orderly relationship to itself and its own intellections.

If one is to posit a relationship between these two texts, I must say that I am inclined to regard the Gnostic as derivative from the Platonist. I view the Gnostics as very much the magpies of the intellectual world of the second century, garnering features that take their fancy both from the Jewish and Christian scriptures, and from the metaphysics of contemporary Platonism, though admittedly giving to these garnerings their own distinctive world-negating twist. This position of mine will certainly be seen as tendentious by devoted students of Gnosticism, and in respect of a feature of Sethian Gnosticism which I will get to presently (the internal structure of the Barbelo), I concede that it raises interesting problems, but I would still wish to maintain that, as regards analogies with Platonism, it is the Gnostics who are derivative.

But let us return to our consideration of the first principle. A number of other texts may be adduced to reinforce that from the *Apocryphon of John*. In *Allogenes* (61. 8 ff.) we find a similar characterization of the first principle, which lays great stress on the *non-essential* way in which all epithets which may be applied to it must be taken as relating to it:

And I beheld the first, which is unrecognizable to all, the deity better than perfect, through a manifestation thereof, along with the triply-powered that exists in all.[13]

. . . Now, its possession of any given non-essential property resides in its mode of existing, either in existing and being about to be, or in being active, or in understanding and being alive—although in an incomprehensible way, it does not possess intellect, life, reality,[14] or unreality. And it has any given non-essential property along with its essential existent property without its being distinguished[15] in any way, at the time that it causes something undertaken, or

---

[13] This is a reference to the second principle, the Barbelo, which has a triadic structure, as we shall see.

[14] The three features, or aspects, of the Barbelo—as, of course, of the Nous, at least in Platonism from Porphyry onwards.

[15] The Coptic can apparently mean this, but it is obscure. It can also mean 'left behind', which makes little sense.

purifies, or receives, or bestows;[16] likewise, without its being active?[17] in any way, whether through its will alone or in bestowing or in receiving from another. Nor has it any will, neither one deriving from itself, nor one bestowed through another. It is not toward its own self that it proceeds; yet neither does it, in itself, bestow anything out of itself, lest it become active?[18] in some other way. Accordingly, it does not need intellect or life, or indeed anything at all: for in its lacking nothing, and being unrecognizable, that is, in its non-existent substantiation (*hyparxis anousios*),[19] it is superior to the totality of things, in its silence and stillness . . .

It is neither divinity nor blessedness nor perfection. Rather, each of these is an unrecognizable non-essential property of it, and not its essential property. Rather it is some other, superior to blessedness, divinity, and perfection.

Again, this goes on some while longer, but enough has been quoted, I think, to make the point clear. What we have is a first principle not unlike the Plotinian One, not least in its transcendence of *ousia* (though Plotinus does grant his One a will, at least in *Enn.* 6. 8), which yet in some ineffable way stands at the head of a whole process of creation.[20]

It is not itself, however, an actively creative principle. The key to the cosmogonic process rests with the primal emanation of the first principle, the Barbelo. This curious term seems to be a garbled version of a Late Egyptian (Coptic) word *berber*, meaning 'boiling over', or 'overflow', combined with the ending -*ō*, meaning 'great'.[21] This is a

---

[16] I confess that the exact sense of this eludes me. It may have lost something in translation into Coptic. It may be a reference, though, to such epithets as 'good', 'pure', or 'beneficent', all of which will have a purely causal sense.

[17] A word is lost here, but this must be approximately the sense.

[18] Again, a word is lost. See previous note.

[19] In the Coptic, *tihyparxis n-atshōpe*, which corresponds to a parallel phrase in *Zostrianos*, 79. 6–7, *n-hyparxis n-atousia*, showing the original Greek adjective was *anousios*. This, notably, is never used as an epithet of the supreme principle in surviving texts of later Platonism (only, by Proclus, in connection with matter); the Neoplatonic epithet for the One is *hyperousios*.

[20] We find a similar first principle presented, as the summit of an elaborate ascent through thirteen 'seals', in the tractate *Marsanes* (*NHCX* 1. 4. 17 ff. and 7. 24 ff.). This is given the title of 'the Silent One who is unknowable', which is superior to a second principle called 'the Invisible, Three-powered (*tridynamos*) One, unbegotten, pre-eternal, non-existent (*anousios*)'. Oddly, the Silent One itself is not described as *anousios*, but rather (at 7. 24) as 'He who is' (probably rendering the LXX and Philonic epithet of God, *ho ōn*). This gives evidence of a troublesome variability in terminology, but, sadly, *Marsanes* survives in a rather fragmentary state, so we may not be getting the full picture. On the face of it, however, this distinction of two Ones, the second somehow presiding over a triad, is interestingly reminiscent (or anticipatory) of the metaphysical system of Iamblichus. The second One, incidentally, in turn generates the Barbelo. Cf. the useful discussion in B. A. Pearson, 'The Tractate Marsanes (NHC X) and the Platonic Tradition', in *Gnosis: Festschrift für Hans Jonas* (Göttingen, 1978), 373–84.

[21] It appears, as a variant, in the form 'Barbērō' in Epiphanius' account of Gnostic

tempting etymology, since it yields a very suitable meaning. One would
have to assume a slight differentiating sound-change from 'R' to 'L',
which may have been stimulated partly from a desire to avoid confusion
with either *barbaros* or *borboros*, 'mud' (which latter is indeed a confusion which was happily made anyhow by ill-intentioned folk, as is
attested by St Epiphanius, who calls one group of Gnostics whom he
attacks 'Borborites'[22]).

At any rate, this second principle arises from the first by a process
rather similar to that of Intellect arising from the One in Plotinus'
system. In the *Apocryphon of John*, we find the first principle indulging
in thought, 'and its thinking produced something, and the thinking was
disclosed, standing plainly in its presence in the brilliance of its light.
This is the first power, which exists prior to all others, and which was
shown forth out of its thinking, that is, the perfect forethought (*pronoia*)
of the *plēroma*' (4. 26–32). It is this *pronoia*, when it 'jells', so to speak,
and takes its stand over against its creator, that is the Barbelo.

This is certainly reminiscent of the evolution of Nous from the One,
through the intermediacy of an indefinite outpouring from the One that
is pre-Nous, except that Plotinus would not have spoken of the One as
thinking.[23] What it may in fact more closely resemble (if only we knew
more about the details of it), is the process by which the Second Intellect
derives from the First in the system of Numenius.[24] Indeed, I would be
inclined to see Numenius, rather than Plotinus, as the philosophical
éminence grise behind these documents.[25] This conjecture becomes rather

doctrine at *Against Heresies*, 26. 10. 10 (though Epiphanius otherwise gives the usual form
of the name), which would support this etymology. It must be admitted, however, that
there is another possible etymology of the name which has found widespread favour (cf.
H. Leisegang, *Die Gnosis* (Stuttgart, 1955), 186): *b' arbē eloh*, 'in four is God', which would
not suit my position so well, as adumbrating a tetrad of some sort, rather than a triad. On
the other hand, such an etymology, even if sound, does not necessarily have any relevance
to the nature of the Barbelo in developed Gnostic systems. It may simply be a reference to
the four letters of the Hebrew YHWH.

[22] *Panarion* 26. 3. 5–6: 'Indeed, the blasphemous assembly full of enormous recklessness,
the anthologizing and narration of its filthy conduct, and the filthy perversity of their
beggarly obscenity truly pollute the ears, so that quite naturally they are called by some
"Borborites".'

[23] See, on the complexities of this process, the useful monograph of John Bussanich,
The One and its Relation to Intellect in Plotinus (Leiden: Brill, 1988), and Dominic O'Meara,
Plotinus: An Introduction to the Enneads (Oxford: Clarendon Press, 1993), chs. 4–6.

[24] On which see J. M. Dillon, *The Middle Platonists* (London, 1977; 2nd edn., 1996),
366–72, and Michael Frede, 'Numenius', *ANRW* 2. 36. 2, 1054–70.

[25] The difficulty about postulating any dependence on Plotinus is simply that some of
these documents, in which this metaphysical system is already present, such as *Zostrianos*
and *Allogenes*, were already being used by Gnostics attached to Plotinus' circle (Porph.

more tenuous, unfortunately, with the salient feature of the Barbelo that I have been alluding to at various points, and now wish to discuss briefly, its triadic structure.

As with the Chaldaean Oracles, the Gnostic documents provide evidence of a tendency to see the second entity in the system as embodying a triad of some sort.[26] In *Apoc. Joh.* (5. 10–35) this appears to be a tetrad, or even more, but that, I think, is a misleading impression.[27] What is stated is that Barbelo, when it hypostasizes itself, makes a series of requests of the 'invisible virgin spirit' (as the first principle is here termed). First it asks for *prognōsis*, 'prior knowledge' (which I take to be the basic condition of its being able to operate as an authoritative creator god, and performer of the Father's will), and then asks in turn for the three qualities of incorruptibility (*aphtharsia*), eternal life (*zōē aiōnios*), and truth (*alētheia*), all of which then become hypostasized (as does *prognōsis*) as aeons. The schema appears in a more obvious form elsewhere, though, as in *Allogenes* 59. 1–37, where the Foreigner, in turning inward towards cognition of the Barbelo, is exhorted to approach the powers within it in a certain order, first Blessedness (*makariotēs*), then Vitality (*zōotēs*), and lastly Essentiality (*ousiotēs*), after which he will grasp the whole essence of the Barbelo. In the *Gospel of the Egyptians* (4. 51. 15–52. 24), on the other hand, we learn that the Great Invisible Spirit emanated three powers, 'which it emitted from its bosom in silence[28] and by its forethought (*pronoia*): the Father, the Mother, and the Son', each of which then generates an ogdoad of aeons. To confuse the issue, the Barbelo now appears as the first of the Mother's aeons, but this has to be an aberration, perhaps signifying that the essence of the Barbelo as generative principle can be seen to reside in the 'female' moment of the intelligible realm. The whole realm (which is initially called Doxomedōn-Domedōn) is referred to as Barbelo just below, at 4. 54.

VP 16), so that one would have to postulate (as has, indeed, been done, but I think implausibly) that what we possess as emerging from Nag Hammadi are 'revised', post-Plotinian versions of the documents mentioned by Porphyry.

[26] Or, in the case of the theological system of the *Marsanes* (see above, n. 20), the second and third entities.

[27] It must be said at the same time that a tetrad *is* also a feature of the Barbelo (cf. *Apoc. Joh.* 8. 2–20; *Gosp. Eg.* 63. 8–14; *Zostr.* 29. 1–19) but that is something distinct, in the form of a set of four 'luminaries', which are given 'angelic' titles, Harmozēl, Oroiaēl, Daueithai, and Elēlēth, but which are also expressed as abstractions, Intelligence, Loveliness, Perception, and Prudence.

[28] Probably intended to be hypostasized here, as Sigē. This is certainly the case when one comes to the Valentinian system, as expounded by Ptolemaeus (*ap.* Irenaeus, *Heres.* 1. 1. 1).

20—or at least Barbelo is portrayed as taking a controlling interest in it. At *Zostrianos* 14, 1 ff. the Barbelo is presented as the source of three basic powers, Essentiality, Blessedness, and Life.

In the Alice-in-Wonderland world of the Gnostics, this is about as near a consistent pattern as we are going to get. However one slices it, and whatever other complexities may also manifest themselves, there is clear evidence, at the level of the secondary divinity in the system, of a triad of aspects, and those aspects, or 'moments', can be equated reasonably well with what appears to us to be the later Neoplatonic triad (envisaged unofficially by Plotinus,[29] but definitely formalized by Porphyry). Unfortunately, however, there is really no sign of such a development as this in Platonism before Plotinus. On the other hand, there is some sign that Origen knew of a graded system of influences emanating from a triad which he takes as Father, Son, and Holy Spirit, but which he handles rather awkwardly, indicating (to me) that he is borrowing it from some alien source,[30] and, since the Platonist (apart from Ammonius Saccas) to whom he relates most closely is Numenius, I am prepared to propose that Numenius had in fact developed some system of this sort.[31] The alternative, I fear, is to admit that the Gnostics (and Chaldaeans) made this substantive contribution to the later Neoplatonic system, and even to that of Plotinus himself.

But I fear I have strayed rather from our proper subject, which was monism, and have instead slipped into an investigation of trinities. The overall burden of this paper, however, to reiterate, is that, beneath all the proliferation of subordinate entities, Gnosticism presents us with a clearly monistic system, where the first principle has, at the highest level, no more than a shadowy female consort (in the form of his 'silence', or his 'forethought'), and no countervailing entity or force not of his own making. Nor does the form of monism manifesting itself in the Gnostic texts seem to me to owe much to Christianity, though I am not sure what its provenance is. The Gnostic first principle, the Great Invisible Spirit, is a far more transcendent and impersonal entity than the Jewish or

[29] Cf. A. H. Armstrong, 'Eternity, Life, and Movement in Plotinus's Accounts of *Nous*', in *Le Néoplatonisme* (Paris: CNRS, 1971).

[30] See my essay, 'Origen's Doctrine of the Trinity and Some Later Neoplatonic Theories', in D. J. O'Meara (ed.). *Neoplatonism and Christian Thought* (Albany, NY: SUNI, 1982), 19–23 (= *The Golden Chain*, Essay 21).

[31] A triad of divinities is of course attested for Numenius, in the form of Father, Demiurge and World Soul (which Proclus declares that he denominated, rather bombastically, Grandfather, Father, and Grandson (fr. 21 Des Places)), but that is not germane to our present enquiry, being more akin to Plotinus' system of hypostases than to a triad of aspects of the hypostasis of Nous.

Christian God—which indeed, in the person of Yahveh as portrayed in the Old Testament, is demoted to the administration of the material world, and mocked at as a boaster and a clown.[32]

SELECT BIBLIOGRAPHY

ARMSTRONG, A. H., 'Dualism: Platonic, Gnostic, and Christian', in R. T. Wallis and J. Bregman (eds.), *Neoplatonism and Gnosticism* (Albany, NY: SUNI, 1992), 33–54.

DILLON, J. M., *The Middle Platonists* (London: Duckworth, 1977; 2nd edn., 1996).

GRANT, R. M., *Gnosticism and Early Christianity* (2nd. edn., New York: Harper & Row, 1966).

JONAS, H., *The Gnostic Religion* (3rd. edn., Boston: Beacon Press, 1970).

LAYTON, B., *The Gnostic Scriptures* (New York: Doubleday, 1987).

PAGELS, E., *The Gnostic Gospels* (New York: Random House, 1979).

PEARSON, B. A., 'The Tractate Marsanes (NHC X) and the Platonic Tradition', in *Gnosis: Festschrift für Hans Jonas* (Göttingen: Vandenhoeck & Ruprecht, 1978), 373–84.

ROBINSON, J. M., (ed.), *The Nag Hammadi Library in English* (San Francisco: Harper & Row, 1977).

RUDOLPH, K., *Die Gnosis: Wesen und Geschichte einer spätantiken Religion* (Leipzig: Koehler & Amelang, 1977; Eng. tr. *Gnosis*, R. McL. Wilson (Edinburgh: T. & T. Clark, 1983).

SCHOEDEL, W. R., 'Gnostic Monism and *The Gospel of Truth*', in B. Layton (ed.), *The Rediscovery of Gnosticism*, i. *The School of Valentinus* (Leiden: Brill, 1980), 379–90.

---

[32] Sakla, one of his chief titles, means 'fool' in Aramaic, while Samaël, another common epithet, means 'the blind god'.

4

f Theos Hypsistos between Pagans, Jews, and Christians

STEPHEN MITCHELL

1. THE ORACLE FROM OENOANDA

In 1971 George Bean published an oracle inscription from the city of Oenoanda in northern Lycia.[1] Within a few months Louis Robert lectured on the text at the Académie des Inscriptions et Belles Lettres in Paris and wrote one of his finest articles on these six hexameter verses, 'Un oracle gravé à Oenoanda'.[2] Ramsay MacMullen, in a footnote to his *Paganism in the Roman Empire*, saluted the achievement of both scholars: 'Professor Robert's discussion and the work of original discovery by G. E. Bean are enough to restore one's faith in scholarship.'[3] Since then the oracle from Oenoanda has occupied an obligatory and worthy place at the centre of all discussions of late Roman paganism.[4]

This discussion of the cult of Theos Hypsistos has grown out of a lecture prepared for the inaugural conference of the University of Wales Institute of Classics and Ancient History held at Gregynog in July 1994 on the topic 'What is a god?' It has subsequently been given as a seminar paper in London and Oxford, and I have benefited from the discussion of all three audiences, as well as from the comments of Polymnia Athanassiadi and of Fergus Millar. The issues which are raised by the material require much fuller treatment than is possible even in a lengthy article. I hope to develop the discussion in a monograph. I am grateful to a reader for drawing my attention to the Sorbonne thesis by N. Belauche, *Contribution à l'étude du sentiment religieux dans les provinces orientales de l'empire romain. Les divinités "hypsistos"* (1984), and her remarks in *Le serment: Signes et fonctions* (CNRS Paris, 1991), 159–68, but I have not seen these.

[1] G. E. Bean, *Journeys in Northern Lycia 1965–67*, D. Ak. Wien phil.-hist. Klasse 104 (1971), 20–2 no. 37.

[2] L. Robert, *CRAI* 1971, 597–619 (*Opera Minora Selecta*, v. 617–39).

[3] *Paganism in the Roman Empire* (1981), 147 n. 65.

[4] Note in particular, M. Guarducci, *Rendiconti dell' Accademia nazionale dei Lincei* 8.27 (1972), 335, *Epigrafia Greca*, iv (1978), 109–12; C. Gavallotti, 'Un epigrafe teosofica ad Enoanda', *Philologus*, 121 (1977), 95–105; G. H. R. Horsley, *New Documents illustrating Early Christianity*, ii (1978), 39; H. W. Parke, *The Oracles of Apollo in Asia Minor* (1985); R. Lane Fox, *Pagans and Christians* (1985), 168–71, 190–200, reviewed by G. Fowden, *JRS* 78 (1988), 178–9; D. S. Potter, *Prophecy and History in the Crisis of the Roman Empire: An Historical Commentary on the Thirteenth Sibylline Oracle* (1990), 351–5.

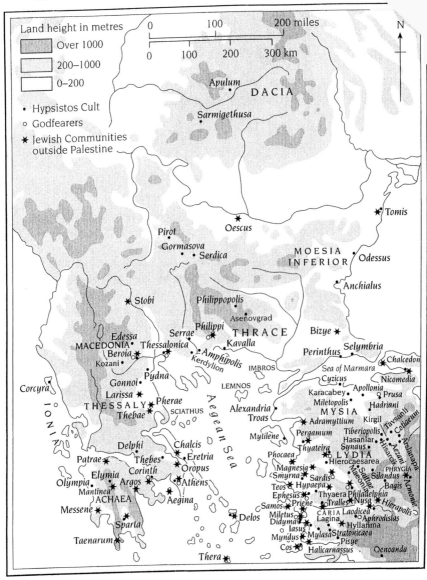

Land height in metres
- Over 1000
- 200–1000
- 0–200

- Hypsistos Cult
- Godfearers
- Jewish Communities outside Palestine

N

Olbia

Tanais

Rostov on the Don

Sea of Azov

CRIMEA

Panticapaeum

Gorgippia

Black Sea

Amastris
Tium
Sinope

PAPHLAGONIA

Trapezus

Hadrianopolis

PONTUS

Malus
Dorylaeum
Ancyra
Sebastopolis
Kuyucak
GALATIA Tavium
Nacolea
Holanta
Hanisa

ARMENIA

Synnada
Pisidian
Antioch
Caesaria
CAPPADOCIA

Iconium
COMMAGENE
LYCAONIA

0   100   200 miles

0   100   200   300 km

Land height in metres
- Over 1000
- 200–1000
- 0–200

- • Hypsistos Cult
- ○ Godfearers
- ✱ Jewish Communities outside Palestine

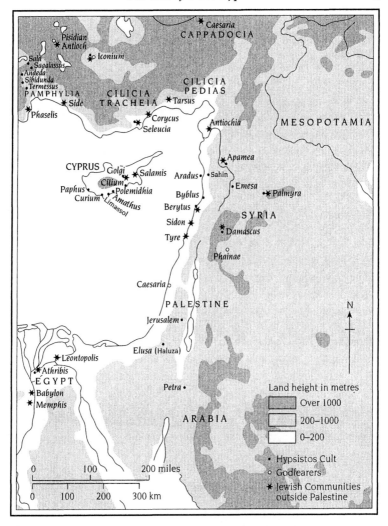

CAPPADOCIA

Caesaria

Pisidian
Antioch

Iconium

Sala
Sagalassus
Andeda
Sibidunda
Termessus
PAMPHYLIA   CILICIA
Side   TRACHEIA

CILICIA
PEDIAS

Tarsus

Phaselis

Corycus
Seleucia

Antiochia

MESOPOTAMIA

CYPRUS *Golgi*
Cilium   *Salamis*   *Aradus* *Sahin*
Paphus   *Polemidhia*
Curium   *Amathus*
Limassol

Apamea

Byblus   *Emesa*   *Palmyra*

Berytus

Sidon

SYRIA

Tyre

Damascus

Phainae

Caesaria

PALESTINE

N

Jerusalem

Elusa (Haluza)

Leontopolis
Athribis
EGYPT
Babylon
Memphis

Petra

ARABIA

Land height in metres

Over 1000

200–1000

0–200

0   100   200 miles

0   100   200   300 km

• Hypsistos Cult

○ Godfearers

✳ Jewish Communities
  outside Palestine

The interest of this text is far from being exhausted. Discussion has rightly focused on the theological implications of the verses, for they purport to reveal nothing less than the nature of god himself. But what god was being worshipped at Oenoanda, and under what circumstances? The verses run as follows:

[Α]ὐτοφυής, ἀδί | δακτος, ἀμήτωρ, | ἀστυφέλικτος, |
οὔνομα μὴ χω | ρῶν, πολυώνυμος, | ἐν πυρὶ ναίων, |
τοῦτο θεός· μεικρὰ | δὲ θεοῦ μερὶς ἄνγε||λοι ἡμεῖς.
τοῦτο πευ|θομένοισι θεοῦ πέ|ρι ὅστις ὑπάρχει, |
Αἰ[θ]έ[ρ]α πανδερκ[ῆ | θε]ὸν ἔννεπεν, εἰς | ὃν ὁρῶντας
εὔχεσθ᾽ ἠῴ|ους πρὸς ἀντολίην ἐσορῶ[ν]|τα[ς].

Born of itself, untaught, without a mother, unshakeable, not contained in a name, known by many names, dwelling in fire, this is god. We, his angels, are a small part of god. To you who ask this question about god, what his essential nature is, he has pronounced that Aether is god who sees all, on whom you should gaze and pray at dawn, looking towards the sunrise.

Two written sources of late antiquity quote the first three lines of the text. They demonstrate that the speaker was Apollo himself and indicate the oracle's provenance. One is the late fifth-century *Theosophy of Tübingen*, a collection of pagan oracles incorporated into a larger work called 'On True Belief', which Christians cited to show that even the pagan gods acknowledged the truth and superiority of the Christian faith. The first three lines of the Oenoanda text are there reproduced as the conclusion of sixteen hexameter verses, which are presented as Apollo's reply to the question posed by a certain Theophilos, whether he or another was god.[5] The other is a passage of the *Divine Institutions* of Lactantius, written in the 320s, which states that these lines were part, to be precise the beginning, of an oracle of twenty-one verses pronounced at the oracular Apolline sanctuary of Claros.[6]

There are difficulties in reconciling the six-line inscribed version of

---

[5] H. Erbse, *Fragmente griechischer Theosophien* (1941, 2nd edn. 1995), 169 is the most recent edition; further bibliography in Robert, *CRAI* 1971, 605: ὅτι Θεοφίλου τινὸς τοὔνομα τὸν Ἀπόλλωνα ἐρωτήσαντος, σὺ εἶ θεὸς ἢ ἄλλος, ἔχρησεν οὕτως.

[6] Lactantius, *Div. Inst.* 1. 7: *Apollo enim, quem praeter ceteros divinum maximeque fatidicum existimant, Colophone residens, quo Delphis, credo, migraverat Asiae ductus amoenitate quaerenti cuidam quis aut quid esset omnino Deus respondit viginti et uno versibus, quorum hoc principium est,* αὐτοφυής, ἀδίδακτος, ἀμήτωρ, ἀστυφέλικτος, | οὔνομα μηδὲ λόγῳ χωρούμενος, ἐν πυρὶ ναίων, | τοῦτο θεός· μεικρὰ δὲ θεοῦ μερὶς ἄνγελοι ἡμεῖς. The variant reading at the beginning of the second hexameter occurs also in the *Theosophy of Tübingen* version, and is doubtless due to Christian influence, which removed the polytheistic overtones of πολυώνυμος from the oracle (Robert, *CRAI* 1971, 608). For a third late source, which cites the oracle, see below § 5.

the oracle with the longer and different forms in which it was known to Lactantius and to the compiler of the *Theosophy*. David Potter has suggested that the first three lines of the Oenoanda text, found also in the other versions, were effectively an oracular commonplace, and that the three texts were independent of one another.[7] But although the resounding negatives of the first line belong to an established tradition of Platonic theological philosophy, and the vocabulary and concepts can be paralleled elsewhere in the religious ideas of the second and third centuries AD, both in style and substance the oracle is not a commonplace utterance, but an impressive and memorable reply to a specific and pointed question. It was this that caused it to be cited by diverse later writers. Oracles that were repeated in different contexts invited contempt, not compliance.[8] Robin Lane Fox has argued that the compilers of the *Theosophy of Tübingen* produced a faulty version of the original by confusing and stitching together similar but unconnected texts.[9] This is more convincing. At all events, the change of speaker between lines 1–3 and lines 4–6, combining first-person quotation with third-person summary of the text, supports the argument that the original form of the oracle was lengthier than the inscribed version. There is therefore no inherent difficulty in reconciling six lines at Oenoanda with the twenty-one known to Lactantius. The full text was too long to be inscribed in the location which the Oenoandans chose for it, so they opted for a summary, doubtless authorized by the priests at Claros, of the part of the text which affected their immediate concern, the rite of worship.[10]

The importance of the physical location of the inscription was brilliantly clarified by Alan Hall, who showed that the oracle was set up in an archaeological context which takes us to the very site of the ritual which it prescribes. The epigraphic text comprises sixteen short lines on a relief of an altar. This is carved on one of the blocks of the inner face

[7] This is also the view of R. Merkelbach and J. Stauber, 'Die Orakel des Apollon von Klaros', *Epigraphica Anatolica*, 27 (1996), 41–5: 'Wahrscheinlich sind die Verse nicht nur einmal benützt worden, sondern hundertmal. Man ermesse, was dies für die Ausbreitung des Monotheismus bedeuten konnte.'

[8] Potter, *Prophecy and History*, 352–5. Word-for-word repetition was a sure way to discredit an oracle's value; compare Oenomaus of Gadara's withering comments on the subject, quoted by Eusebius, *Praep. Ev.* 5. 22 (J. Hammerstaedt, *Die Orakelkritik des Kynikers Oenomaos* (1988) fr. 14 with commentary). Robert, *CRAI* 1971, 610–14 and Lane Fox, *Pagans and Christians*, 170 discuss the language and philosophical associations of the text.

[9] In a lecture to the conference held in Oxford in 1995 on the tenth anniversary of the death of Louis Robert.

[10] Compare Robert, *CRAI* 1971, 614–15. *Pace* Potter, *Prophecy and History*, 354 the text occupies the entire altar relief, which had been prepared for it.

PLATE 1. The oracle of Apollo at Oenoanda (Catalogue 233).

of the Hellenistic city wall of Oenoanda, above and to the right of an arched doorway which led into the back of the round tower in the southern section of this wall (Pl. 1). The last line of the oracle prescribed prayer addressed to the rising sun, and the wall section where the block was placed, which runs north-eastwards along a prominent ridge, was the first part of the whole site of Oenoanda to be struck by the sun's rays

PLATE 2. The open-air sanctuary of Theos Hypsistos at Oenoanda on the inner side of the hellenistic city wall.

PLATE 3. Chromatis dedicates a lamp to Theos Hypsistos (Catalogue **234**).

at dawn. The sanctuary, where the faithful gathered for worship, was the semicircular open area in front of the oracle inscription (Pl. 2; see below §3). As the verses told them, they would have stood facing east, with their backs to the tower and the text, gazing up at heaven and offering their prayers to all-seeing Aether.[11]

[11] A. S. Hall, 'The Klarian oracle at Oenoanda', *ZPE* 32 (1978), 263–8. The photographs shown here were taken during further field work at Oenoanda in 1994.

The oracle stated that this god could not be contained in a name and therefore was known by many names. His divine personality was not equated with any of the gods of the Olympian pantheon, not even with Zeus. He was elevated beyond that status, and his superiority to other pagan deities was made explicit: Apollo and his fellow gods were only a small part of him, and acted as his angels, his divine messengers. The emphatic reduction in the status of the traditional pagan gods is an important feature of the text. This was the crucial device by which Hellenic paganism could be reconciled with a monotheistic system of belief. But in ancient ritual it was necessary to name an object of worship, even when there were doubts about the nature of the god in question,[12] and the god at Oenoanda had a conventional name or title. This is revealed by the only other inscription carved in a similar fashion on the old city wall at Oenoanda, the dedication by a woman, Chromatis, of a lamp to Theos Hypsistos, the highest god (**234**). The votive offering was appropriate to the god's divine nature. The lamp stood in a small niche, carved at the top of the low relief of an altar, and the next block of the wall had a ledge cut along its upper edge where a row of lamps could be placed (Pl. 3). Chromatis' dedication was the humble earthly counterpart to the deity's divine fire.

Lamps and fire were essential to a cult which was associated with the upper air of heaven and with the sun. An inscription from Alexandria virtually conflates Theos Hypsistos with Helios in the dedicatory formula 'For god the highest, who sees all, and for Helios and the Nemeseis', since the adjective ἐπόπτης, which is here applied to Theos Hypsistos, was more usually attributed to Helios, the sun.[13] This association is complete on the text of an altar from Pergamum, which has been restored as a dedication to Helios Theos Hypsistos (**186**). Theos Hypsistos received lamps from devotees at a village in northern Lydia (**169**). A restored text from the territory of Phrygian Tiberiopolis appears to mention the offering of a fire shovel and perhaps of a lamp (**225**). The dedication of an altar at Pergamum to 'the Lord God who exists for eternity', surely Hypsistos, included a lantern-stand and a lantern (**188**).[14] The remains of a sanctuary which has come to light in Serdica in Thrace include a limestone altar with four lamps carved into its upper surface, and over sixty lamps were recovered from the sanctuary on

---

[12] See E. Fraenkel, *Commentary on Aeschylus' Agamemnon* (1950), ii. 99–100.

[13] See **284** from Alexandria. The idea corresponds evidently to the αἰθὴρ πανδερκής of the oracle. For Helios who sees all, cf. S. Mitchell, *Anatolia: Land, Men, and Gods in Asia Minor* (1993), ii. 47.

[14] See P. Trebilco, *Jewish Communities in Asia Minor* (1991), 163.

Delos.[15] The significance of lamps and torches in cult ritual is also stressed in the patristic sources to be discussed in §2.

The Oenoanda oracle text illustrates the central theological ideas and prescribes a form of worship appropriate to the cult of Theos Hypsistos. Although the essence of the divinity was beyond reach in the upper air of heaven, the Aether, it was tangibly embodied in the element of fire and in light, whether from the sun or from a humble oil-lamp. By dedicating a lamp in the sanctuary it was possible for even the most insignificant devotee to establish a direct link with the eternal heavenly fire.

2. THE HYPSISTARIANS

More than any other cult of the Roman world, the worship of Theos Hypsistos has been taken to illustrate the predisposition among pagans of the second and third centuries AD to worship a single, remote, and abstract deity in preference to the anthropomorphic figures of conventional paganism. In other words it has a key place in discussions of monotheism in the later Roman Empire. The external characteristics of this worship are well illustrated by the evidence from Oenoanda. They can also be reconstructed in some detail from a group of passages in the patristic literature, adduced by Emil Schürer a century ago in a classic study of the worship of Theos Hypsistos in the Bosporan kingdom.[16]

In his *Panarion*, the medicine-chest of remedies against poisonous heresies, published in 376, Epiphanius, the bishop of Salamis in Cyprus, provided a description of the religious practices of groups known to him as Messaliani or Euphemitai.[17] Epiphanius has a discursive style and is not always a reliable guide to the heresies which he describes, but this account might have been drawn directly from the scene which we can reconstruct at Oenoanda. Since it also raises several points which correspond with other epigraphic and archaeological evidence for the cult, it must be quoted at some length.

After the preceding sects there has arisen yet another . . . to which belong both men and women who have been deceived. They are called Messalians, which means 'those who pray'. But there have been for some time now, from the days

---

[15] M. Taceva-Hitova, *Balkan Studies*, 19 (1977), 59–75 pl. 5; for Delos see below at n. 30.

[16] E. Schürer, 'Die Juden im bosporanischen Reich und die Genossenschaften der σεβόμενοι θεὸν ὕψιστον ebendaselbst', *Sb. Berl.* (1897), 200–25.

[17] Epiphanius, *Panarion*, ed. K. Holl, *Griechische Christliche Schriftsteller*; Selected translation, including this passage by P. R. Amidon, *The* Panarion *of St. Epiphanius, Bishop of Salamis: Selected Passages* (1990), 355–9.

of Constantius to the present, still others called Euphemites or Messalians, a sect which I think it likely that the one we are considering here has striven to imitate. But those others have arisen from pagans; they do not adhere to Judaism, nor are they Christians, nor do they come from the Samaritans. They are simply pagans who admit the existence of gods but worship none of them; they adore one God only, whom they call the Almighty. They also construct for themselves certain houses or spacious areas, like *fora*, which they call *proseuchai*. Of old there were certain places of prayer among the Jews which were outside the city, and among the Samaritans, as we find as well in the Acts of the Apostles, where Lydia, a seller of purple goods, met those with Paul, even as sacred scripture relates when it says, 'We supposed there was a place of prayer.' The apostles approached and taught the women who had gathered on that occasion. There is also a place of prayer in Shechem, in what is now called Neapolis, outside the city about two miles distant in the plain, which has been copied by the Samaritans, who imitate the Jews in everything, and which is shaped like a theatre and thus is open to the sky.

Now these earlier Messalians, who derive from pagans and who appeared on the scene before those at present who derive from the Christian religion, have themselves constructed on the one hand certain small places in certain regions which are called *proseuchai* or *eukteria*, while in other locations they have built for themselves something like proper churches, where they gather at evening and morning with much lighting of lamps and torches and lengthy singing of hymns and acclamations to God by the zealous among them, through which hymns and acclamations they fondly think to conciliate God. It is ignorance in its blindness and self-conceit that has arranged all these things for those that have gone astray. One of their places of worship was struck by lightning a while ago, I cannot say where; it may have been in Phoenicia that we heard that it happened. Some zealous officials as well killed many of them because they were counterfeiting the truth and mimicking the church, although they were neither Christians nor derived from the Jews. I believe that general Lupicinus was one of those who punished these Euphemites who derive from the pagans. And from this there arose a second source of error for them. For some people took the bodies of those that were killed at that time on account of this sort of pagan lawlessness and buried them in certain places where once again they chant the same acclamations and call themselves the Martyrians because of those martyred for their idols (Epiphanius, *Panarion* 80. 1–2, trans. Amidon).

Despite some evident confusion, this passage distinguishes an earlier group from a later sect which had defected from Christianity in the time of Constantius. The former were pagans:

ἀλλ' ἐκεῖνοι μὲν ἐξ Ἑλλήνων ὡρμῶντο, οὔτε Ἰουδαϊσμῷ προσανέχοντες οὔτε Χριστιανοὶ ὑπάρχοντες οὔτε ἀπὸ Σαμαρειτῶν, ἀλλὰ μόνον Ἕλληνες ὄντες δῆθεν, καὶ θεοὺς μὲν λέγοντες, μηδενὶ μηδὲν προσκυνοῦντες, ἑνὶ δὲ μόνον δῆθεν τὸ

σέβας νέμοντες καὶ καλοῦντες παντοκράτορα, τινὰς δὲ οἴκους ἑαυτοῖς κατα-
σκευάσαντες ἢ τόπους πλατεῖς, φόρων δίκην, προσευχὰς ταύτας ἐκάλουν.

Epiphanius compares these places of prayer to extra-mural Jewish
sanctuaries, the one where Paul won over the god-fearing Lydia near
Philippi, the other in a plain two miles outside Neapolis in Palestine,
built by the Samaritans in the form of an open-air theatre. The
Messalians had built similar open-air places of prayer as well as using
buildings which resembled churches: . . . ὡς προσευχὰς καλούμενα καὶ
εὐκτήρια, ἐν ἄλλοις δὲ τόποις φύσει καὶ ἐκκλησίας ὁμοίωμά τι
ποιήσαντες, καθ' ἑσπέραν καὶ κατὰ τὴν ἕω μετὰ πολλῆς λυχναψίας καὶ
φώτων συναθροιζόμενοι.[18] Although this account classifies these groups
as Hellenes, they have obvious connections with the Jews. The term
pantokrator applied to the deity is virtually restricted to Jewish or
Christian worship,[19] and *proseuche* occurs almost exclusively in Jewish
contexts.[20] The last point was acknowledged by Epiphanius himself, who
noted the similarity between the Messalian *proseuchai* and Jewish places
of prayer both in Gospel times and in his own day. The Messalians also
had close affinities with Christian believers, as appears not only from the
fact that some of them 'derive from the Christian religion', but also from
their adoption of a martyr cult.

The best-known witness to the Hypsistarians in the fourth century is
Gregory of Nazianzus. He explicitly acknowledged the affinity between
the worshippers of Hypsistos and the Jews in the oration which he
delivered at the funeral of his father in 374. This gave an account of the
elder Gregory's early beliefs, before he was converted to Orthodox
Christianity by a party of bishops travelling to attend the Council of
Nicaea in 325:

[18] Epiphanius, *Pan.* 80. 1–2.
[19] For *pantokrator*, see Schürer, *Sb. Berl.* (1897), 221; D. Feissel, *BCH* 104 (1980), 463–5;
Horsley, *New Docs.* i. 137; 3. 118. A cult of Zeus Pantokrator has recently been identified in
Bithynia, *I. Nicaea* ii. 1. 1121; 2. 1512. The editor of these inscriptions, S. Şahin, has rightly
pointed out the relationship of this cult to the worship of Theos Hypsistos.
[20] For *proseuche*, see L. Robert, *Opera Minora Selecta*, iii. 1611; E. Schürer, *The History of
the Jewish People in the time of Jesus Christ* (ed. G. Vermes and F. Millar; henceforth Schürer²), ii (1979), 425–6 n. 4 and 439–40 n. 61. The word is used to denote the
sanctuaries of Theos Hypsistos in the Bosporan kingdom (**85, 88**). It occurs on Delos (**109**),
in Galatia (**202**), at Athribis in Hellenistic Egypt (**285**, see the commentary of Horsley, *New
Docs.* iii. 121 and iv. 201). It also appears on a dedication from Amastris in Paphlagonia
which has not been listed in the catalogue of the Hypsistos texts but which may be
associated with the cult: C. Marek, *Stadt, Ära, und Territorium in Pontus-Bithynia und
Nord-Galatia* (1993), 165 no. 27: θεῷ | ἀνεικήτῳ | Ἀσβαμεῖ κα[ὶ] | (τ)ῇ κυρίᾳ προσ|ευχῇ
εὐξάμενος καὶ | ἐπιτυχὼν ἀνέθηκα Αὐ|ρήλιος Πρω|τόκτητος, | εὐχαριστή|[ρι]ο[ν].

ἐκεῖνος τοίνυν . . . ῥίζης ἐγένετο βλάστημα οὐκ ἐπαινετῆς . . . ἐκ δυοῖν
ἐναντιωτάτοιν συγκεκραμένης Ἑλληνικῆς τε πλάνης καὶ νομικῆς τερατείας, ὧν
ἀμφοτέρων τὰ μέρη φυγὼν ἐκ μερῶν συνετέθη. τῆς μὲν γὰρ τὰ εἴδωλα καὶ τὰς
θυσίας ἀποπεμπόμενοι, τιμῶσι τὸ πῦρ καὶ τὰ λύχνα· τῆς δὲ τὸ σάββατον
αἰδούμενοι καὶ τῆς περὶ τὰ βρώματα ἔστιν ἃ μικρολογίαν τὴν περιτομὴν
ἀτιμάζουσιν. Ὑψιστάριοι τοῖς ταπεινοῖς ὄνομα, καὶ ὁ παντοκράτωρ δὴ μόνος
αὐτοῖς σεβάσμιος.

He was a branch sprung from a root not at all to be admired . . . The cult was a
mixture of two elements, Hellenic error and adherence to the Jewish law.
Shunning some parts of both it was made up from others. Its followers reject the
idols and sacrifices of the former and worship fire and lamplight; they revere the
sabbath and are scrupulous not to touch certain foods, but have nothing to do
with circumcision. To the humble they are called Hypsistarians, and the
Pantokrator is the only god they worship.[21]

The similarities between this account and Epiphanius' rambling description, published only two years later, are obvious. It is not unlikely that
the latter had collected information about the sect from Gregory
of Nazianzus himself, just as he had gleaned facts about the fire-
worshipping Magusaioi of Cappadocia from Basil of Caesarea.[22] Gregory,
understandably deferent to his father's early allegiance, showed more
sympathy to the Hypsistarians than Epiphanius to the Messalians. 'By
their way of life they anticipate the faith and only lack in name what they
possess in attitude.'[23]

In a passage of the *Contra Eunomium* the other Cappadocian Gregory,
the bishop of Nyssa, contrasted the true piety of those who acknowledged the Christian God, Father of all, undying and unique, with that
of those who feigned another god beside the Father. They were to be
counted among the Jews and the so-called Hypsistiani, who acknowledged god as 'highest' and as pantokrator, but denied him the role of the
Father:

ὁ γὰρ ὁμολογῶν τὸν πατέρα πάντοτε ⟨κατὰ τὰ αὐτά τε⟩ καὶ ὡσαύτως ἔχειν, ἕνα
καὶ μόνον ὄντα, τὸν τῆς εὐσεβείας κρατύνει λόγον, βλέπων ἐν τῷ πατρὶ τὸν υἱόν,
οὗ χωρὶς πατὴρ οὔτε ἔστιν οὔτε λέγεται. εἰ δὲ ἄλλον τινὰ παρὰ τὸν πατέρα θεὸν
ἀναπλάσσει, Ἰουδαίοις διαλεγέσθω ἢ τοῖς λεγομένοις Ὑψιστιανοῖς· ὧν αὕτη ἐστὶ
πρὸς τοὺς Χριστιανοὺς διαφορά, τὸ θεὸν μὲν αὐτοὺς ὁμολογεῖν αὐτὸν εἶναι
τινά, ὃν ὀνομάζουσιν ὕψιστον ἢ παντοκράτορα· πατέρα δὲ αὐτὸν εἶναι μὴ

[21] Gregory of Nazianzus, *Or.* 18. 5 (*PG* 35. 990).
[22] Basil, *Ep.* 258 reflected in Epiphanius, *Expositio Fidei, Panarion* 3. 2. 12, *PG* 42. 804C.
See Mitchell, *Anatolia*, ii. 73; P. Rousseau, *Basil of Caesarea* (1994), 19 n. 58.
[23] Gregory Naz. *Or.* 18. 6 (*PG* 35. 992B), trans. L. P. McCauley, *Funeral Orations by Saint
Gregory Nazianzen and Saint Ambrose* (1953), 123.

παραδέχεσθαι· ὁ δὲ Χριστιανός, εἰ μὴ τῷ πατρὶ πιστεύοι, Χριστιανὸς οὐκ
ἐστίν.[24]

Although this description is not as specific as those of Epiphanius and
Gregory of Nazianzus, it is striking that it omits any mention of the
pagan associations of the cult. The followers of Hypsistos are mentioned
in the same breath as the Jews, and by implication their beliefs were close
to those of true Christians.

At the beginning of the fifth century Cyril of Alexandria gave very
similar information to Epiphanius', reporting on groups of self-styled
'god-fearers' (θεοσεβεῖς) in Palestine and Phoenicia. Their beliefs, he
claimed, were similar to those of the Midianites in the time of Moses, in
that they worshipped ὕψιστος θεός, but believed in other gods, including
Earth and Heaven, the Sun and the Moon, and the brightest stars.[25] The
reference to Phoenicia may pick up Epiphanius' allusion to the
religiously motivated massacre of Messalians carried out by the *magister
militum per Orientem* Flavius Lupicinus in the mid-360s, which had
caused the sect to honour the victims in Christian fashion as martyrs.[26]
Cyril observed that they adhered strictly neither to Jewish nor to pagan
customs, but were torn and divided between the two cultures. Their
designation as 'god-fearers', virtually the technical term from the first
century AD and throughout late antiquity for Jewish sympathizers, is
further evidence for this link with Judaism. Its significance will be discussed below in §6.[27]

All these descriptions of the worship of the 'Highest God' were
written by orthodox Christian bishops, who were opposed not only to
pagan and Jewish beliefs, but to anything that they could construe as
heretical. The designations 'Hypsistarii' and 'Hypsistiani' which they
applied to the followers of the cult, while logical enough, were not, as far
as we know, adopted by the worshippers themselves. Like the first-
century followers of Jesus in Palestine and Antioch, they were known
by a label which outsiders had applied to them. Evidence from earlier
periods (to be considered in detail in §6) confirms the report of Cyril of
Alexandria that they called themselves *theosebeis*, 'god-fearers'. The most

---

[24] Gregory of Nyssa, *Refutatio Confessionis Eunomii*, 38 (W. Jaeger, *Greg. Nys.* ii. 327) [*In
Eunomium* 2 (*PG* 45. 482)].

[25] *De adoratione in Spiritu et Veritate* 3. 92 (*PG* 68. 281C): προσεκύνουν μὲν γὰρ . . .
ὑψίστῳ θεῷ . . . , προσεδέχοντο δὲ καὶ ἑτέρους τάχα που θεούς, ἐναριθμοῦντες αὐτῷ τὰ
ἐξαίρετα τῶν ἄστρων ἐπισημότερα. Compare Origen, *Contra Celsum* 5. 4–6, which refers
to very similar beliefs.

[26] *PLRE* 1. 520: Flavius Lupicinus 6.

[27] See Schürer, *Sb. Berl.* (1897), 222–3.

hostile description comes from the pen of Epiphanius, who appears to have had least contact with the sect and who had the liveliest interest in condemning it as a dangerous heresy. We might reasonably suspect him of malice and the two Gregories of providing incomplete if not outright misinformation. However, there is no need to be sceptical about the factual basis of all four accounts. Gregory of Nazianzus had good reason to be familiar with Hypistarian doctrine, for it had been his father's original faith. Epiphanius' description corresponds remarkably precisely with the evidence from Oenoanda. Furthermore, parallels to the use by the patristic authors of the terms παντοκράτωρ, προσευχή, θεοσεβεῖς, and ὕψιστος itself can be found in inscriptions both of Jews and of worshippers of Theos Hypsistos. In short: these Orthodox Christian accounts of the beliefs and practices of Hypsistarians (Gregory of Nazianzus' terminology has prevailed) and their status *vis-à-vis* Jews and Christians are precise and credible. They can also be confirmed at many points by archaeological and epigraphic evidence.

3. THE ARCHAEOLOGICAL AND EPIGRAPHIC EVIDENCE FOR
THEOS HYPSISTOS: A METHODOLOGICAL SURVEY

Epiphanius knew that Messalians worshipped both in buildings like churches, including a shrine in Phoenicia which was struck by lightning,[28] and at locations resembling Jewish open-air sanctuaries, such as the theatre-like place of prayer near Neapolis, or its first-century predecessor near Philippi in Macedonia. Four sanctuaries of Hypsistos have now been archaeologically identified, and these claims can be tested.

One is buried between the streets of modern Sofia in Bulgaria, the ancient Serdica, and the architecture of the shrine is beyond recovery. It appears from the sculptural remains, including the figure of a deity supported by an eagle and two altars with lamps carved into their upper surfaces, that the sanctuary was not unpretentious. We should probably think of an enclosed rather than an open-air sanctuary, since altars with lamps were probably located inside rather than outside a building.[29]

It is easier to envisage the open-air sanctuary in the Pnyx at Athens. Fifty-eight niches designed to hold dedicatory offerings have been identified in the vertical scarp to the east of the bema. Twelve dedications to Hypsistos have been found in the Pnyx itself, and several others,

[28] *Pan.* 80. 2. 3.
[29] M. Taceva-Hitova, *Thracia*, iv (1977) (*non vidi*); *Balkan Studies*, 19 (1978), 60–1 with pls. 4–5.

98 S. Mitchell

discovered elsewhere in Athens, are likely to have originated there before being dispersed around the city. All date to the second or third centuries AD, a period when the original function of the Pnyx as a place of assembly had been given up. But the theatre-like form of the site was ideally suited for open-air communal worship and matches Epiphanius' use of the adjective θεατροειδής to describe the place of prayer outside Neapolis.[30] We can envisage a similar arrangement at Oenoanda. Although the rocky slope outside the city wall is badly weathered and eroded, it is clear that there was a roughly semicircular level space, with a radius of about 25 metres, in front of the door to the tower where the oracle was engraved. This too could have been a small, open-air 'theatre', where a group of worshippers could gather.

A structure on the island of Delos, which was in use between the first century BC and the second century AD, seems to have been specifically designed for the cult. The building was an assembly hall, typical of communal centres in this period, where associates might meet for cult or other purposes.[31] It is identified as a shrine by three dedications to Theos Hypsistos, one to Hypsistos and by another inscription mentioning an offering ἐπὶ προσευχῇ (106–9). On the strength of the last text, the structure has been interpreted as a synagogue used by the Jews on Delos. This is undoubtedly correct, but we should not neglect the point that the sanctuary is also a Greek one, containing dedications set up by persons with Greek names for Theos Hypsistos. It is also significant that over sixty lamps were found in the building, many adorned with pagan, but none with Jewish motifs.[32] The texts from this building present an interesting contrast with two Hellenistic inscriptions found in a different location on Delos, set up by 'The Israelites who pay the first fruits to the sacred Gerizim', who clearly belonged to a Samaritan community.[33] We may compare the situation reported at Tarsus in late antiquity, where there were separate synagogues for the Jews and the Samaritans.[34]

[30] J. Travlos, A Pictorial Dictionary of Ancient Athens (1971), 569–72; B. Forsen, 'The Sanctuary of Zeus Hypsistos and the Assembly Place on the Pnyx', Hesperia, 62 (1993), 414–43. The inscriptions are collected in the appendix below, nos. 1–23.

[31] See A. Plassart, 'La Synagogue juive de Délos', Mélanges Holleaux (1913), 201–15; Schürer² iii. 1. 70–1; Ph. Bruneau, Recherches sur les cultes de Délos (1970), 480–93; A. T. Kraabel, ANRW 2. 19. 1 (1979), 491–4; P. Trebilco, Jewish Communities in Asia Minor (1991), 133–4; L. M. White, 'The Delos Synagogue Revisited: Fieldwork in the Graeco-Roman Diaspora', Harvard Theological Review, 80 (1987), 133–60. See W. Ameling, in R. Jütte and A. P. Kustermann, Jüdische Gemeinden und Organisationsformen von der Antike bis zur Gegenwart (1996), 34.   [32] Kraabel, ANRW 2. 19. 1, 492–3.

[33] For the inscriptions of the Israelites, see Ph. Bruneau, '"Les Israélites de Délos" et la juiverie délienne', BCH 106 (1982), 465–504 (SEG 32 (1982), 809–10).

[34] Palladius, in the Life of John Chrysostom, PG 47. 73.

Other buildings for the cult are attested epigraphically. An inscription from Sciathos may imply a building (**118**) and one from Odessos refers to a gateway to a sanctuary dedicated to Zeus Hypsistos (**81**). A devotee from Phrygia paid for columns and a propylon, which suggests the monumental entrance to a colonnaded area enclosing either a small temple or an open sanctuary around an altar (**215**).[35]

While archaeological data remain scarce, the number of inscriptions for the cults of Zeus and Theos Hypsistos is large and expanding rapidly. The geographical range which they cover is huge, extending from Achaea and Macedonia to the eastern parts of Asia Minor and to the edge of the Syrian desert, from Rostov on the Don to the Nile Delta. The cultural contexts in which the inscriptions have been found are also extremely varied. The cult made an impact in cosmopolitan Athens, on the fringes of the Hellenized world in the Bosporan kingdom, and in the traditional rural environment of inner Anatolia. Hypsistos was one of the most widely worshipped gods of the eastern Mediterranean world.

In the discussion that follows I have deliberately considered dedications to Theos Hypsistos, Zeus Hypsistos and simply Hypsistos as a whole. This is not because they can be regarded as formally identical. Logically we can only assert the identity of two distinct entities in relation to a single, shared archetype. But there can be no such archetypes for ancient (or modern) gods, who must be regarded simply as collective representations of the human imagination.[36] Zeus Hypsistos and Theos Hypsistos are not two ways of denoting the same reality. On the other hand, at the practical level of cult, the association between them was extremely close. In many sanctuaries, most notably at Athens and at Carian Stratonicaea, all three possible designations were used by a variety of worshippers. On other occasions symbols associated with Zeus, especially the figure of an eagle, were carved on monuments for Theos Hypsistos. It is both convenient and analytically profitable to focus on the 'hypsistarian' nature of these cults, and treat them together, rather than to split them and stress their differences.[37] This is not to say that significant conclusions may not also be drawn from the different designations used by worshippers in various contexts.

[35] Compare the fragmentary text from Alexandria, **283**.

[36] Compare J. K. Davies, 'The Moral Dimension of Pythian Apollo', in A. B. Lloyd (ed.), *What is a God? Studies in the Nature of Greek Divinity* (1997), 43–64 at 43.

[37] All the more so as the term *hypsistos* is only applied very rarely to other Graeco-Roman deities.

In another respect I have lumped together material which has been kept separate in earlier studies. Hypsistos or Theos Hypsistos was a name often given to the Jewish God, but the terms are also at home in pagan contexts. A major focus of scholarly enquiry has been to distinguish Jewish from pagan examples of the worship of Theos Hypsistos, and to conduct separate enquiries into the two groups of evidence, implying or assuming that they represent two different strands of religious belief and practice, stemming from widely different traditions. This exercise has not been entirely fruitless or unhelpful. However, its main value has been unwittingly to illustrate the difficulties of this procedure, and to show how fragile and disputable the criteria for distinguishing the two groups are. It has thus obscured a crucial issue. The 200 surviving inscriptions which specifically refer to Theos Hypsistos are strikingly uniform. It is an important question to ask not what differentiates them, but what they have in common. We need to find out why worshippers chose to address their god by a name that fitted both pagan and Jewish patterns of belief. Instead of assuming that the inscriptions need to be sorted into Jewish and pagan groups we should try to see if they make sense as a single body of material, treated on its own terms.

In a large number of cases the pagan credentials of the cult are unambiguously clear from the fact that the god is named not Theos but precisely Zeus Hypsistos.[38] This tendency is particularly marked in old Greece and in Macedonia, and in the most Hellenized parts of Asia Minor. So, outside the sanctuary on the Pnyx at Athens,[39] there is not a single certain dedication to Theos Hypsistos from mainland Greece, the Roman province of Achaia, and out of twenty-five inscriptions from Macedonia nineteen are for Zeus compared with six for Theos Hypsistos (four from Thessalonica (55–8) and two others (37, 43)). We should not be surprised that Hellenic influence on the cult was strongest precisely in Greece itself. It is, however, worth noting that the most informative inscription for the cult in Macedonia, the dedication of a stele to Zeus Hypsistos in 250 by an association of worshippers, indicates that one of the cult officials was an *archisynagogos*, implying that the group worshipped in a synagogue.[40] The use of these terms occurs very rarely

---

[38] Schürer, *Sb. Berl.* (1897), 209 collected classical references to Zeus Hypsistos: Pindar, *Nem.* 1. 60; 11. 2; Aeschylus, *Eum.* 28; Sophocles, *Philoctetes* 289; Theocritus 25. 159. There seem to be no overtones of monotheism in these passages.

[39] Forsen's *Hesperia* article carries a misleading title. Fewer than a quarter of the Athenian dedications are to Zeus Hypsistos.

[40] J. M. R. Cormack, 'Zeus Hypsistos at Pydna', *Mélanges helléniques offerts à Georges Daux* (1974), 51–5; Horsley, *New Docs.* no. 5 (51).

outside Jewish or Judaizing contexts.[41] Zeus predominates in the small sample from the coastal cities of Caria (**129–34, 137–9**) and inland at Carian Stratonicaea, where the eighteen Hypsistos dedications (**140–57**), most of them associated with the indigenous Anatolian cult of a divine angel, consist of fifteen to Zeus Hypsistos, two to Theos Hypsistos (**147, 153**), and one to Hypsistos alone (**154**). Direct Macedonian influence on the cult in Caria is not to be ruled out.[42]

On the other hand the overall total of dedications to Theos Hypsistos or simply to Hypsistos outnumbers that for Zeus by 197 to 81, more than two to one, and in some of the areas where the cult was most popular, Phrygia, Lydia, Cyprus, and Crete for example, no texts for Zeus Hypsistos are found at all. Even in Athens, the twenty-three dedications published to date comprise only three or four for Zeus (**4, 8, 14; 21** is uncertain), three for Theos Hypsistos (**1, 3, 13**), and the remainder simply for Hypsistos.

Of course in some cases worshippers clearly associated Theos Hypsistos with Zeus, and used an iconographic symbol to mark this. The eagle appears on dedications to Theos Hypsistos at Philippopolis (**65**), Mytilene (**115**), Chersonesus in Crete (**121**), on five of the inscriptions from Tanais (**88, 90, 92, 96, 100**), at Tralles (**158**), Thyateira, a Macedonian foundation (**176**), Nicomedia (**190–1**), and Amastris (**195**), and sculptures of eagles were found in the sanctuary at Serdica, although the inscriptions are all for Theos Hypsistos (**69–73**).[43] But it is also striking that even when dedications explicitly named the god as Zeus Hypsistos, he was only rarely portrayed in anthropomorphic form.[44] An exception that illustrates the rule is the stele from Miletupolis in Mysia (**185**), which depicts Zeus with his thunderbolt. Uniquely in this case Zeus Hypsistos is also described as βρονταῖος, and his divine character has been assimilated with that of Zeus Brontaios, who was regularly portrayed in anthropomorphic form.[45] Normally there was a strong tendency to abstraction.

[41] See T. Rajak and D. Noy, 'Archisynagogoi: Office, Title and Social Status in the Graeco-Roman Synagogue', *JRS* 83 (1993), 75–93; Horsley, *New Docs.* iv. 213–20. For non-Jewish synagogues, see Horsley, *New Docs.* iii. 43; iv. 202.

[42] A. D. Nock, *Essays on Religion and the Ancient World*, i. 422 (The Guild of Zeus Hypsistos).

[43] M. Taceva-Hitova, *Balkan Studies*, 19 (1978), 60–1 with fig. 4. **74** for Zeus Hypsistos comes from a village on Serdican territory, not from the city sanctuary.

[44] Exceptions are the relief from Cyzicus, decorated with figures of Zeus, Artemis (?), and Apollo (**182**) and a bearded bust of Zeus on the dedication from Byblus (**269**).

[45] For Zeus Brontaios see A. B. Cook, *Zeus*; L. Robert, *Hellenica*, 7. 30–4 especially for Mysia and the Propontic region. Zeus Brontaios was to be distinguished from the strictly Phrygian deity, Zeus Bronton, for which see C. W. M. Cox and A. Cameron, *MAMA* 5, pp. xxxviii–xliv; T. Drew-Bear and C. Naour, *ANRW* 2. 18. 3 (1990), 1992–2013.

The pagan associations of Theos Hypsistos are also to be noted in the contexts where he was linked with another divinity: the *Meter Theon* at Beroia (37), the *Meter Oreia* at Nisa in Lycia (232), Nemesis at Thessalonica (54), Helios and Nemesis at Alexandria (284), Zeus, Ge, and Helios at Gorgippia (85), the goddess Larmene at Saittai in Lydia (172), and Mên Ouranios at Andeda in Pisidia (228).

But it is illegitimate to assume that all the worshippers at a given sanctuary identified the god with Zeus, simply because some did so. Most of the devotees at Athens preferred to address the divinity simply as Theos Hypsistos or simply Hypsistos. Conversely the majority at Stratonicaea regarded him as Zeus. Those who did not conform to the pattern at these sanctuaries are not likely to be guilty of confused religious sentiments or sloppy expression. Rather they chose a designation that would have seemed self-evidently correct and appropriate, and which tells us something about their personal religious convictions. The presence of one dedication to Zeus Hypsistos at Seleuceia on the Calycadnus (241), at Nicomedia (190), or at Zermigethusa (77) does not imply that the term Theos Hypsistos found on other dedications there should be interpreted as a mere approximation to a full and proper description. Worshippers in these cases chose not to identify their god with the Hellenic Zeus.

Both Theos or Zeus Hypsistos are associated with other divine beings who do not fit within the familiar framework of Greek polytheism. These usefully widen the framework of enquiry. The dedications mostly to Zeus Hypsistos at Carian Stratonicaea introduce a lesser divinity, variously designated as (*to*) *theion* (141, 143–8, 155–6), *theion basilikon* (149, 152, 154, 157), or *theios angelos* (142, 150, 151, 153). The presence of this heavenly angel or messenger appears as an adjunct to the cult of Theos Hypsistos elsewhere in Asia Minor and links the worship of Zeus Hypsistos at Stratonicaea firmly to a well-documented aspect of the indigenous religious culture of Anatolia. Angels, as we have seen, were an essential part of the theological picture of the Oenoanda oracle. The name showed that the god dwelt in a high and remote place, Aether, beyond human reach.[46] The other pagan gods, including the speaker,

---

[46] Note the adjective ἐπουράνιος, heavenly, which occurs on an inscription from Galatia (202). Angels and other gods are simply οὐράνιος (142, 228) and this term could also serve for Zeus or Theos Hypsistos (269, 279). Compare Schürer, *Sb. Berl.* (1897), 214 n. 1, who cites a passage of Philo of Byblus (preserved in Eusebius, *Praep. Ev.* 1. 10. 9) on a Phoenician deity Samemramos (Semiramis) ὁ καὶ Ὑψουράνιος. According to Origen, *Contra Celsum* 5. 4, Celsus supposed that angels ἀναβαίνειν μὲν προσάγοντας τὰς τῶν ἀνθρώπων ἐντεύξεις ἐν τοῖς καθαρωτάτοις τοῦ κόσμου χωρίοις ἐπουρανίοις ἢ καὶ τοῖς

Apollo himself, are identified as messengers of Hypsistos. Many other Asia Minor inscriptions of the second to fourth centuries AD mention angels, and have been much discussed recently. Angels hold an important place in Jewish theology,[47] but it is important to note that they appear as a common feature of pagan, Jewish, and Christian worship in Asia Minor.[48] The famous 'angel of Rubes' appeared as a Jewish guardian spirit in a Christian cemetery of Phrygian Eumeneia.[49] St Paul warned against the worship of angels in his letter to the Colossians, indicating that the practice was current in southern Phrygia in the mid-first century. Theodoret's commentary on Colossians, written in the fifth century, indicates that Paul's admonitions were in vain, for he observes that the disease of angel worship survived until his own time in large parts of Phrygia and Pisidia.[50]

Angel worship was an important symptom of monotheistic belief. This is shown with particular clarity by a Lydian inscription, dated to 256/7, which can be associated with the cult of Theos Hypsistos:

Στρατόνεικος Κακολεις τοῦ Ἑνὸς
καὶ Μόνου θεοῦ [ἱ]ερεὺς καὶ τοῦ Ὁ-
σίου καὶ Δικαίου μετὰ τῆς συμβίου
Ἀσκληπιαίας εὐξάμενοι περὶ τῶ[ν]
τέκνων εὐχαριστοῦντες ἀνέσ-
τησαν. ἔτους τμα' (AD 256/7)

The relief shows the mounted messenger above the couple, while the woman appears to be placing an offering on an altar.[51] The wording of the text is strikingly emphatic. Although in late Roman paganism the simple acclamation ΕΙΣ ΘΕΟΣ might merely convey the meaning that a god had unique qualities, rather than that he was literally unique,[52] the designation of Stratonicus as 'priest of the *One and Only God*' leaves no

τούτων καθαρωτέροις ὑπερουρανίοις. This whole passage should be read with the worship of Theos Hypsistos in mind.

[47] A. R. R. Sheppard, *Talanta*, 12/13 (1980–1), 77–100 who concentrates on the Asia Minor evidence. See also the older studies of F. Cumont, *Rev. Hist. Rél.* 36 (1915), 159–82; M. Simon, *CRAI* 1971, 120–32.

[48] See esp. C. P. Jones, *Phoenix*, 36 (1982), 264–71; Horsley, *New Docs.* v (1989), 72–3; M. Ricl, *Epigraphica Anatolica*, 19 (1992), 99–101 (with special reference to Hosios and Dikaios); G. Petzl, 'Die Beichtinschriften Westkleinasiens', *Epigraphica Anatolica* 22 (1994), 5.

[49] L. Robert, *Hellenica*, 11/12 (1960), 429–35; A. R. R. Sheppard, *AS* 29 (1979), 169–80.

[50] Col. 2: 16; Theodoret, *PG* 82. 614, 619; cf. Origen, *Contra Celsum* 5. 4–5 condemning Phrygian angel worship.

[51] *TAM* 5. 1 246; M. Ricl, *Epigraphica Anatolica*, 18 (1991), 3 no. 2, pl. 1.

[52] E. Petersen, *ΕΙΣ ΘΕΟΣ. Epigraphische, Formgeschichtliche und Religionsgeschichtliche Untersuchungen* (1926).

doubt that he be identified as a believer in the monotheistic theology of the Oenoanda oracle. The god in this case can only be Theos Hypsistos, who was widely worshipped in the same part of northern Lydia (163–74).[53] In the context of this text 'Hosios and Dikaios', the Phrygian god of justice, must be regarded as an angel, as he was elsewhere. An inscription from the same region identifies Hosios Dikaios precisely as an angel,[54] and at a Phrygian sanctuary near Cotiaeum the pair Hosios and Dikaios (or Hosion and Dikaion) were worshipped by a group of followers who called themselves the φιλανγέλων συνβίωσις.[55] A series of Lydian monuments depicts this angelic messenger of justice as a rider with a cloak billowing out behind him.[56] One of the lengthy series of confession texts from northern Lydia, dating to 164/5, indicates that an angel was supposed to have transmitted a message from the god Mên Axiottenos to a delinquent who had stolen clothing from a bathhouse.[57]

The theological hierarchy of the Lydian inscription and of the Oenoanda oracle is exactly matched by a group of acclamations recorded on inscriptions from Asia Minor and the Aegean, which clearly relate to a form of monotheistic worship without specifically naming Theos Hypsistos. A text from Saittai in Lydia reads Εἷς θεὸς ἐlν οὐρανοῖς, Ι μέγας Μὴν Ι Οὐράνιος, Ι μεγάλη δύlναμις τοῦ ἀlθανάτου θεοῦ.[58] This is a direct counterpart to the inscription from the small Pisidian city of Andeda set up by a priest of Mên Ouranios as a dedication to Theos Hypsistos (228; see §5). Worshippers of the highest god in regions where the cult of Mên was very widespread thus found a way of accommodating the lesser divinity into their scheme of belief. A stele from Arvalia, south of Ephesus, offers another acclamation of the supreme god in the company of two familiars, with the wording Μέγα τὸ ὄνομα τοῦ θεοῦ, Ι μέγα τὸ Ὅσιον, Ι μέγα τὸ Ἀγαθόν,[59] and these are closely matched in a short text from Thasos, reading Μέγα τὸ Ὅσεον,

[53] See C. Naour, *Epigraphica Anatolica*, 2 (1983), 116–17.

[54] *TAM* 5. 1. 185; Ricl, *Epigraphica Anatolica*, 18 (1991), 2 no. 1; originally published by L. Robert, *Anatolia*, 3 (1958), 120 (*OMS* 1. 419).

[55] A. R. R. Sheppard, *Talanta*, 12/13 (1980–1), 87–9 no. 8 (*SEG* 31 (1981), 1130); Ricl, *Epigraphica Anatolica*, 18 (1991), 24–5 no. 48.

[56] Ricl, *Epigraphica Anatolica*, 18 (1991), pls. 1–2 nos. 2, 3, 4, and 7. Compare the rider god depicted on a stele of 104 from Tanais, *CIRB* 1259 illustrated by J. Ustinova, *History of Religions*, 31 (1991), 156 fig. 1. She suggests that this represents Theos Hypsistos in person, but see below, p. 117 n. 106. The rider is the god's messenger.

[57] *TAM* 5. 1. 159; Petzl, 'Die Beichtinschriften Westkleinasiens' 3; another angel, of Mên Petraeites, appears in his no. 38.

[58] *TAM* 5. 1. 75; see the discussion of Peterson, *ΕΙΣ ΘΕΟΣ*, 268–70.

[59] J. Keil, *JÖAI* 11 (1908), Beiblatt 154–6 no. 1 (*I. Ephesos* 7. 1. 3100).

μέγα τὸ Δίκαιον.[60] The acclamation which most clearly reveals this conception of a single god, served by angels of justice, is on an unpublished inscription from Phrygian Aezani: 'One God in Heaven! Great is the Holy! Great is the Just!'[61]

It was relatively unusual for religious acclamations of this sort to be inscribed on stone. This group of texts from the Aegean and the western parts of Asia Minor, which are certainly associated with the cult of Theos Hypsistos, confirms the observation of Epiphanius, that acclamations were a distinctive feature of Hypsistarian worship.[62]

Taken as a whole, the inscriptions give an impressive, and probably not fundamentally misleading picture of the geographical spread of the cult, but our understanding of the overall picture needs to take the 'epigraphic habit' and accidents of discovery into account. The discovery of a large number of inscriptions in a single sanctuary, as at Athens, Stratonicaea, or Tanais, of course reveals these places as significant centres. But isolated texts should often be interpreted as the surviving representatives of similar groups, and may come from sanctuaries of equal significance. Furthermore little or nothing should be deduced from the absence of dedications in particular parts of Asia Minor or the Levant. The presence of only a single inscription from Cappadocia (242), the home of the only 'Hypsistarian' identified in the literary sources, the father of Gregory of Nazianzus, is simply explained by the fact that few inscriptions of any sort have been found in the region. The relative infrequency of Greek inscriptions in Syria, compared at least to their abundance in Asia Minor, presumably explains why Theos Hypsistos is attested only sporadically in the 'Semitic' cultural area of the Roman East, although the Jewish associations of the cult as well as the references in the patristic sources to worshippers at Neapolis, and generally in Palestine and Phoenicia, as well as a reference in Epiphanius to Messalian emigrants from Mesopotamia to Syrian Antioch,[63] suggest that they occurred widely in the region.

A large number of the dedications to Theos Hypsistos were very modest monuments, set up by ordinary people, and they are found indifferently in city and countryside. The god had an exceptionally wide appeal. Furthermore the pattern of worship revealed by the texts was in no way esoteric and in most respects resembled the worship of

---

[60] *IG* 12. 8. 613.
[61] See Mitchell, *Anatolia*, ii. 45.
[62] For inscribed acclamations relating to cults, see Robert, *Hellenica*, 10. 85–8.
[63] *Pan*. 80. 3. 7.

other gods during the same period. Like other pagan deities, he was frequently called ἐπήκοος in the hope that he would give ear to men's prayers.[64] The familiar formulas κατὰ ἐπιταγὴν (**37, 58**) and κατὰ κέλευσιν (**231, 232**) or κατὰ χρηματισμόν (**244**) show that vows were made in response to the instructions of dreams and oracles (**55, 133, 158, 190, 228**), in the usual fashion. Dedications from Phrygia in central Asia Minor, emanating from a world of peasant agriculture, display ears or sheaves of corn, the banal symbol of the god's concern for fertility and the harvest (**213, 216, 218, 227**, cf. **219** ὑπὲρ βοῶν σωτηρίας).[65] Agricultural prosperity was the concern of any god in this milieu, all the more so if he were regarded as the highest divine being. After all St Paul, when he addressed the people of Lystra in Lycaonia, assured them that his God had always been among them: 'He sends you rain from heaven and crops in their seasons, filling your hearts with nourishment and good cheer.'[66] While the specific attributes of agricultural well-being were appropriately displayed on votive monuments, and help to modify the perception of the god as a remote and abstract being, unconcerned with everyday human welfare, they no more serve to characterize the nature of Theos Hypsistos in the round than Paul's matter-of-fact address to the people of Lystra amounts to an exhaustive statement of Pauline theology.

Theos Hypsistos received prayers not simply from peasants for good harvests, but also from worshippers suffering from illness, injury, or infertility. At Athens almost all the votives were set up by women who sought relief from ailments which may be identified from the reliefs they displayed (**5–12, 14–15, 22**, compare the unprovenanced **289**).[67] The god's role as healer is also explicit in texts from Delos and Aezani (**107, 209**), in the bronze plaque which depicted with remarkable realism the eye malady of an Ephesian woman (**159**), and in three dedications from Golgi in Cyprus (**257–9**). It is probably implied by several inscriptions set up by individuals on behalf of family members (**28, 38, 80, 142, 151** (and indeed all the Stratonicaea group), **166, 210, 243, 248**). Other texts comprise vows of thanks made to the god after surviving the hazards of war (**68, 183**) or a lengthy journey (**55, 116, 218**), and dedications made by

---

[64] O. Weinreich, Θεοὶ ἐπήκοοι, *Ath. Mitt.* 37 (1912), 1–68, esp. 21–2 (*Ausgewählte Schriften*, 1. 131–95, esp. 152–3). Ears are actually represented on a number of texts, **79, 141**. Compare the bronze votive hands, **266–7**.

[65] This aspect is particularly stressed by T. Drew-Bear and C. Naour, *ANRW* 2. 18. 3 (1990), 2032–43.

[66] Acts 14: 8–18.

[67] B. Forsen, *Tyche*, 5 (1990), 9–12.

humbler individuals on behalf of their masters or rulers (**46, 56, 60, 68**). There is one significant exception to this pattern. Although Theos Hypsistos might be associated with corporeal anthropomorphic deities, such as the *Thea Larmene* (**172**) or the angelic messengers who were depicted on votive stelai in Lydia, there was no distinctive iconography of the god. Unlike other deities Theos Hypsistos did not appear to men in human form. No epiphanies are recorded in the inscriptions or in other texts. Apparently the only tangible presence of Theos Hypsistos recorded by any of the monuments is, quite simply, a footprint. An inscription from Pisidian Termessus (**231**), dedicated to θεῷ ἐπηκόῳ ὑψίστῳ . . . κατὰ κέλευσιν αὐτοῦ was carved on an altar which supported a bronze representation of a left foot. This in turn was identified by the text: σὺν τῷ ἕποντι ἴχνει τοῦ θεοῦ. It remains unclear whether this was the foot of Theos Hypsistos or of one of his messengers.[68]

Indigenous concepts of divinity in Asia Minor could readily embrace the notion of a god as an abstract neuter being, as is clear from the many references to Hypsistos' messenger as *to theion*,[69] but this did not prevent most worshippers from imagining Theos Hypsistos to be male. It is refreshing to note at least one nod in the direction of sexual parity, some-thing also to be observed in early Christian worship in Asia Minor,[70] in the single dedication set up in a Lydian village (by a man) to Thea Hypsiste (**167**). We are dealing, however, with an incorporeal being: the upper air of heaven of the Oenoanda oracle or, in satirical mode, the clouds worshipped by the god-fearing father mocked by Juvenal.[71]

Apart from the literary descriptions which mention prayers to the rising and setting sun and the lighting of lamps, both forms of worship which are confirmed by the inscriptions, there is sparse evidence for ritual. The Lydian stelai relating to the angel cults depict worshippers raising their hands,[72] the most common gesture of prayer, which is

---

[68] See K. von Lanckoronski, *Städte Pamphyliens und Pisidiens*, ii (1890), 16 fig. 27; O. Weinreich, *Ath. Mitt.* 37 (1912), 36–9 (*Ausgewählte Schriften*, i. 166–8); K. Dunbabin, *JRA* 3 (1990), 88 and 95. A section of a column shaft which I noted at Pogla in Pisidia in 1993, had room to support a statue of a foot on top and carries the inscription Ἀρτέμιδ[ος] Ι τὸ ἴχνος Ι κατὰ χρηματισ]μόν

[69] See esp. the Stratonicaea texts (**141–57**) and a pair from Lydia (**171–2**). The Phrygian justice god was sometimes rendered in the neuter as Hosion Dikaion, M. Ricl, *Epigraphica Anatolica*, 19 (1992), 74. See L. Robert, *Anatolia*, 3 (1958), 113–18 for a fundamental discussion.

[70] Susannah Elm, *Virgins of God: The Making of Asceticism in Late Antiquity* (1994).

[71] Juvenal 14. 96–106; see below § 6; cf. Aristophanes, *Nubes*.

[72] Ricl, *Epigraphica Anatolica*, 18 (1991), 55 pl. 1 nos. 2a, 3, and 4.

recalled on two votive texts for Theos Hypsistos from Berytus (**266-7**), and expressly mentioned on an inscription from Alexandria (**284**). No text or document found to date associates Theos Hypsistos in any way with animal sacrifice.

This survey of the evidence serves to outline the cult's main characteristics. The lack of any representations of the god and the absence of animal sacrifice from the rituals distinguish the worship of Hypsistos from most other pagan cults in Greece, Asia Minor, and the Near East. All the other features which the epigraphic evidence presents may easily be paralleled from the worship of other divinities during the period. To this degree the cult of Theos Hypsistos conformed to the normal pattern of religious activity in the east Roman world.

4. CHRONOLOGY

Earlier discussions of pagan monotheism in general and of Theos Hypsistos in particular have taken the cult to be a phenomenon which developed in the later Roman period. This is a judgement based on the chronological distribution of the epigraphic evidence. Two of the earlier attestations found in Asia Minor come from Miletus during the 140s, where a member of the city council, Ulpius Carpus, known from the *Theosophy of Tübingen* to have consulted Apollo's oracle at Didyma on a matter concerning the worship of Sarapis, was prophet and priest of 'the highest and most holy god' (**135-6**). The followers of this cult included members of two humble groups who honoured Ulpius Carpus precisely in his priestly capacity, the association of municipal gardeners and the 'fleet of razor-fish prickers'.[73] One of the latest items, dated to 308/9, is the inscription from a village between Aezani and Cotiaeum, in up-country Phrygia, which records the gift of columns and a propylon for a sanctuary of Theos Hypsistos (**215**). These texts place a convenient chronological frame around the bulk of the documentation. Most of the inscriptions reviewed in the previous section belong to the second and third centuries AD. However, it is crucial to stress that the nature of the documentation itself seriously skews the chronological picture. The fact that the great majority of the inscriptions for Theos Hypsistos belong to the later imperial period cannot be taken as an indication that the cult was first introduced, or even became more popular then. It is a simple truth that the epigraphic habit was not introduced to many of the

---

[73] See L. Robert's dazzling elucidation in 'Trois oracles de la Théosophie et un prophète d'Apollon', *CRAI* 1969, 594-9 (*OMS* v. 610-15).

regions where the cult was widespread until the second century AD, and in those areas where inscribed documentation is available the cult of Hypsistos is solidly attested much earlier.

To look no further than the firmly dated inscriptions, it is clear that Theos Hypsistos was worshipped in Thrace at Selymbria in AD 25 (**68**), and at Thessalonica in 74/5 (**55**). In and around the Black Sea he was worshipped at Amastris on the south coast in 45 (**195**), in the Bosporan kingdom at Gorgippia in 41 (**85**), and at Tanais in 68 (**89**). Zeus Hypsistos is attested at Kavalla in Thrace between 36 and 48 (**60**) and the cult probably dates back to the Hellenistic period in Macedonia (**41**) and perhaps to the second century BC in Caria (**129–31, 134, 137**). In Egypt there are Jewish dedications to Theos Hypsistos from the mid-second century BC (**283, 285**). The papyrus which documents the guild of Zeus Hypsistos at Philadelphia in the Fayum dates to between 69 and 57 BC (**287**). It is not unreasonable to presume that the cult had a similarly long pedigree in Anatolia, before its first epigraphic appearance around the middle of the second century. The earliest inscription mentioning Hosios and Dikaios, found in Mysia, should be dated to the first century AD if not earlier.[74] St Paul reproached the Colossians for angelolatry between 50 and 60 and the practice was still alive in the fifth century when Theodoret commented on the practice. The phenomenon of the angel cult and the religious mentality which went with it was not confined to the period when it is most frequently attested by inscriptions, namely between *c*.150 and 300. The chronological distribution of the documents reveals the increased use of inscriptions in the second and third centuries, but nothing of significance about the increased popularity or development of the cults of angels and of Theos Hypsistos between these dates.[75] These cults were not a development of the second and third centuries, but occurred at least sporadically during the late Hellenistic or early imperial periods. This is confirmed by the literary evidence, which begins with parts of the Septuagint dating to the third century BC and resurfaces in the patristic literature of late antiquity, periods for which there is little or no epigraphic documenion. The belief in a remote and incorporeal deity, within a system of belief that tended

---

[74] G. Petzl, *Epigraphica Anatolica*, 20 (1992), 143–6.

[75] See R. MacMullen's famous article on 'the epigraphic habit', *AJPhil.* 103 (1982), 233–46. The point is made in connection with the cult of Hosios and Dikaios by G. Petzl, 'Ein frühes Zeugnis für den Hosios-Dikaios-Kult', *Epigraphica Anatolica*, 20 (1992), 143–7 with pl. 15. He dates this newly published text from central Mysia to no later than the 1st cent. AD; none of the 110 other inscriptions relating to the cult collected in M. Ricl's corpus (*Epigraphica Anatolica*, 18 (1991), 1–70) is certainly earlier than 200.

towards monotheism, was widespread in the Hellenistic period and around the time of the birth of Christ, as well as during the Roman empire and in late antiquity across the whole area where Theos Hypsistos inscriptions occur.

5. THEOS HYPSISTOS AND THE JEWS

Since Schürer's day the cult has attracted special attention from students of Judaism. The Jewish God was named Theos Hypsistos as early as the third century BC. Over 110 occurrences of the term have been noted in the Septuagint, and it was widely used in the Jewish Pseudepigrapha.[76] Marcel Simon on the basis of the evidence from the Old and New Testaments and the second and third Sibylline oracles, which emanate from Jewish circles, deduced that the full form Theos Hypsistos, in contrast to the simple Hypsistos, was usually used by or attributed to non-Jews, as a way of referring to the Jewish god.[77] Paul Trebilco concludes that 'Hypsistos was used as a way of designating Yahweh in the intertestamental period and as an appropriate name for God which could be put in the mouth of pagans in Jewish literature.'[78] Theos Hypsistos or Hypsistos alone is used to denote the Jewish God in the New Testament by Mark, by Luke in his Gospel and in Acts, and in the Epistle to the Hebrews.[79] The most revealing of the New Testament contexts is the passage describing Paul's presence at Philippi. As Paul and his companions (including the author Luke) were approaching the place of prayer outside the city, a female slave, possessed by a demon, came up to them, and shouted out that they were slaves of the highest god, δοῦλοι τοῦ θεοῦ τοῦ ὑψίστου.[80] There are good grounds for thinking that the place where this confrontation occurred was a sanctuary of Theos Hypsistos (see below, §6). The historicity of this episode is supported by the fact that the cult of Theos Hypsistos is well attested epigraphically in cities of Aegean and Propontic Thrace around the middle of the first century AD (**55, 60, 68**; see §4).

Philo of Alexandria used the term Hypsistos to denote the Jewish

[76] Schürer, *Sb. Berl.* (1897), 224–5.

[77] M. Simon, 'Theos Hypsistos', *Ex orbe religionum. Studia Geo. Widengren* (1972), 372–85. Trebilco, *Jewish Communities*, 130 agrees, and suggests that the full formula ὁ θεὸς ὁ ὕψιστος may have been adopted by Gentiles, while ὕψιστος alone occurs in purely Jewish contexts.

[78] Trebilco, *Jewish Communities*, 129.

[79] Lk. 1: 32, 35, 76; 6: 35; 8: 28; Mk. 5: 7; Acts 7: 48; 16: 17; Heb. 7: 1.

[80] Acts 16: 17.

God.[81] The temple at Jerusalem was known as ὁ τοῦ ὑψίστου Θεοῦ νεώς,[82] and in the famous edict which granted them important privileges, preserved by Josephus, Augustus allowed the Jews of Asia to follow their own customs in accordance with ancestral law, as they had observed them in the time of Hyrcanus, high priest of θεὸς ὕψιστος. This text preserves Augustus' own designation, which in turn would have corresponded with the terminology used by the Jews of Asia in their petition to him.[83] Inscriptions which name the Jewish God as Theos Hypsistos range in place and date from Egypt in the second century BC (**285**) to Asia Minor in the third century AD (**207**). A further indication of the relationship between Theos Hypsistos and the Jewish God can be found in a passage of Malalas, writing in the sixth century, who cited precisely the opening of the Oenoanda oracle in the belief that it was a Delphic response to the question, supposedly put by the Pharaoh of Egypt, about who was the first of the gods and who was the great God of Israel.[84]

As already noted in §3, modern discussion of the inscriptional evidence has focused on a single issue. When we encounter a text for Theos Hypsistos, should it be treated as pagan, or as Jewish or Judaizing? There is a large literature on the subject, which need not be reviewed in full here. Paul Trebilco's careful recent discussion in his *Jewish Communities in Asia Minor* is a representative example, which takes account of the earlier bibliography. His argument starts from the premiss that pagan and Jewish Theos Hypsistos inscriptions have to be distinguished, and concludes with the claim that Jewish use of the title decreased as it became more current among pagans, precisely to avoid the dangers of syncretism.[85] The chronological argument about declining

[81] Philo, *Leg. ad Gaium* 278; *In Flaccum* 46.

[82] Philo, *Leg.* 278. Julian gave the Jews permission to rebuild τὸν ναὸν τοῦ Ὑψίστου Θεοῦ, Lydus, *De Mens.* 4. 53 cited in Bidez and Cumont, *Iuliani Imperatoris Epistulae et Leges* (1922), 192 no. 134. [83] Josephus, *AJ* 16. 163.

[84] Malalas pp. 65–6, cited by Potter, *Prophecy and History*, 352.

[85] Trebilco, *Jewish Communities*, 127–44: 'The problem with the inscriptions is therefore to discover when the term is used by Jews to refer to Yahweh and when it is used by pagans to refer to a pagan divinity (127) . . . No evidence has arisen from this study to suggest that Judaism in Asia Minor was ever compromised by paganism . . . A. D. Nock noted that we are on a religious frontier . . . However, perhaps the most important fact is that the frontier existed (142–3) . . . The term [Theos Hypsistos] was not easily understood by pagans with the meaning intended by Jews. This explains the reluctance to use the term which we found in both Josephus and Philo. Just as significant as the use of the title for Yahweh in inscriptions by Jews is the fact that its use seems to have declined during the period under investigation here (143) . . . We can suggest, therefore, that in both Asia Minor and elsewhere the syncretistic dangers of the title were recognised and it was avoided (144).'

Jewish use is extremely precarious,[86] but there are more serious problems inherent in the basic premiss.

The difficulty lies in the fact that most 'pagan' or 'Jewish' examples of the term Theos Hypsistos are formally indistinguishable from one another and that the arguments for assigning them to either category are rarely decisive. The presence of an influential Jewish community at Sardis led many to believe that the Theos Hypsistos inscriptions from Sardis' Lydian hinterland were Jewish. The excavators of the Sardis synagogue re-examined the question and concluded the reverse, rightly stressing the clear pagan associations of most of the Lydian texts.[87] That was a fair conclusion, but even so perhaps a little too clear-cut. L. Robert pointed out that the confession texts from the region, which are critically important for understanding the religious mentality of Roman Lydia, contain features, notably the practice of εὐλογία, singing the god's praises, which are closely paralleled only in Jewish practice.[88] It is not inconceivable that the beliefs of the Jewish colonists, who arrived at Sardis at the end of the third century BC, influenced the native cults of Lydia, especially in those contexts where the indigenous deities, for instance the Anatolian god Mên, exercised an 'Old Testament' function as dispenser of divine justice.[89] It is noteworthy that the adjective εὐλογητός is applied almost certainly to Theos Hypsistos in an inscription from the territory of Thracian Philippopolis (67) as well as in texts from Gorgippia and Tanais, where other Judaizing features are very prominent (84–7).[90]

The difficulties of distinguishing between pagan and Jewish dedications are acutely posed by other cases from Asia Minor. One of the largest Jewish communities of Phrygia, which dates back certainly to the later first century AD and probably to the settlement of Jews in Lydia and Phrygia by Antiochus III, was at Acmonia.[91] The tombstone of an unknown citizen found in a village on Acmonia's territory ends with the curse, that if anyone disturb the grave he shall have to reckon with τὸν

[86] The texts from Acmonia (206–7) are acknowledged as clear counter-examples. So too is the inscription from Galatia (202).

[87] A. T. Kraabel, GRBS 10 (1969), 81–93; cf. L. M. White, HTR 80 (1987), 133–60 at 141–7.

[88] L. Robert, Nouvelles inscriptions de Sardes, i (1964), 23–33 no. 2 (= Petzl, Beichtinschriften, no. 101) at 28–30; Hellenica, 11/12. 392–6.

[89] See Mitchell, Anatolia, ii. 31–6.

[90] See Schürer, Sb. Berl. (1897), 205–6.

[91] Mitchell, Anatolia, ii. 35; for an excellent survey of the Jews in Asia Minor, see W. Ameling, 'Die jüdischen Gemeinden im antiken Kleinasien', in R. Jütte and Abraham P. Kustermann (eds.), Jüdische Gemeinden und Organisationsformen von der Antike bis zur Gegenwart (1996), 29–55.

θεὸν τὸν ὕψιστον καὶ τὸ ἀρᾶς δρέπανον (**207**).[92] Another text from the same village is a dedication to Theos Hypsistos by a certain Epictetus (**206**). The juxtaposition of the two texts has led commentators to conclude that the dedication is Jewish. On the other hand, another village in the same city territory has produced a dedication to Theos Hypsistos with no other Jewish inscription (**205**). This has accordingly been taken for pagan.[93] But the judgement is entirely arbitrary, deriving not from any intrinsic distinguishing feature of either text, but from the chance discovery of an epitaph ending with a Jewish curse in the village where one of them was found. One can have no confidence in its correctness.

A similar problem is posed by two inscriptions from the Bozova in Pisidia. One, from Sibidunda, records the dedication of a bronze incense burner to Theos Hypsistos and Hagia Kataphyge, the Highest God and Sacred Refuge (**230**; there is a photograph in Mitchell, *Anatolia*, ii. 35 fig. 16). *Kataphyge* is the term used in the Septuagint's rendering of the Psalms for divine refuge, and this has led to the reasonable conclusion that the inscription is a Jewish or Judaizing text.[94] But another votive inscription found at Andeda, a few kilometres away in the same Pisidian valley, was set up in response to an oracle by Quintus Numerius, priest of Mên Ouranios for Theos Hypsistos (**228**; see §3 above). By the usual criteria, this text is equally clearly pagan, yet in truth the distinction between the two inscriptions is hair-fine. The dedicatee in each case is the same god, called by the same name. Mên of the Heavens and 'Sacred Refuge', both associated with the Highest God, had their origins in different cultures and in different religious traditions, but can we seriously suggest that they represented different modes of belief and religious thinking to their worshippers? Was the Theos Hypsistos of the Sibidunda text conceptually and culturally alien from his namesake at Andeda? The proposition is hard to believe.

Epigraphy often aspires to be a precise science, and it is not surprising that epigraphers should wish to draw firm lines of demarcation. But this

[92] The last expression, 'the sickle of a curse' is a cryptic reference to a passage in the Septuagint version of the book of Zechariah 5: 2–4. It is important to note that the reference to the sickle occurs only in the Greek version of the book, for the Hebrew original refers not to a sickle, *meggal*, but to a flying scroll, *megilla*, on which was written a curse which would drive every thief and perjurer from the land; the Jews of Acmonia, we may be certain, studied their holy books in Greek, not Hebrew. See J. Strubbe, 'Jewish Poetical Tomb Inscriptions', in J. W. van Henten and P. W. van der Horst, *Studies in early Jewish Epigraphy* (1994), 70–128 at 87–9, and Trebilco, *Jewish Communities in Asia Minor*, 75–6.

[93] So the discoverer of these inscriptions, T. Drew-Bear, *GRBS* 17 (1976), 247–9.

[94] See esp. J. and L. Robert, *Bull. ép.* 1961, 750; 1965, 412; Trebilco, *Jewish Communities*, 136.

aim is not always appropriate. A. D. Nock, publishing the papyrus for the guild of Zeus Hypsistos, remarked long ago of cults of Hypsistos that 'we are on a religious frontier', and again that 'in (certain) cases we can clearly see the impact of Jewish or judaising culture; perhaps we should in others, but it is not possible to be dogmatic; the ground quakes under our tread'.[95] Louis Robert expressed the same uncertainties even more graphically:

Il est difficile d'atteindre à la précision . . . dans le monde religieux de cette Asie Mineure du IIIe siècle de notre ère où se coudoient les religions: chrétiens orthodoxes (des laxistes et des intégristes) et hérétiques de toutes les sectes, montanistes et gnostiques, juifs et judaisants avec les doctrines d'une intensité très différente que peuvent exercer les doctrines ou les pratiques juives sur les païens et les chrétiens, païens syncrétisants et tenants de cultes qui sont ailleurs travaillés par des mouvements rénovateurs, adorateurs du Saint et du Juste, de divinités solaires.[96]

We are evidently dealing with an area of belief where Jews, Judaizers, and pagans occupied very similar territory. Jewish borrowing from or assimilation to pagan practice is demonstrated by clear cut epigraphical formulations. In the Bosporan communities documents record manumissions which took place in an apparently Jewish place of prayer, a προσευχή, in which the subject was dedicated θεῷ ὑψίστῳ παντοκράτορι εὐλογητῷ. Yet they conclude with an oath sworn by Zeus, Ge, and Helios (**85, 89**). The Jewish influence is beyond dispute, yet the religious affiliation was loose enough to allow the pagan oath.[97] This and other inscriptions from the Bosporan kingdom, where we encounter a ritual framework which seems largely Jewish, although coloured by pagan touches, provide counterparts to the confession texts from Lydia, where a pagan ritual environment may be marked by Jewish influence.

In the light of this cross-fertilization between Jews and pagans, and the meeting of separate religious cultures in the worship of Theos Hypsistos, it is not easy to be confident about the Jewish character of a dedication from a Galatian village east of Ancyra offered to μεγάλῳ θεῷ ὑψίστῳ καὶ ἐπουρανίῳ καὶ τοῖς ἁγίοις αὐτοῦ ἀγγέλοις καὶ τῇ προσκυνητῇ προσευχῇ (**202**).[98] The adjective ἐπουράνιος is an emphatic reminder of the divine hierarchy. The highest god dwelt in a distant heavenly sphere with his angelic associates. We recall the Mên Ouranios of the Theos Hypsistos

---

95 *Essays on Religion and the Ancient World*, i. 425, 428.
96 *Hellenica*, 11/12. 438.
97 Note the comments in Schürer² iii. 1. 37.
98 As I was in 1982 when I published this text as *RECAM* ii. 209b; cf. *SEG* 31 (1981), 1080.

inscription from Andeda, and the Lydian texts which regarded Mên as an angel (above, pp. 102–5). This highest god with his angels and his place of prayer stands as close to the god of the sanctuary of Oenoanda, described by Apollo's oracle as Aether, as he does to Jehovah. Here is a text which can be placed right in the centre of the common ground. The cult of Theos Hypsistos had room for pagans and for Jews. More than that it shows that the principal categories into which we divide the religious groupings of late antiquity are simply inappropriate or misleading when applied to the beliefs and practices of a significant proportion of the population of the eastern Roman empire.

6. THE *THEOSEBEIS*

In the account of Paul's second journey Luke described the activities of the missionaries in the Roman colony of Philippi in Macedonia, where they spent several days.

τῇ τε ἡμέρᾳ τῶν σαββάτων ἐξήλθομεν ἔξω τῆς πύλης παρὰ ποταμόν, οὗ ἐνομίζομεν προσευχὴν εἶναι, καὶ καθίσαντες ἐλαλοῦμεν ταῖς συνελθούσαις γυναιξί. καί τις γυνὴ ὀνόματι Λυδία, πορφυρόπωλις πόλεως Θυατείρων, σεβομένη τὸν Θεόν, ἤκουεν.

Lydia was converted and baptized. The narrative then resumes,

ἐγένετο δέ, πορευομένων ἡμῶν εἰς τὴν προσευχήν, παιδίσκην τινὰ ἔχουσαν πνεῦμα πύθωνα ὑπαντῆσαι ἡμῖν, ἥτις ἐργασίαν πολλὴν παρεῖχε τοῖς κυρίοις αὐτῆς μαντευομένη. αὕτη, κατακολουθοῦσα τῷ Παύλῳ καὶ ἡμῖν, ἔκραζε λέγουσα, Οὗτοι οἱ ἄνθρωποι δοῦλοι τοῦ Θεοῦ τοῦ ὑψίστου εἰσίν, οἵτινες καταγγέλλουσιν ὑμῖν ὁδὸν σωτηρίας.

After several days Paul exorcized the spirit from her.[99] This is precisely the passage cited by Epiphanius as evidence for the Jewish extra-mural open-air places of prayer which were imitated in his day by Messalian, Hypsistarian worshippers. Furthermore, the story concerning the woman of Thyateira, Lydia, identified her as one of the 'worshippers of the God' or 'god-fearers', and this links her to the many groups of σεβόμενοι or φοβούμενοι τὸν Θεὸν who appear elsewhere in the New Testament. These have been identified as Jewish sympathizers, who attended the synagogues without being members of the Jewish community.

New epigraphic discoveries and several recent discussions have resolved much of the controversy surrounding the status of the god-

---

[99] Acts 16: 13–18. Recent discussion of the second part by P. Trebilco, 'Paul and Silas – "Servants of the Most High God"', *Journal for the Study of the New Testament*, 36 (1989), 51–73.

fearers attested in the New Testament, who are known from inscriptions as θεοσεβεῖς.[100] Analysis of the relevant passages in Acts shows that the σεβόμενοι or φοβούμενοι τὸν Θεὸν are to be equated with the Hellenes mentioned on other occasions, non-Jews who attended the synagogues where Paul preached and who represent a significant proportion of his adherents.[101] These groups are attested collectively at Pisidian Antioch and at Iconium in Galatia, at Thessalonica and Beroea in Macedonia, and at Athens; and there is a general reference to their presence in Asia.[102] Individuals can be identified in the persons of Cornelius the centurion at Caesarea, described as εὐσεβὴς καὶ φοβούμενος τὸν Θεόν, Lydia at Philippi, Titus Iustus at Corinth, and perhaps also Timothy of Derbe, the son of a Jewish mother and a Gentile father, whom Paul had circumcised to avoid giving offence to the Jews.[103] Luke's very specific evidence is backed up by observations in other early imperial authors, but especially by Josephus. Judaizers or Greek adherents to Jewish cult were to be found in Antioch and elsewhere in Syria.[104] These were not simply token sympathizers, but committed and well organized, for the wealth stored in the temple at Jerusalem was due to contributions τῶν κατὰ τὴν οἰκουμένην Ἰουδαίων καὶ σεβομένων τὸν Θεόν, the latter including worshippers from Europe and Asia.[105]

The connection between Theos Hypsistos and the class of σεβόμενοι τὸν Θεὸν recurs explicitly at two other points in the documentation, taking us forward to the third and fifth centuries respectively. Four of the much-discussed dedications from Tanais to Theos Hypsistos were made by a group called the εἰσποιητοὶ ἀδελφοὶ σεβόμενοι θεὸν ὕψιστον (96, 98, 100, 101). These 'adopted brothers who worship the Highest God' appear on texts dated between 212 and 240, most probably to the decade 220–30. The group appears to be formally identical to the collective of

---

[100] See F. Millar's up-to-date revision in Schürer² iii. 1. 150–76. J. Reynolds and R. Tannenbaum, *Jews and Godfearers at Aphrodisias* (1967), 53 have argued that the *theosebeis* and the *sebomenoi* or *phoboumenoi ton theon* should not be identified with one another, contending that the latter are absent from the inscriptions, while the former are not attested as a class by literary texts later than the Septuagint. This is not the case. *Sebomenoi* is the term used in the inscriptions of Tanais (96, 98, 100, 101), while Cyril of Alexandria attests the use of *theosebes* in the relevant sense (§ 2). The identity of the two groups is taken as self-evident by M. Simon, 'Gottesfürchtiger', *Reallexicon für Antike und Christentum*, xi (1981), 1060–70, Millar in Schürer² iii. 1. 166, and Trebilco, *Jewish Communities*, 164–6.

[101] Trebilco, *Jewish Communities*, 147–52; cf. Mitchell, *Anatolia*, ii. 8.

[102] Acts 13: 50; 14: 1; 17: 4, 12, 17; cf. 19: 10 referring to congregations in Asia.

[103] Acts 10: 1–2; 16: 14; 18: 7; 15: 28.

[104] Josephus, *BJ* 2. 18. 2, 463; 7. 3. 3, 45.

[105] Josephus, *AJ* 14. 7. 2, 110. For the correct interpretation of this passage, see Trebilco, *Jewish Communities*, 147–8.

worshippers known from other inscriptions as the σύνοδος of θιασεῖται or θιασῶται. Schürer saw that this terminology established a connection between the cult associations of Tanais and the god-fearers of the New Testament, and also with individuals described as *metuentes* by a number of inscriptions from the Latin West.[106] The regularity with which the god-fearers appear alongside Jewish groups of the Diaspora implies that they were not casual groups of Jewish sympathizers but regularly organized bodies of worshippers. This is fully consistent with the Tanais evidence, which implies that the god-fearers were formally incorporated into associations. The verb εἰσποιεῖν is almost always used in Geek with the sense of adopting a child into a household, or admitting someone to a family, a procedure which must have been matched by the *thiasoi* at Tanais.[107]

The link occurs for the third time at the beginning of the fifth century in the account of Cyril of Alexandria, who observed that the worshippers of Theos Hypsistos in Palestine and Phoenicia called themselves *theosebeis* (see §2).

The inscriptions which mention *theosebeis* mostly date between the second and fourth centuries. By far the most informative of these is the long text from Aphrodisias, which lists contributions to a Jewish foundation made by ninety Jews (eighty-seven *Ioudaioi* and three proselytes) and sixty-five *theosebeis*.[108] The social range extends from nine members of the city council across a fascinating range of urban artisans and traders. As Fergus Millar has observed of the detailed status designations of this text, 'it would be difficult to imagine clearer evidence that *theosebeis* could be categorized as a formal group attached to a Jewish community, and distinguished both from Jews and from full proselytes.'[109] *Theosebeis* appear in isolation on gravestones from Rhodes,[110] from Cos,[111] and from Bursa Museum,[112] They had reserved seats with the

---

[106] *Sb. Berl.* (1897), 200–25. It will be seen from the whole thrust of my argument that I cannot accept the conclusions of J. Ustinova, 'The *thiasoi* of Theos Hypsistos in Tanais', *History of Religions*, 31 (1991), 150–80, who rejects Schürer's reading of the evidence and concludes, *inter alia*, that 'the Jews of the diaspora lived in the pagan environment for generations, with no attempts being undertaken to find a religious compromise with the gentiles' (p. 163). However, her speculations about the Iranian religious background to the religious traditions of Tanais, including a tendency to solar monotheism, may help to explain why, as it seems, almost all the inhabitants of 3rd-cent. Tanais worshipped Theos Hypsistos.   [107] LSJ 9th edn. s.v.

[108] J. M. Reynolds and R. Tannenbaum, *Jews and God-Fearers at Aphrodisias* (1987); *SEG* 36 (1986), 970, cf. 1583. I believe that the inscription more probably belongs to the fourth than to the second century, but this is not the place to argue the case in full.

[109] Schürer² iii. 1. 166.   [110] *IG* 12. 1. 893: Εὐφροσύνα θεοσεβὴς χρηστὰ χαῖρε.

[111] Paton and Nicks, *Inscriptions of Cos*, no. 258: Εἰρήνη θεοσεβὴς χρηστὴ χαῖρε.

[112] *I. Prusa* no. 115; cf. Trebilco, *Jewish Communities*, 146: Ἐπιθέρσῃ τῷ θεοσεβεῖ καὶ

118   S. Mitchell

Jews in the fifth row of the theatre at Miletus,[113] and explicitly joined the Jews in synagogues at Panticapaeum,[114] Tralles,[115] Sardis,[116] and Philadelphia in Lydia.[117] The individuals in question range across the entire social spectrum. The god-fearer at Tralles was Claudia Capitolina, daughter and wife of a Roman senator.[118] The report of Josephus that Poppaea, the wife of the emperor Nero, was a *theosebes* is entirely credible.[119] There were other western adherents: Agrippa son of Fuscus from Phaenae in Syria, who died in Rome in the second century,[120] and Rufinus, *theosebes*, who shared knowledge of the sacred (i.e. Jewish) laws and wisdom and was commemorated by a Greek epitaph probably of the fourth century from Lorium in Latium.[121] The term was transcribed into Latin script in the form *teuseves* on a South Italian epitaph,[122] but generally in the West the term was translated and rendered as *metuens*. Examples are recorded in Rome,[123] in North Italy at Pola,[124] and in Numidia.[125]

Θεοκτίστῳ τὰ τέκνα Μαρκιανὸς καὶ Ἐπιθέρσης μετὰ τῶν ἀδελπῶν ἐκ τῶν εἰδείων μνήμης χάριν. The name Theoctistos is another clue to the religiosity of this family (cf. L. Robert, *Nouvelles inscriptions de Sardes* (1964), 57), but there is no argument to support the view that it was Christian, as suggested by T. Corsten in his commentary.

113 H. Hommel, *Ist. Mitt.* 25 (1975), 167–95 provides the fullest discussion of the inscription: τόπος τῶν Εἰουδαίων τῶν καὶ θεοσεβιῶν. I follow Schürer and many others in understanding καὶ τῶν (contra Robert, *Nouvelles inscriptions de Sardes*, 41 n. 4).

114 CIRB 71; a manumission conducted in the συναγωγὴ τῶν Ἰουδαίων καὶ θεὸν σεβῶν (the last word conflating θεοσεβῶν and θεὸν σεβομένων).

115 L. Robert, *Études anatoliennes* (1937), Καπετωλῖνα ἡ ἀξιόλογ. καὶ θεοσεβ. ποήσασα τὸ πᾶμ βάθρον ἐσκουτλῶσα τ[ὸν] ἀναβασμὸν ὑπ[ὲρ] εὐχῆς ἑαυτῆς [καὶ τῶν] πεδίων τε καὶ ἐγγόνων. εὐλογία. The text undoubtedly refers to her benefactions to a synagogue.

116 L. Robert, *Nouvelles inscriptions de Sardes* (1964), 39 nos. 4 and 5. Four further texts are referred to in Trebilco, *Jewish Communities*, 252 n. 60. I am persuaded by H. Botermann, *Zeitschrift für Neutestamentliche Wissenschaft*, 81 (1990), 103–21, that none of the evidence for the Sardis synagogue is earlier than the 4th cent.

117 IGR iv. 1340; L. Robert, *Études anatoliennes* (1937), 410–11: [τ]ῇ ἁγιοτ[άτῃ σ]υναγωγῇ τῶν Ἑβραίων Εὐστάθιος ὁ θεοσεβὴς ὑπὲρ μνίας τοῦ ἀδελφοῦ Ἑρμοφίλου τὸν μασκεύλην ἀνέθηκα ἅμα τῇ νύμφῃ μου Ἀθανασίᾳ.

118 References, bibliography, and discussion in Schürer² iii. 1. 166; Trebilco, *Jewish Communities*, 155–62.

119 Josephus, *AJ* 20. 195. M. H. Williams, *JTS* 1988, 97–111.

120 Frey, *Corpus Inscriptionum Iudaicarum* 500: Ἀγρίππας Φολύσκου Φαινήσιος θεοσεβής.

121 D. Noy, *Jewish Inscriptions of Western Europe*, i (1993), no. 12: ἐνθάδε ἐν εἰρήνῃ κεῖτε | Ῥουφεῖνος ἀμύμων | θεοσεβὴς | ἁγίων τε νόμων | σοφιῆς τε συνίστωρ κτλ.

122 *Jewish Inscriptions of Western Europe* 1, no. 113 (Venosa, 4th–5th cent.).

123 CIL 6. 29759 = CIJ 1² 285; 29760 = CIJ 1² 524; 29763 = CIJ 1² 529; 31839 = CIJ 1² 5.

124 CIL 5. 88 = CIJ 1² 642 = Noy, *Jewish Inscriptions of Western Europe*, i, no. 9.

125 CIL 8. 4321. Cf. Schürer, *Sb. Berl.* (1897), 219; the references are collected in Schürer² iii. 1. 168 n. 74.

Theosebes was a specific, 'technical' term used to describe themselves by the worshippers of Theos Hypsistos.[126] It served to identify them both among themselves and to the outside world. The prefix *theo-* should not be understood in a loose sense as referring to any god, but precisely to the highest, the one and only god, whom they revered. This observation applies also to the growing use of proper names with the same prefix, especially in imperial times. Individuals who chose to call themselves Theoctistes, Theodorus, Theodoulos, or by a host of similar names, were in very many cases declaring their devotion to the cult.

The evidence for the cult of Theos Hypsistos and for the god-fearers of the inscriptions and the literary sources runs in strict parallel. Dedications for Theos Hypsistos occur at almost all the places where god-fearers appear (Cos, Aphrodisias, Miletus, Tralles, Philadelphia, in the Bosporan kingdom, Rome). More important, given the randomness of epigraphic survival, the geographical distribution of the two sets of evidence is virtually identical, covering Syria, Asia Minor, old Greece and Macedonia, and the north shore of the Black Sea. The *theosebeis* are only missing from Egypt, where Theos Hypsistos occurs, while Theos Hypsistos is little attested in the Latin West. The followers of the god, however, may be identified in Africa with the groups known as *Caelicoli* (see §7). The chronological span of the two phenomena also matches closely. Most of the testimonia for the god-fearers, like those for Theos Hypsistos, occur between the first and fourth centuries, but the Septuagint version of 2 Chronicles, written around 200 BC, contains a passage referring to Jews, god-fearers, and proselytes in the phrase πᾶσα συναγωγὴ Ἰσραὴλ καὶ οἱ φοβούμενοι καὶ οἱ ἐπισυνηγμένοι,[127] while a passage in the *Jewish Antiquities* suggests that *theosebeis* were identifiable at the time of the Maccabean revolt. These correspond to the earliest Hellenistic attestations of Theos Hypsistos in inscriptions and literary sources.[128] At the other end of the time range, not only do several of the inscriptions for god-fearers, including, I believe those from Aphrodisias and Sardis, belong to the fourth century or later, but the crucial passage of Cyril of Alexandria, which reveals *expressis verbis* that the worshippers

---

[126] This is not to deny that in classical literary usage, *theosebes* was often used more loosely, simply to mean pious. However, the technical meaning became increasingly dominant, just as the adjective *eusebes*, which had been universally used to denote piety towards the pagan gods, was increasingly taken over to describe their own faith by Christians.

[127] LXX, 2 Chron. 5. 6; see Reynolds and Tannenbaum, *Jews and Godfearers at Aphrodisias*, 65. Interestingly there is no equivalent in the Hebrew text to οἱ φοβούμενοι.

[128] Josephus, *AJ* 12. 284. See **283, 285, 287**.

of Theos Hypsistos called themselves *theosebeis*, dates to the early fifth century.

The most telling argument for identifying the worshippers of Theos Hypsistos with the god-fearers is, quite simply, that their beliefs and practices precisely coincided. The clearest summary of the beliefs of *theosebeis* comes from a western source, Juvenal's fourteenth Satire, in which he mockingly deplores the bad influence on his son of a western god-fearer, *metuentem sabbata patrem*. Juvenal's father worshipped no god but the clouds and the heavenly spirit (*numen caeli*), abstained from pork, and observed the sabbath. Juvenal hazarded that the son would outdo him and undergo circumcision, repudiating Roman for Jewish law.[129]

Juvenal's sketch is confirmed by an impeccable source. In a striking passage of the *Contra Apionem*, extolling the virtues of Jewish against Greek practices, Josephus wrote: 'The masses have long since shown a keen desire to adopt our religious observances, and there is not one city, Greek or barbarian, not a single nation to which our custom of abstaining from work on the seventh day has not spread, and where the fasts and lighting of lamps and many of our prohibitions in the matter of food are not observed.'[130] There is an uncanny parallel between this account and Gregory of Nazianzus' description of his father's beliefs (already quoted above in §2): 'The cult was a mixture of two elements, Hellenic error and adherence to the Jewish law. Shunning some parts of both it was made up from others. Its followers reject the idols and sacrifices of the former and worship fire and lamplight; they revere the sabbath and are scrupulous not to touch certain foods, but have nothing to do with circumcision.'[131] The conclusion is clear. The *theosebeis* of Josephus (not named as such but clearly identifiable in the *Contra Apionem* passage) were the direct ancestors of the Hypsistarians of late antiquity. Their religious position appears to have changed little in the intervening centuries.

This equation should lead us to change our interpretation of the religious position of the *theosebeis* in one crucial respect. It is now the standard view among scholars that the god-fearers were non-Jewish

---

[129] Juvenal, 14. 96–106. Further references to the adoption of Jewish customs in pagan Roman circles are collected in Schürer² iii. 1. 161 n. 50.

[130] Josephus, *CAp.* 2. 39. 282; translation from Schürer² iii. 1. 161. Reynolds and Tannenbaum, *Jews and Godfearers at Aphrodisias*, 49 treat this passage as an obvious exaggeration. The catalogue of evidence for Theos Hypsistos shows that it is close to being the literal truth.

[131] Gregory of Nazianzus, *Or.* 18. 5 (*PG* 35, 990); see above § 2.

sympathizers with Jewish beliefs, Gentile attenders of Jewish synagogues. That is certainly also the clear perspective of Josephus, writing as a Jewish apologist, and of Juvenal, abhorring the corruption of Roman by Jewish ways, writers who not only provide the evidence to define their position and status, but also offer an implicit or explicit moral judgement on it, whether favourable or hostile to the Jews. Modern commentators have been keen to follow their lead, in particular to interpret the Jews themselves as the genuine, rigorist adherents of the law, in contrast to the laxist tendencies of the god-fearers. The former are judged to have been immune to the temptations of syncretism; only the Hellenes have shifted their ground.[132] But in the arena of secular life it is transparently clear that diaspora Jewry in the Hellenistic and imperial periods achieved a remarkable level of integration into the social and political life of the Greek cities and other indigenous communities of the Near East.[133] The argument of this paper shows that this integration also took place in religious practice. The Jews of the Dispersion had found a common religious language with a vast number of Gentile worshippers, and they forged a shared tradition, current throughout the eastern Mediterranean, of monotheistic worship. By any definition this was one of the most spectacular demonstrations of religious syncretism that the ancient world has to offer.

7. CHRISTIANS AND THE INFLUENCE OF THEOS HYPSISTOS

As it becomes possible to recognize the contours of this religious landscape, it becomes more urgent to locate the origins and spread of Christianity within it. This is not the place to launch yet another reappraisal of the missionary strategy of the early Church and St Paul's role within it. It is enough to say that Luke's entire account of Paul's mission emphasizes the critical importance of his appeal to the Gentiles, more specifically to the Hellenes and God-Worshippers to be found in the shadow of the Diaspora synagogues. The passionate arguments about whether converts should be circumcised acquires specific relevance when applied to religious communities which were precisely divided between Jews, who had been circumcised, and god-fearers, who

---

[132] So L. H. Feldman, *Jew and Gentile in the Ancient World* (1993), *passim*, but especially 342–82. Trebilco, *Jewish Communities* handles the issue with more subtlety.

[133] See now the excellent synthesis of the evidence by W. Ameling, 'Die jüdischen Gemeinden im antiken Kleinasien', in R. Jütte and Abraham P. Kustermann (eds.), *Jüdische Gemeinden und Organisationsformen von der Antike bis zur Gegenwart* (1996), 29–55.

had not. It was the ready-made association of the two groups in all the cities visited by Paul which provided ideally fertile ground where the seeds of the new faith could be scattered. The god-fearers were fully at home with monotheistic belief, familiar with the religious ideas of the Jews and with Old Testament prophecy, but not wedded to them by uncompromising religious fundamentalism. They also had their own, non-Jewish traditions, to which Paul could also appeal. When he apparently stood trial on the Areopagus at Athens,[134] he started his defence by pointing out an altar dedicated ἀγνώστῳ θεῷ and reminded them that the Lord who created the cosmos, master of heaven and earth, did not dwell in temples built by man. If the location of this episode was indeed the hill of the Areopagus, he was standing directly in front of the cult place of Theos Hypsistos, the God 'not admitting of a name, known by many names'.[135]

What stance did Christians of the middle and later empire take up in this same landscape? The answer provided by inscriptions from rural Asia Minor, the best-documented area of the early Christian world outside Rome, is that they mingled with their non-Christian fellows without friction or confrontation in a territory which was familiar to all of them.[136] Gregory, the father of Gregory of Nazianzus, was urged to Orthodoxy by a group of bishops en route to Nicaea in 325. He is a symbolic figure. Before 325 his beliefs and religious practices would hardly have been a matter of public issue. As a worshipper of Theos Hypsistos, a follower of the 'one and only god', he should have been at ease in Christian company, even at times of persecution when the measures taken by the emperors, Diocletian, Galerius, and Maximinus, may briefly have made life as uncomfortable for Hypsistarians as they did for Christians. But the religious politics of Constantine forced people to define their allegiances much more sharply. The True Church had to be distinguished from its rivals; Orthodoxy needed to be defined and established. Nicaea represented the critical turning point; the moment when the elder Gregory had to choose.

The Christian epigraphy of the third and fourth centuries offers clues to support this reconstruction. A doggerel verse inscription from the neighbourhood of Iconium contains the epitaph of Gourdos, priest of Theos Hypsistos, who slept in death 'like a dove' (237). The phraseology

---

[134] Acts 17: 16–34 with T. D. Barnes, 'An Apostle on Trial', *JTS* 20 (1969), 407–19.

[135] Barnes believes that the trial was on the Areopagus; C. J. Hemer, *New Testament Studies*, 20 (1973/4), 341–50 argues cautiously for the NW corner of the agora.

[136] Mitchell, *Anatolia*, ii. 37–43, 57–64.

is all but Christian, and it is likely that another inscription, put up for his *threptos* by an Aurelius Gourdos, concerns the same man. In this text he is unambiguously identified as a Christian priest.[137] He should be equated spiritually with another priest from Mysia, whose epitaph says that 'he had gained the greatest honour among all mankind, had brought joy to the holy people of the highest god, and charmed them all with sacred songs and readings, and who sleeps now in the immaculate place of Christ' (184).

The most influential sect throughout much of central Anatolia in the fourth century was the Novatian church. The Novatians were rigorists whose cult included many Judaizing features, to the extent that most of their rural followers celebrated Easter to coincide with the Passover.[138] A major Church Council of the mid-fourth century which met at Laodicea on the Lycus addressed the problems of Phrygian Christians who celebrated Jewish festivals.[139] The theological and cultural background of these rural Novatians has been brilliantly detected in one of the grandest of their epitaphs, the verse inscription compiled for a priest, Eugenius, which begins with the lines: 'First I shall sing a hymn for God, who oversees everything; second I shall sing a hymn for the first angel, who is Jesus Christ. Great is the remembrance on earth for the dead Eugenius.'[140] The name of Christ is concealed in the formula τισαι τ(ι)σιν. This was a Greek transcription of the Aramaic number ninety-nine (*tisa tisin*), which by the device known as isopsephism rendered the word *Amen*, equivalent to Christ. This riddling was a Jewish trait and the epitaph is a Judaeo-Christian inscription, precisely reflecting the religious environment of third- and fourth-century Lycaonia. It treated Christ not as a being who encroached on the uniqueness of God, but as the first of His angels. The Novatian Church's ritual calendar was harmonized with that of the Jews.[141] 'Pagan' or Judaizing worshippers of

[137] J. R. S. Sterrett, *An Epigraphical Journey in Asia Minor*, Papers of the American School of Classical Studies at Athens 2 (1883/4 publ. 1888), no. 197; W. M. Ramsay, *Luke the Physician* (1908), 390.

[138] Mitchell, *Anatolia*, ii. 98.

[139] C. Hefele and H. Leclercq, *Histoire des Conciles*, i. 2 (1907), 989–1028; Trebilco, *Jewish Communities*, 101–3; Mitchell, *Anatolia*, ii. 98.

[140] W. M. Calder, *Anatolian Studies pres. to W.M. Ramsay* (1923), 76 no. 4; D. M. Robinson, *TAPA* 57 (1926), 209 no. 20a. There is indispensable commentary by H. Grégoire, *Byzantion*, 21 (1924), 699–701 and 2 (1925), 449; A. Wilhelm, *Akademieschriften*, ii. 373; and L. Robert, *Hellenica*, 11/12. 434 n. 2, who refers to J. Barbel, *Christus Angelus. Die Anschauung von Christos als Bote und Engel in der gelehrten und volkstümlichen Literatur des christlichen Altertum* (Bonn, 1941), *non vidi*. See Mitchell, *Anatolia*, ii. 101–2.

[141] The canons of the Church Council held at Laodicea on the Lycus in 340 attempted to outlaw Judaizing behaviour in the Christian community.

Hypsistos were not only easily accommodated within this scheme of ritual and belief, they may even have helped to dictate its theological framework. Imperial legislation and Christian fundamentalism, the least savoury legacy of the Constantinian revolution, sharpened the divide between religious groupings in the fourth and fifth centuries, but certainly did not alienate all the inhabitants of rural communities from one another. Christians and Jews were buried together in third-century Phrygia, where a Jewish guardian angel protected a Christian grave (see above, § 5). In the territory of Tavium in eastern Galatia and at Seleuceia and Corycus in Rugged Cilicia Jewish graves were inserted at random into Christian cemeteries.[142] The ancient world is not lacking in examples of religious polarization, and of religious groups of all persuasions separating themselves off from the rest of the population. However, this is not a model of behaviour which can readily be applied to large parts of the eastern Roman world, and especially of Asia Minor, which was arguably the main seed-bed of Christian expansion in the third and fourth centuries.

If we move from the modest epitaphs and votive monuments of rural Asia Minor to religious politics at the highest level, it is possible to descry recognizably similar features. This is not the occasion to explore the issue of Constantine's Christian convictions at length, but Constantine's conversion, if such it was, from a worshipper of Apollo, the sun-god, via a vision of a solar halo which he took to resemble a cross, to committed Christianity, makes sense in this context.[143] The cult of Theos Hypsistos was palpably linked by many followers with worship of the sun (**186, 284**). Constantine's early religious experiences occurred in the Latin West, where the cult of the sun had made more headway than the worship of the abstract Theos Hypsistos. An eastern Constantine might well have started as a Hypsistarian.

This was true of high-ranking contemporaries. In the spring of 314, when confronted with the obduracy of the Donatists, Constantine wrote to Aelafius, the vicar of Africa, asking him to provide both Catholic bishops and their Donatist rivals with permits to use public transport to travel from Africa across Spain to the council held at Arles. The governor is referred to as *summi dei cultor*, worshipper of the highest

---

[142] *RECAM* ii, nos. 504–12, discussed by K. Bittel, *Bogazköy*, v. 110–11. *MAMA* 3. 222, 262, 440 (pre-Constantinian), 205, 237, 295, 344, 448, 607, 679, on which see M. H. Williams, 'The Jews of Corycus', *Journal for the Study of Judaism*, 25 (1994), 274–86.

[143] For Constantine's conversion see P. Weiss, 'Die Vision Constantins', *Festschrift A. Heuss* (Frankfurter Historische Studien 13, 1993), 143–69 (brilliant and convincing).

god. Constantine assumed accordingly that he would sympathize with the emperor's aim not to allow contention and dispute in the Church to lurk unseen, in case this provoked God's wrath not merely against the human race in general but specifically against Constantine himself.[144] The phraseology does not suggest that the *vicarius* of Africa was a Christian of Constantine's own, still hardly formed Christian persuasion. *Summus Deus* is the term used to translate Theos Hypsistos and to designate the Jewish God in the Latin version, dating probably to the fifth century, of the *Assumption of Moses*, an apocryphal text of Hellenistic or early imperial origin.[145] The text of Constantine's letter, taken at face value, implies that Aelafius was a western worshipper of Theos Hypsistos. He and Constantine, both before and after the latter's conversion, occupied ground which was not yet exclusively reserved for Christians. Adherents of Aelafius' beliefs continued to be found in the fifth century. Two constitutions of 408 and 409, known from the Theodosian Code, were concerned to outlaw a heretical Judaizing group known as the *Caelicolae*.[146] The Beza Latin translation used precisely this term to translate σεβόμενοι when it appears in Acts 13: 50 and 17: 40, and we should assume, with Schürer, that their beliefs were very similar to, if not identical with those of the god-fearers of the eastern provinces. They were certainly to be found in North Africa, for Augustine in a letter reported that he had been detained from carrying out an episcopal ordination by having to conduct an interview with a leader of the sect, who was reported to have seduced many of its followers into a sacrilegious second baptism.[147]

8. CONCLUSIONS

What significance should be attached to the cult of Theos Hypsistos? Who was this god? His worship from the Hellenistic period until the fifth century was found in town and country across the entire eastern

[144] 'Nam cum apud me certum sit, te quoque dei summi esse cultorem, confiteor gravitati tuae, quod nequaquam fas esse ducam, ut eiusmodi contentiones et altercationes dissimulentur a nobis, ex quibus forsitan commoveri possit summa divinitas non solum contra hominum genus sed etiam in me ipsum' (*CSEL* xxvi. 204–6, tr. J. Stephenson, *A New Eusebius*, no. 263).

[145] Schürer, *Sb. Berl.* (1897), 215 citing *Assumptio Mosis* 6. 1; see further Schürer[2] ii. 1. 278.

[146] Schürer, *Sb. Berl.* (1897), 223–4; *CTh.* 16. 5. 43; 8. 19 (both issued in the names of Theodosius and Honorius).

[147] Augustine, *Ep.* 44. 13: 'Sed quia ordinandi episcopi necessitas nos inde iamiamque rapiebat, diutius cum illo esse nequivimus. Iam enim miseramus ad maiorem Caelicolarum, quem audieramus novi apud eos baptismi institutorem exstitisse et multos illo sacrilegio seduxisse.'

Mediterranean and the Near East. It was not the preserve of an intellectual or cultural elite. On the contrary, worshippers came mostly from the
humbler levels of society. Theos Hypsistos made contact with humans
not through direct epiphany, but through dreams or oracles, or by the
intercession of messengers. In Lydia these angels were envisaged as
heavenly riders, but were addressed as abstractions, the Just, the Holy, or
the Divine. Holiness and divine justice were qualities of direct relevance
to human conduct, for in the villages of Lydia and Phrygia, beyond the
reach or the notice of secular civic and imperial authority, justice in
palpable and concrete form was meted out in the sanctuaries of the
gods.[148]

The origins of the cult extend at least as far back as the second
century BC, and already at this period the worship of Hypsistos was to be
found not merely among the Jews of Israel but also in Egypt and in the
Aegean region. It is, perhaps, a formal possibility that, just as Jews of the
Diaspora were responsible for transmitting specific aspects of their
ritual, such as εὐλογία, to the pagan communities around them, so they
could have spread and implanted the entire basis of the cult in the local
populations which they encountered. On this interpretation Jewish
belief would have formed the basis for all Hypsistarian worship. But this
reconstruction is historically and sociologically highly implausible. The
cult of Zeus Hypsistos in Greece and Macedonia surely developed from
local roots, although the import of the terminology of the synagogue
suggests that it absorbed Jewish influence. The concept of a highest god
and his angels is likely to have evolved independently in the unhellenized
communities of the interior of Asia Minor and on the north shore of the
Black Sea. In the first case it drew on an indigenous tradition which
favoured both monotheism and an ascetic religious morality;[149] in the
second it may owe something to abstract Iranian ideas of divinity which
had influenced the Sarmatian peoples of South Russia.[150] It developed
firmer outlines as a result of cross-fertilization with the ideas of Jewish
or Judaizing groups, producing a religious culture which spanned the
pagan–Jewish divide. The Jewish influence was particularly effective in
focusing religious ideas. We may compare the effect that Christian
doctrines and practices had on late paganism, providing sharper con-

---

[148] The epigraphic documentation for this entire phenomenon is now conveniently
available in Petzl, 'Beichtinschriften', and M. Ricl, 'Hosios kai Dikaios. Première partie:
catalogue des inscriptions', *Epigraphica Anatolica*, 18 (1991), 1–70, and 'Hosios kai Dikaios.
Seconde partie: Analyse', *Epigraphica Anatolica*, 19 (1992), 71–102.

[149] Mitchell, *Anatolia*, i. 187–95.

[150] So Ustinova, 'The *thiasoi* of Theos Hypsistos in Tanais', 173–6.

tours and a clearer definition to polytheistic belief.[151] Jewish communities served as a powerful role model. They were well-defined, set apart by dietary laws, by the practice of circumcision, and by observance of the sabbath, as well as by the traditions preserved in their holy books.[152] The worshippers of Theos Hypsistos, the *theosebeis* as they called themselves, acquired many Jewish characteristics but did not contemplate full conversion. It remained important to them to remain a part of the non-Jewish world, to preserve the religious, moral, and intellectual traditions which they had inherited in their Greek or native communities. Conversely, Jews of the Diaspora could not prevent their own beliefs and sense of cultural and religious identity being influenced by the Gentile neighbours, whose way of life they shared. Most important of all, shared worship threw the two groups together. This was the environment in which the earliest Christian missions were undertaken, and the beliefs and doctrinal positions of Christians, Jews, and god-fearers continued to overlap throughout antiquity.

Although the epigraphic evidence is a poor guide to the chronological evolution of the worship of Theos Hypsistos, it does allow one to measure the success of this quasi-monotheistic worship against that of other cults during the same period. No other indigenous Greek, Anatolian, or Near Eastern deity has so dense a distribution over so wide an area. Theos Hypsistos had the specific advantage of not being tied to civic or imperial institutions. It was not linked, like the worship of the emperors or the main civic deities, to sporting or musical competitions, grand festivals, lavish euergetism, or even to animal sacrifice. It was therefore ideally equipped to weather the storms of economic recession, social change, and the militarization of the Roman world in the third and fourth centuries. The persistence of monotheism, like the demise of polytheistic paganism, owed much to economic as well as to psychological and cultural conditions.

The worship of Theos Hypsistos had another crucial advantage over the traditional pagan cults. The notion of a supreme and abstract deity, supported by lesser divine beings, already developed in Jewish theology and the books of the Old Testament, found a perfect expository partner in Neoplatonic philosophy. This enabled a popular cult to evolve into a highly sophisticated theological system, which appealed to intellectuals and the educated elite as well as to ordinary people. The parallel with the

---

[151] See G. W. Bowersock, *Hellenism in Late Antiquity* (1990).

[152] Josephus, *Contra Apionem*, 1. 38–44 cited by F. Millar, *The Roman Near East* (1993), 338 is the *locus classicus*.

way in which Christianity laid down firm roots in the third and fourth
centuries, by developing sophisticated and convincing philosophical
explanations of its simple doctrines, is obvious, irresistible, and entirely
apt. The Oenoanda oracle is simply the tip of an iceberg of surviving
literature which can be used to illustrate this development. The oracular
shrines of Claros and Didyma helped to disseminate this philosophical
theology among the followers and sympathizers of the cult. Furthermore, the process of theological explanation and discussion helped make
room for Christians and Jews to climb aboard. Didyma's oracles contain
pronouncements about Jehovah and even about Christ, as well as about
Zeus, Aether, and pagan wonder-workers like Apollonius of Tyana.[153]
The cult of Theos Hypsistos and the monotheistic conceptions of a widespread and popular religious culture were the seed-bed into which
Jewish and Christian theology could readily be planted. Without them,
the transformation of ancient patterns of belief from pagan polytheism
to the predominantly monotheistic systems of Judaism, Christianity,
and Islam would not only have been far less tidy and unidirectional than
it was, it might not have occurred at all.

APPENDIX: DOCUMENTARY EVIDENCE FOR
THEOS HYPSISTOS AND ZEUS HYPSISTOS

Most of the documentation of the cult is epigraphic. For this list of inscriptions,
I have followed the regional geographical arrangement of *SEG*. I have not tried
to edit the material in detail, but have provided a simple text of the inscriptions
and an indication, sometimes very approximate, of their date. Some of the longer
texts have been abbreviated, to save space. Decoration and details of the monuments have been noted where these are of clear relevance to the cult. The
references have been confined to the most accessible publications, where further
bibliographical information may generally be found. For earlier collections of
the evidence, see Schürer, *Sb. Berl.* 1897, 209–13; F. Cumont, *RE* 9. 1 (1916), 444–
50; A. B. Cook, *Zeus* 2. 2 (1925), 873–90; H. Schwabl, *RE Suppl.* 12 (1974), 1477–80.

Mainland Greece

1. Athens (N. slope of Acropolis), *IG* 2² 4782, II AD. Ionic capital supporting a
seated eagle Ἀγαθῇ Τύχῃ | Ἰουλ. Ἀσκληπιανὴ | θεῷ ὑψίστῳ ὑπὲ[ρ] | Μαξίμου
τοῦ υἱ[οῦ] | εὐχαριστήριον ἀνέθ[ηκεν]

[153] See especially Robert, *CRAI* 1969, 568–99 (*OMS* v. 584–619), whose notes contain
many essential references to a vast literature on the subject; Lane Fox, *Pagans and
Christians*, 256–61; and A. D. Nock, 'Oracles théologiques', *Essays on Religion and the
Ancient World*, i. 160–8.

2. Athens (Pnyx), *IG* 2² 4783, II AD. Relief showing two breasts. Διονυσία Ὑψίστῳ | εὐχήν

3. Athens (Roman agora), *IG* 2² 4784, II AD. Relief showing two footprints Εὐτυχία εὐχὴν θεῷ | Ὑψίστῳ ἀνέθηκα

4. Athens (Pnyx), *IG* 2² 4798, I–II AD. Σύντροφος Ὑψίστῳ Διὶ | χαριστήριον

5. Athens (Pnyx), *IG* 2² 4799, I–II AD. Relief of an eye. Εὔοδος Ὑψίστῳ εὐχήν

6. Athens (Pnyx), *IG* 2² 4800, I–II AD. Relief of a vulva. Ὀλυνπιὰς ὑψίστῳ εὐχήν

7. Athens (Pnyx), *IG* 2² 4801, I–II AD. Relief showing a face from the eyebrows downwards. Τερτία ὑψίστῳ | εὐχήν

8. Athens (Pnyx), *IG* 2² 4802, imperial. Relief showing a breast. Ὀνησίμη εὐχὴν | Διὶ ὑψίστῳ

9. Athens (Pnyx), *IG* 2² 4803, I–II AD. Relief showing a breast. Εὐτυχὶς Ὑψίστῳ εὐ|χήν

10. Athens (Pnyx), *IG* 2² 4804, I–II AD. Relief showing a breast. Εἰσιὰς Ὑψ[ίστῳ] | εὐχ[ήν]

11. Athens (Pnyx), *IG* 2² 4805, I–II AD. Relief showing two eyes. Φιλη`ᾶτιν` | [ε]ὐχὴν ἀνέ[θ]ηκεν

12. Athens (Pnyx), *IG* 2² 4806, I–II AD. Relief showing two arms. Κλαυδία Πρέπουσα | εὐχαριστῶ Ὑψίστῳ

13. Athens (Pnyx), *IG* 2² 4807, I–II AD. –]α θεῷ ὑψί[στῳ ε]ὐχήν

14. Athens (from foot of N. slope of Acropolis), *IG* 2² 4808, I–II AD. Relief showing eyes and a nose. Εἰσιδότη Διὶ ὑψίστῳ

15. Athens (from foot of N. slope of Acropolis), *IG* 2² 4809, I–II AD. Relief showing two breasts. Εὐτυχία | Ὑψείστῳ | εὐχήν

16. Athens (from foot of N. slope of Acropolis), *IG* 2² 4810, I–II AD. Εὔπραξις | εὐχήν

17. Athens (Peiraeus), *IG* 2² 4811, I–II AD. Εὐοδία Ὑψίστῳ εὐ|χήν

18. Athens (agora), *SEG* 19. 225, I–II AD. Χρυσάριν Ὑψίστῳ εὐχήν

19. Athens (agora), *SEG* 19. 226, I–II AD. Γράτ⟨α⟩ Ὑψί⟨σ⟩τ|ῳ εὐχήν

20. Athens (agora), *SEG* 16. 184, I–II AD. Ὑψίστ[ῳ] | εὐχὴ[ν] | Μοιραγένης

21. Athens (Pnyx), *SEG* 37 (1987), 142, imperial. [Διὶ ὑψ]ίστῳ | [εὐχὴ]ν Ζωσί[μη θ]εραπευ[θεῖ]σα

22. Athens, *SEG* 40 (1990), 201, I AD? Nude male torso from waist to mid-thigh. [Κό]σμο[ς] | ['Υψ]ίστῳ | [εὐ]χή[ν]

23. Athens, *IG* 2² 4738, I–II AD. Γλαῦκος | Τρύφαινα | Λέων | [Υ]ψίστῳ | [εὐχὴν] ὑπέρ | – –

The sanctuary of Hypsistos on the Pnyx at Athens is discussed by Cook, *Zeus* 2. 2. 876–80 and B. Forsen, 'The Sanctuary of Zeus Hypsistos and the Assembly Place on the Pnyx', *Hesperia*, 62 (1993), 414–43. Fifty-eight niches to receive votive reliefs or inscriptions are visible cut in the scarp to the east of the bema on the Pnyx. Almost all the surviving dedications were set up by women in connection with some illness or affliction from which they had suffered, and many depict parts of the anatomy. These are reviewed by B. Forsen, *Tyche*, 5 (1990), 9–12.

130   S. Mitchell

24. Sparta, *IG* 5. 1. 240, imperial? Relief showing two eagles. Διὶ ὑψίστῳ | εὐχήν
25. Sparta, *SEG* 11. 683, II AD. Ἀφροδείσιλος δοῦλος | Κλαυ. Πρατο|λάου τοῦ
Βρα|σίδου Διὶ ὑ[ψ]|ίστῳ εὐχήν]
26. Sparta, *SEG* 11. 684, II AD. Διὶ | ὑψίστῳ | Νεικέρως | εὐχ[ήν]
27. Sparta, *SEG* 11. 685, II AD. Διοκλῆ[ς] | Διὶ ὑψίστῳ | εὐχήν
28. Sparta, *SEG* 11. 686, II AD. [–]θενα Σω|[ζο]ύσης ὑπὲ|ρ Εὐπορίαν τὴν |
θυγατέρα Διὶ ὑψίστῳ εὐχήν
29. Sparta, *SEG* 11. 687, II AD. Hand holding a thunderbolt. [Διὶ] ὑψίστῳ εὐ[χήν]
30. Sparta, *SEG* 11. 688, II AD. [Διὸς ὑψ]ίστ[ου ?]
31. Delphi, *SEG* 14. 425, I–II AD. Relief showing a crescent moon. Τυχικὸς Τ. |
[Φ]λ. Μεγαλὶ[ν]ου δοῦλος | [Δ]ιὶ (*vel* [θε]ῷι) ὑψίστῳ
32. Corcyra, *IG* 9. 1. 718, imperial. [– –] | ΦΑΙΑΚΟΣΥΝΗ Διεὶ ὑψίστῳ | εὐχήν
Pausanias 5. 15. 5 reports that there were two altars for Zeus Hypsistos at
Olympia, and remarks on the cult at Corinth (2. 2. 8) and Thebes (9. 8. 5).

Thessaly

33. Gonnoi, B. Helly, *Gonnoi II. Les inscriptions* no. 157, imperial. Διὶ ὑψίστῳ |
Νικόβουλο[ς]

Macedonia

34. Beroia, J. M. R. Cormack, *JRS* 31 (1941), 21, imperial. Διὶ [ὑψ]ίσ[τῳ] | οἱ περὶ
Ἔρωτα Εὐβιότου διάκ[ο]νοι | (names follow)
35. Beroia, J. M. R. Cormack, *JRS* 31 (1941), 19, AD 236. Διεὶ ὑψίστῳ ΑΓΑΙΣ κατ᾿
εὐχὴν ἀνέθηκε | εὐτυχῶς. ἔτους ζξσ΄ Δαισίου ηι΄
36. Beroia, *SEG* 35 (1985), 714, II–III AD. Stele with male bust above eagle in
wreath. Διὶ ὑψίστῳ | Πό. Κορνήλιος Ῥοῦφος | καὶ οἱ ὑπ᾿ αὐτὸν διάκονοι |
κριτεύοντος Σεξ. Ποπιλλίου | Φιλ[–]
37. Beroia (Lefkopetra), G. H. R. Horsley, *New Docs.* 5 (1989), 138, I–II AD.
Ἀ[ρ]ιάγνη Μητ[ρὸς θεῶν] | ἱερόδουλος κατ᾿ ἐπιταγὴν θεοῦ ὑ[ψί]στου | μετὰ
υἱοῦ Παραμό|νου τὴν ἐπιτ[αγ]ὴν | ἀπέδωκεν τῷ θεῷ
38. Edessa, *SEG* 40 (1990), 537, I BC. Stele decorated with an eagle on a garland.
Ζωίλος Ἀλεξάνδρου | ὑπὲρ τῶν παιδίων | Διὶ ὑψίστῳ.
39. Edessa, J. M. R. Cormack, *ABSA* 58 (1963), 24 no. 7, II AD. Πο. Αἴλιος Δι[ὶ]
ὑψίστῳ | Τερεντιανὸς Ἀττικὸς κατ᾿ ὄναρ
40. Edessa, A. B. Cook, *Zeus* 2. 878 n. 9, imperial. Διὶ ὑψίστῳ εὐχὴν Μάρκος
Λιβούρνιος Οὐάλης
41. Edessa, P. Perdrizet, *BCH* 22 (1898), 347 no. 2, Hellenistic? Χάρης
Ἀλεξάνδρου καὶ Δημήτριος | Χάρητος Διὶ ὑψίστῳ
42. Elymia, T. Rizakis and G. Touratsoglu, Ἐπιγραφὲς Ἄνω Μακεδονίας (1985)
no. 17 (*SEG* 35 (1985), 698), imperial. Δειὶ ὑψ[ίστῳ –] Αἰλείου [εὐχήν]
43. Kerdylion, nr. Amphipolis, *BCH* 19 (1895), 110, I–II AD. Μ. Λευκείλιο[ς] |
Μασκλᾶς θεῶ[ι] | ὑψίστωι χαριστήριον
44. Kozani (Malei), T. Rizakis and G. Touratsoglu, Ἐπιγραφὲς Ἄνω Μακεδονίας
(1985) no. 20, imperial. Διὶ ὑψίστῳ | Ὀρέστης | Λιμναίου

45. Kozani (Malei), T. Rizakis and G. Touratsoglu, Ἐπιγραφὲς Ἄνω Μακεδονίας (1985) no. 21, imperial. Διὰ ὑψίστῳ Ἀμύ|νταιs

46. Kozani (Malei), T. Rizakis and G. Touratsoglu, Ἐπιγραφὲς Ἄνω Μακεδονίας (1985) no. 22, imperial. Χρυσέρως Φιλίππου | ἀνπελουργὸς Διὰ ὑψίσ|τῳ εὐχαριστήριον ὑπὲ[ρ] | κυρίου· ἀπονομάζει | δὲ αὐτῷ ἀμπέλων δύω ὄρχου|s ἐκ τῶν πε|κουλαρίων

47. Kozani (Malei), T. Rizakis and G. Touratsoglu, Ἐπιγραφὲς Ἄνω Μακεδονίας (1985) no. 9, imperial. Διὰ ὑψίστῳ | Ἀρτεμ[ᾶς] | καὶ Νεικ[ά]|νωρ οἱ [Νει]|κάνορος | εὐ|χήν

48. Kozani (Malei), T. Rizakis and G. Touratsoglu, Ἐπιγραφὲς Ἄνω Μακεδονίας (1985) no. 10, imperial. Ἀλέ|ξαν|δρος | Ῥυμε|τάλ|κου | ὁ καὶ | Ῥῆλος | Διὰ | ὑψίσ|τῳ | εὐχή

49. Kozani (Aiani), T. Rizakis and G. Touratsoglu, Ἐπιγραφὲς Ἄνω Μακεδονίας (1985) no. 7 (SEG 34 (1984), 641), imperial. Statuette of eagle. Δεὶ ὑψίσ⟨τ⟩ῳ | Ἀτρείδης | Καπύλλου | εὐχήν

50. Kozani (Ano Komi), SEG 34 (1984), 646, imperial. Δειὶ ὑψ[ίστῳ] | ΑΙΔΩΙΟΝ – | – –

51. Pydna, Horsley, New Docs. 1. 26–7, AD 250. Ἀγαθῇ Τύχῃ | ἔτους βηs' Σεβ. | τοῦ καὶ ηρτ' Δαισίου ηι' ἐν Πύδνῃ | οἱ συνελθόντες | θρησκευταὶ ἐπὶ θεοῦ | Διὸς ὑψίστου ἔθεν|το τήνδε τὴν στήλην, | λογιστεύοντος Οὐρ|βανιανοῦ Βιλίστου, | ἄρχοντος Αὐρ. Νιγερ[ί]|ωνος ὑπὸ ἀρχσυνάγωγον Αὐρ. Κηπίωνα τὸν | πρὶν Πιερίωνος καὶ προστάτου | Αὐρ. Σεβήρου κτλ.

52. Serrai (Verge), SEG 30 (1980), 591, AD 154 or 270. Plaque with relief showing bull's head with an eagle on top. Διὰ ὑψίστῳ | Διαζειπα | Δυτουλου | ἔτος βτ' | Πανήμου σ'

53. Serrai (Verge), SEG 30 (1980), 592, II–III AD. Διὰ ὑψίστῳ Τοκης ὁ καὶ Ἰσίδωρος

54. Thessalonica or the vicinity, IG 10. 2. 62, II AD? Διὰ ὑψίστῳ θεὰν δικαίαν Νέμεσιν | Κο. Οὐρβανὸς ἀνέθηκεν | εὐχήν

55. Thessalonica, IG 10. 2. 67, AD 74/5. θεῷι ὑψίστωι | μεγίστωι σωτῆρι | Γ. Ἰούλιος Ὥριος | κατ᾽ ὄνειρον χρη|ματισθεὶς καὶ σω|θεὶς ἐκ μεγάλου κιν|δύνου τοῦ κατὰ θάλασσαν εὐχαριστήριον | ἐπὶ ἱερέως | Μ. Οὐητίου Πρόκλου | ἔτους βκσ'

56. Thessalonica, IG 10. 2. 68, I AD. θεῷι | ὑψίστωι | ὑπὲρ Τ. Φλαουίου | Εὔκτιμένου υἱοῦ | Ἀμύ[ν]τα τοῦ | [τρικλει]νάρχου | [οἱ ὑπογε]γραμμένοι | [συνκλ]ίται (list of names)

57. Thessalonica, IG 10. 2. 71, I–II AD. [–θε]ῷι ὑψίστωι | [Τερ]έντιος Ἑρμ[–]

58. Thessalonica, IG 10. 2. 72, I–II AD. θεῷι ὑψίστῳ κατ᾽ ἐπιταγὴν Ἰουεσ[–]

59. Trebeni, T. Rizakis and G. Touratsoglu, Ἐπιγραφὲς Ἄνω Μακεδονίας (1985) no. 27, imperial. Μαικηνᾶς Διὰ ὑ|ψίστωι εὐχήν

Thrace

M. Taceva-Hitova, Thracia, 4 (1977), 271–301 lists and discusses 21 instances in Thrace (SEG 27 (1977), 1281); see also Balkan Studies, 19 (1978), 59–75, Eastern

Cults in Moesia Inferior and Thracia (1983), 190–215

60. Kavalla (from quarries at Nea Karvali), *SEG* 38 (1987), 597 no. 3, AD 36–48.
Dedication to Ζεὺς ὕψιστος by superintendent and workmen at quarries ὑπὲρ
κυρίου βασιλέως Θρακῶν Ῥοιμητάλκα Κότυος καὶ τῶν τέκνων αὐτοῦ
61. Kavalla (near Nea Karvali), *SEG* 40 (1990), 572, imperial. [–ὑψ]ίστῳ |
[ἀνέθη]κεν Ταρσᾶς | [χ]αλκεύς
62. Pautalia (Zelenigrad), *IGBulg.* 4. 2111, II–III AD. θεῶι ὑψί[στωι] | ὑπὲρ
Αὐφιδίων οἴκων | [– Αὐ]φίδιο[ς –]
63. Perinthus, *BCH* 24 (1900), 161 no. 1, imperial. θεῷ ὑ|ψίστῳ | Σαβεῖλνα δῶρον
64. Perinthus or Selymbria, M. Sayar, unpublished (*I.Perinthos*), imperial.
65. Philippopolis, *IGBulg.* 3. 1. 937, imperial. Marble plaque with relief of an
eagle. θεῷ ὑψίστῳ | ΑΤΠΓ
66. Philippopolis (Asenovgrad), *IGBulg.* 3. 1. 1431, imperial. Ἀγαθῇ Τύχῃ | θεῷ
ὑψίστῳ ἐ|[πηκόῳ –]
67. Philippopolis (Asenovgrad), *IGBulg.* 3. 1. 1432, imperial. [– –]|.εια Ἑλέ|νη
ἀνέθηκεν | εὐλογητῷ εὐ|χήν
68. Selymbria, *IGR* 1. 777, AD 25. θεῶι ἁγίωι ὑψίστωι | ὑπὲρ τῆς Ῥοιμη|τάλκου
καὶ Πυθο|δώριδος ἐκ τῶν κα|τὰ τὸν Κοιλα[λ]ητικὸν | πόλεμον κινδύνου |
σωτηρίας εὐξάμενος | καὶ ἐπιτυχὼν Γάιος | Ἰούλιος Πρόκ[λ]ος χαρι|στ[ήρι]ον
Serdica: a sanctuary of Theos Hypsistos which produced altars, bases, column
capitals, reliefs depicting eagles and the following five inscriptions (note to
IGBulg. 4. 1941; M. Taceva-Hitova, *Balkan Studies*, 19 (1978), 60–1)
69. Serdica, *IGBulg.* 4. 1941, imperial. [θ]εῷ ἐπηκόῳ | ὑψίστῳ Πονπώ|νιος
Θεόδουλος | Λόπου ὑπὲρ ἑαυτοῦ
70. Serdica, *IGBulg.* 4. 1942, imperial. Ἀγαθῇ [Τύχῃ] | θεῷ ὑψ[ίστῳ] | Διζου[–
–] | εὐξάμ[ενος] | ἀνέθηκε
71. Serdica, *IGBulg.* 4. 1943, imperial. Ἀγαθῇ Τύχῃ | Πανθία | θεῷ ὑψίστ(ῳ) |
εὐχαριστή|ριον
72. Serdica, *IGBulg.* 4. 1944, imperial. θεῷ ὑψίστῳ | ἱερεύς
73. Serdica, *IGBulg.* 4. 1946, imperial. [–]ιμος Α[–]|ήτου καὶ [–] |ροβος
Αι[–]|ήτου θεῷ [ὑψί]|στῳ εὐχα[ριστή|ρι]ον
74. Serdica (Gormasovo), *IGBulg.* 4. 2014, I–II AD. Δορζιν|θης Δίνε\|ος Δὶ |
ὑψίσ|τῳ εὐχ|ήν
75. Pirot, Serbia, *AEMÖ* 10 (1886), 238, imperial. Ἀγαθῇ [τύ]χ[η] | θεῷ ἐπηκόῳ
ὑψίστῳ | εὐχὴν ἀνέστησαν | τὸ κοινὸν ἐκ τῶν ἰ|δίων διὰ ἱερέως | Ἑρμογένους
κτλ . . . θία[σος] Σεβαζιανὸς . . .

Dacia

76. Apulum, *CIL* 3. 1090, imperial. *Iovi summo ex|superantissimo | divinarum
hu|manarumque rerum rectori | fatorumque ar|bitro – –*
77. Zermigetusa (for these texts see S. Sanie, *ANRW* 2. 18. 2, 1263–4 nos. 99–101,
see also 1225–6), *I. Dac. Rom.* 3. 2. 222, III AD. Δὶ ὑψίστῳ | ἐπηκόῳ | Αἴλ.
Ἀπολινάριος ἐπίτροπος | καὶ Μαξίμα | εὐχαριστήριον

The Cult of Theos Hypsistos 133

78. Zermigetusa, *I. Dac. Rom* 3. 2. 223, II–III AD. θεῷ ǀ ὑψίστῳ ἐǀπηκόῳ
εὐχαριστοῦǀσα ἀνέθηκα Αἰλία Κασσία

79. Zermigetusa, S. Sanie, *Studii si cercetare di Istorie Veche*, 28 (1977), 135–42
(*SEG* 27 (1977), 422), *I. Dac. Rom.* 3. 2. 224, II–III AD. Votive plaque depicting two
ears. Ἰ. Ἀτείμ[ητος] ǀ θεῷ ὑ[ψίστῳ]

Moesia Inferior

80. Anchialis, *IGBulg.* 1². 371, II–III AD. Διὶ ὑψίστῳ δεσπ[ό]ǀτῃ Πολυ.ρος
ὑ[πὲρ ǀ τ]ῶν τέκνων καὶ ἐǀαυτοῦ εὐχαριστήριον

81. Odessus?, *IGBulg.* 2. 780, II–I BC? Relief shows Zeus and Nymphs. [–]μος ὁ
καὶ Παπίας οἰκοδομήσας τὸν πυ[λῶνα ǀ καὶ καθιερώσ]ας τὸν τόπον Διὶ
ὑψǀ[ίσ]τῳ εὐχήν – –

82. Tomis, D. Pippidi, *St. Clas.* 16 (1974), 260–1, imperial. Ἀγαθ[ῇ Τύχῃ] ǀ
ὑψίστ[ῳ θεῷ? –] ǀκη ἀνέθη[κε –] ǀ Σωσθένο[υς –] ǀ ἱδρο[–]ǀ θιασ[–]αι[–]ǀ
ρε[–]ρον.α[–] ǀ εὐχαριστήρ[ιον]

North Shore of the Black Sea

E. Schürer, 'Die Juden im bosporanischen Reich und die Genossenschaften der
σεβόμενοι θεὸν ὕψιστον ebendaselbst', *Sb. Berl.* 1897, 200–25; E. R. Goodenough,
'The Bosporus Inscriptions to the Most High God', *Jewish Quarterly Review*, 47
(1956–7), 1–44; B. Lifshitz, 'Le culte du Dieu Très Haut à Gorgippia', *Riv. fil.* 92
(1964), 157–61; M. Taceva-Hitova, *VDI* 1 (1978), 133–42 (*SEG* 28 (1978), 1648); I.
Levinskaja, *Anticnaja Balkanistica* (Moscow, 1987), 67–73; J. Ustinova, *HR* 31
(1991/2), 150–80 (*SEG* 42 (1992), 726). I have not always reproduced the texts of
the longer inscriptions in full.

83. Gorgippia, Latyschev, *Inscr. Ant. Orae Sept. Ponti Euxini*, 4. 436b = *CIRB* 1231,
imperial. Two references to θεῷ ὑψίστῳ (l. 4, 15) in a list of names including
Judaizing Sambation.

84. Gorgippia, *SEG* 32 (1982), 790, early I AD. [θεῶι ὑψίστωι παν]τοκράτωρ[ι] ǀ
[εὐλογητῶι βασιλ]εύοντος ǀ [Κότυος τοῦ Ἀσπού]ργου φιλοǀ[καίσαρος καὶ
φιλ]ορωμαίου ǀ [– –] καὶ Μητρότειǀ[μος οἱ τοῦ –] σωθέντες ǀ [ἐκ μεγάλων
κιν]δύνων ἐν τῶι ǀ [– ἔτει ἀνέθηκαν] εὐχήν

85. Gorgippia, Latyschew II, 400 = *CIRB* 1123, AD 41. Manumission document.
θεῷ ὑψίστῳ παντοǀκράτορι εὐλογητῷ, βαǀσιλεύοντος Μιθριδάτου φιλοǀ[–]καὶ
φιλοπάτρǀιδος ἔτους ηλτ' μηǀνὸς Δείου, Πόθος Στǀράβωνος ἀνέθηκεν ǀ τ[ῆι]
προσευχῆι κατ' εὐχ[ῆ]ǀν θ[ρ]επτὴν ἑαυτοῦ, ᾗ ὄνοǀμα Χ[ρ]ύσα, ἐφ' ᾧ ᾖ
ἀνέπαφος καὶ ἀνεπηρέαστο[ς] ǀ ἀπὸ παντὸς κληρον[όμ]ǀου ὑπὸ Δία Γῆν Ἥλιον

86. Gorgippia, *CIRB* 1126, AD 67/8. θεῶι ὑψίστωι παν⟨τα⟩τοκράτορι ǀ
εὐ(λ)ογητῶι, βασιλεύοντος βασιλέǀλως Ῥησκουπόριδος, φιλοκαίσαρος ǀ καὶ
φιλορωμαίου, εὐσεβοῦς, ἔτους ǀ δ(ξ)τ' μηνὸς Δαεισίου . . . Νεοκλῆς ǀ
Ἀθηνοδώ[ρου ἀφίημι ἐλευθέρ]ους ὑπὸ Δία, Γῆν, Ἥλιον, etc.

87. Gorgippia, Latyschev 2. 401 = *CIRB* 1125, I AD. [θεῷ ὑψ]ίστ[ῳ πανǀτοκράτ]ορι εὐλογ[ή|τ]ῳ, βασιλεύοντρ[ς] | βασίλεως Τιβερίου Ἰ⟨ω⟩Ιουλίου ⟨λιου⟩ Σαυρομάτου etc. (manumission of a foster-daughter by Timotheus)

88. Panticapaeum, *CIRB* 64, AD 306. θεῷ ὑψίστῳ | ἐπηκόῳ εὐΙχήν. Αὐρ. ΟὐαλέΙριος Σόγους Ὀιλύμπου, ὁ ἐπὶ | τῆς Θεοδοσίας, ΙσεβαστόγνωΙστο[ς], τειμηθεὶς ὑΙπὸ ΔιοκλητιαΙνοῦ καὶ Μαξιμιανοῦ, | ὁ καὶ Ὀλυμπιανὸς | κληθεὶς ἐν τῷ ἐΙπαρχείῳ. ὁ πολλὰ | ἀποδημήσας καὶ | ἀποστατήσας ἔτη | δέκα ἐξ καὶ ἐν πολΙλοῖς θλίψεσι γενόΙμενος, εὐξάμενος, | ἐκ θεμελίου οἰκοΙδομήσας τὴν προσευχὴν ἐν τῷ γχ′

89. Tanais, Latyschev 2. 437 = *CIRB* 1261, earliest of Tanais group. [θε]ῷ ὑψίστωι ε[ὐχήν], | [β]ασιλεύοντος βα[σιλέως Τιβερίου] | [Ἰ]ουλίου Ῥοιμητάλκο[υ φιλοκαίσαρος καὶ] | φιλορωμαίου, εὐσε[βοῦς κτλ.] Relief of eagle in gable.

90. Tanais, Latyschev 2. 438 = *CIRB* 1260, AD 156. [Ἀγα]θῆι τ[ύχηι] | θεῷ | ὑψίστῳ ἐπηκόῳ εὐχή· βασιλεύοντος βασιλέως [Τιβερίου] | Ἰουλίου Εὐπάτορος . . . [ἐν τῷ ἔτει] βνυ′. Two eagles holding a garland beneath gable.

91. Tanais, Latyschev 2. 439 = *CIRB* 1260a, mid-II AD. [Ἀγα]θῆι [τύχηι, θεῶι ὑψίσ]τωι, | [βασι]λεύοντ[ος βασιλέως Τιβ] ερίου | [Ἰουλίου Εὐ]πάτ[ορος φιλοκαίσαρο]ς καὶ | [φιλορωμαίου, εὐσεβοῦς] κτλ

92. Tanais, Latyschev 2. 445 = *CIRB* 1277, c. AD 200. θεῷ ὑψίστῳ. ἀγαθῆι τύχηι. | βασιλεύοντος βασιλέως Τιβ. Ἰουλ. Σαυρομάτου | φιλοκαίσαρ[ος κα]ὶ φιλο[ρ]ωμαίου, εὐσεβοῦς, ἡ σύνοδος | ἡ περὶ ἱ[ερέα κτλ. Relief of eagle in gable.

93. Tanais, Latyschev 2. 446 = *CIRB* 1278, AD 220. ἀγα[θῆ]ι τύχηι | θεῶι ὑψίστωι ἐπηκόωι | [ἡ σ]ύνοδος ἡ [περ]ὶ θεὸν ὕψιστον κα[ὶ] | ἱερέα Χόφρασμον κτλ. ([ἐν τῶ]ι ζιφ′ ἔ[τει]

94. Tanais, Latyschev 2. 447 = *CIRB* 1279, AD 225. ἀγαθῇ τύχῃ | θεῷ ὑψίστῳ ἐπηκόῳ ἡ σ]ύνοδος ἡ πε|ρὶ θεὸν ὕψιστον καὶ ἱερέα Χόφρασμον κτλ. (ἐν τῷ βκφ′ ἔτει καὶ μηνὶ Περειτίου κ′)

95. Tanais, Latyschev 2. 448 = *CIRB* 1280, AD 225. ἀγαθῆι τύχη[ι] | θεῳ ὑψίστωι ἐπηκόωι ἡ σύ[]νοΙδος ἡ περὶ θεὸν ὕψιστον καὶ ἱερέΙα Καλλισθένην κτλ. ([ἐν τῷ] βκφ′ ἔ[τει καὶ μ]η]νὶ Περειτ[ίου –)

96. Tanais, Latyschev 2. 449 = *CIRB* 1281, AD 212–29. θεῶι [ὑψίστωι], | βασιλεύοντος β[ασιλέως Τιβερίου] | Ἰουλίου Ῥησκουπό[ριδος φιλοκαίσαρος καὶ φιλορωμ[αίου, εὐσεβοῦς], | ἰσποιητοὶ (ἀ)δελφο[ὶ σεβόμενοι] | [θε]ὸν ὕψιστον ἀν[έστησαν τὸν] | τελ(α)μῶνα ἐνγ[ράψαντες ἑαυτῶν] | τὰ ὀνόματα κτλ. Relief of eagle in gable.

97. Tanais, Latyschev 2. 451 = *CIRB* 1282, AD 228. ἀγαθῇ τ[ύ]χη | [ἡ σύ]νοδος περὶ θεὸν ὕψιστον καὶ ἱερέα | [Δη]μήτριον κτλ. ([ἐ]ν τῷ ϛκφ′ ἔτει καὶ μηνὶ Λώου α′)

98. Tanais, Latyschev 2. 452 = *CIRB* 1283, AD 228. [ἀγαθ)ῇ τύχῃ | θεῷ [ὑ]ψίστῳ εὐ[χήν], | βασιλεύοντ[ο]ς βασιλέως [Τιβερίου] | [Ἰ]ουλίου Κότυος φιλοκα[ίσαρο]ς καὶ φι[λορωμαί]ου εὐσεβοῦς, εἰσποιητοὶ | ἀδ[ελφοὶ σ]εβόμενοι θεόν ὕψιστον, | ἐνγρά[ψαντ]ες ἑαυτῶν τὰ ὀνόματα | περὶ πρεσβύτερον Μ[–] κτλ. (ἐν τῷ εκφ′ ἔτει, Γορπιαίου α′)

99. Tanais, Latyschev 2. 453 = *CIRB* 1284, AD 230. ἀγαθῆι [τύχηι] | θεῷ ὑψίστ[ῳ

The Cult of Theos Hypsistos 135

εὐχήν], | [βα]σιλέως [Τιβ. Ἰουλίου] | Κότυος υἱοῦ με[γάλου βα]|σιλέως
Ῥ[ησ]κουπ[όριδος] | κτλ. (ἐν τῷ ζκφ' | [ἔτει καὶ μ]ηνὶ Δείῳ)
100. Tanais, Latyschev 2. 450 = CIRB 1285, AD 212–29? ἀγαθῆι τύ[χ]ηι | θ[ε]ῶι
ὑψίστ[ωι) ε[ὐ]χήν, | βασ[ιλε)ύοντος βασιλ[έ]ως Τ[ιβερίου] | Ἰου[λίου
Ῥησ]κο̯υ[πόριδο]ς̯, φιλοκαίσα|ρο̯[ς καὶ φι]λορω[μαίου, εὐσεβ]ο̯ῦς, ἰσπ[οι]ι|[ητοὶ
ἀδε]λφοὶ σ[εβόμενοι θεὸ]ν̯ ὕ[ψισ|τον κτλ]
101. Tanais, Latyschev 1. 456 = CIRB 1286, c.220–40 AD. – – – – | εἰ[σποιητοὶ
ἀδελφοὶ σε]βό|με̯ν[ο]ι̣ θ[εὸ]ν̯ ὕψ̣[ιστον ἀν]ε̣|στήσαμε[ν] τὸν [τελαμῶ]να |
ἐνγράψαντες [ἑαυτῶν] τὰ | ὀνόματα περὶ π[ρεσβύτ]ε̣ρον | Ἀττίαν κτλ.
102. Tanais, Latyschev 2. 454 = CIRB 1287, AD 244. ἀγαθῆι τύχηι, | θεῷ [ὑψίστ]ῳ
ἐπηκόῳ εὐχῆι. ἡ σύνοδος περὶ | ἱερέα Π̣άπαν Χρήστου καὶ [σ]υναγωγὸν
Νυμφέρωτα κτλ. (ἐν τῷ αμφ' Πανήμου).
103. Tanais, Latyschev 2. 457 = CIRB 1289, III AD. [θεῷ ὑψίστ]ῳ ἐπηκ[όῳ], |
[βασιλεύοντος] βα̣σι̣[λέως] κτλ
104. Rostov on the Don, CIRB 1316, cf. O. Weinreich, Ausgewählte Schriften, 1.
153, I–II AD. [θεῶι] ὑψίστ[ωι] | ἐπηκόῳ σωθέ[ν]|τες ἐκ μεγάλω[ν] | κινδύνων |
[Β]ίων καὶ Θεόl[δωρος] υἱοὶ Φάν|[να καὶ μ]ητήρ . . .

Aegean Islands

105. Cos, Paton and Hicks, The Inscriptions of Cos (1891) no. 63, I–II AD. Θέανος
θεῷ ὑψίστῳ εὐχήν
105a. Cos, Ann sc. arch. Atene, 22–3 (1944/5, publ. 1952), 31 no. 33 (cf. Bull. ép.
1953, 153), II AD. [Διὶ ὑψίστῳ καὶ Ἥρᾳ [Ο]ὐρανίᾳ καὶ Ποσειδῶνι Ἀσφαλείῳ καὶ
Ἀπόλλωνι καὶ ἄλλοις θεοῖς ὑπὲρ τῆς Κώιων πόλεως οἱ σακκοφόροι οἱ ἀπὸ τῆς
Καλύμνας ἐποίησαν ἐκ τῶν ἰδίων
106. Delos, I. Delos 2331; CIJ 726, 727, I–II AD. Ζωσᾶς | Πάριος | θεῶι |
ὑψίστωι | εὐχήν
107. Delos, I. Delos 2330; CIJ 728, I BC. Λαωδίκη θεῶι | ὑψίστωι σωθεῖlσα ταῖς
ὑφ' αὐτlοῦ θαραπήαις | εὐχήν
108. Delos, I. Delos 2328; CIJ 729, I BC. Λυσίμαχος | ὑπὲρ ἑαυτοῦ | θεῷ ὑψίστῳ |
χαριστήριον
109. Delos, I. Delos 2332; CIJ 730, I–II AD. ὑψίσlτῳ εὐlχὴν Μlαρκία
(Compare Delos, I. Delos 2329; CIJ 726, I BC. Ἀγαθοκλῆς καὶ Λυσίμαχος ἐπὶ
προσευχῆι, with discussion of the Jewish community on Delos by Ph. Bruneau,
BCH 106 (1982), 465–504)
110. Rheneia (Delos), SIG³ 1181; I. Delos 2352, late II BC. ἐπικαλοῦμαι καὶ ἀξιῶ
τὸν θεὸν τὸν | ὕψιστον, τὸν κύριον τῶν πνευμάτων | καὶ πάσης σαρκός κτλ. Two
virtually identical gravestones depicting raised hands. They are illustrated and
discussed by Cook, Zeus 2. 2. 880.
110a. Delos, I. Délos 2306, Hellenistic. Διὶ ὑψίστῳ καὶ θεοῖς οἷς τοὺς βωμοὺς
ἱδρύσατο
111. Euboea, Eretria (Styra), IG 12. 9. 58, imperial. Διὸς ὑψίστου
112. Euboea, Eretria (Styra), IG 12.9. 59, imperial. Ζεὺς ὕψιστος

136   S. Mitchell

113. Imbros, *IG* 12. 8. 78, Hellenistic. Διὶ ὑψίσ[τῳ] | Ἀθηναίῳ[ν] | εὐχήν

114. Lemnus, *IG* 12. 8. 24, II–III AD. ἐπηκόῳ | θεῷ ὑψίστῳ | Βεῖθυς ὁ καὶ Ἄδωνις εὐχήν

115. Mytilene, *IG* 12. 2. 115, I AD? θεῷ ὑψίστῳ ε[ὐ]χ[α]|ριστήριον Μάρκος | Πομπήιος Λυκάων με[τ]|ὰ τῆς συμβίου Φοίβης | καὶ τῶν ἰδίων. Relief shows eagle with spread wings in a wreath of olive leaves.

116. Mytilene, *IG* 12. 2. 119, I AD? Γ. Κορνήλιος | Χρηστίων, Κορ|νηλία Θαλλού|σα, Γ. Κορνήλιος | Σεκοῦνδος χει|μασθέντες ἐν | πελάγει | θεῷ ὑ|ψίστῳ χρηστή|ριον (sic)

117. Mytilene, *IG* 12. 2. 125, II AD. θεῷ | ὑψίστῳ | Π. Αἴλιος Ἀρ|ριανὸς Ἀλέ|ξανδρος | βουλευ(τὴς) | Δακίας κο|λωνείας | Ζερμιζεγ[ε]|θούσης εὐχή[ν] | ἀνέθηκεν

117a. Mytilene, S. Charitonidis, *αἱ ἐπιγραφαὶ τῆς Λέσβου, Συμπλήρωμα* (Athens, 1968), 28 no. 34, imperial. θεῷ ὑψίστῳ εὐχὴν κατ᾽ ὄναρ

118. Sciathus, *IG* 12. 8. 631, Hellenistic? [Διὶ ὑ]ψίστῳ καὶ τῇ πόλει (a reference to a building follows)

Crete

119. Cnossus, *SEG* 41 (1991), 759, I–II AD. θεῷ ὑψί[στῳ –]

120. Cnossus, *I. Cret.* 1. 8. 18, I–II AD. Κόρωνος θε|ῶι ὑψίστωι | εὐχὴν δη|μόσιος

121. Chersonesus, *I. Cret.* 1. 7. 7, I AD. Relief of an eagle. Τερτύλα θεῷ | ὑψίστῳ | εὐχήν

122. Gortyn, *I. Cret.* 4. 241, imperial. [θ]εῷ [ὑψί]στῳ [εὐ]χὴν Εὐ[φ]|ράνωρ αὐ|λητὴς | ὑπὲρ τέ[κ]|νου

123. Gortyn, *I. Cret.* 4. 242, imperial. θεῷ ὑψίστῳ Ζώ|σιμος χρυσοχόος | εὐχήν

124. Sybrita, *I. Cret.* 2. 26. 3, imperial. θεῷ ὑψίστῳ εὐ|χὴν Τυ|χαμένη(ς) | Φιλομούσω

Italy

125. Rome, *IG* 14. 995, I–II AD. θεῶι ὑψίστωι εὐχὴν ἀνέθηκεν | Κλαυδία Πίστη

Spain

126. Valentia, *IG* 14 suppl. 2580, III AD ? On amulet. τὸν θεὸν τὸν ὕψιστον, μή με ἀδικήσ[ῃ]ς

Caria

127. Aphrodisias, J. Reynolds and R. Tannenbaum, *Jews and Godfearers at Aphrodisias*, 138 no. 11 (*SEG* 37 (1987), 853). Μα|ρκια|[ν]ὸς | θεὸ | ὑψίσ|τοι ε[ὐ]|χή

128. Aphrodisias, Reynolds and Tannenbaum, *Jews and Godfearers*, 138–9 no. 12 (*SEG* 37 (1987), 854), I BC/AD ? [–] Τατας | [θ]εῷ ὑψίστῳ | – –

129. Iasos, *I. Iasos* 235, Hellenistic? Boundary stone. Διὸς ὑψίστου

130. Iasos, *I. Iasos* 236, Hellenistic? Boundary stone. Διὸς ὑψίστου

131. Iasos, *I. Iasos* 237, Hellenistic? ὑψίσ[τῳ –] | ιδ[–]

The Cult of Theos Hypsistos 137

132. Didyma, *I. Didyma* 128, imperial. Διεὶ ὑψίστῳ

133. Didyma, *I. Didyma* 129, imperial. Ἑρμίας Δ[ιὶ] | ὑψίστῳ | κατὰ χρη|σμὸν | εὐχαρι|στήριον

134. Miletus, *Ath. Mitt.* 1893, 267 no. 1, Hellenistic? Διὸς | ὑψίστου

135. Miletus, *OGIS* 755, Hadrianic. τὸν ἱερέα τοῦ ἁγιωτά|του [θεοῦ ὑψί]στου σωτῆρος | Οὔλπιον Κάρπον | βουλευτὴν ὁ στατίων | τῶν κατὰ πόλιν κηπου|ρῶν τὸν ἴδιον εὐεργέτη[ν] | ὑπὲρ τῆς ἑαυτῶν σωτηρί[ας]

136. Miletus, *OGIS* 756, Hadrianic. Οὔλπιον Κάρπον | τὸν προφήτην τοῦ | ἁγιωτάτου θεοῦ | ὑψίστου | ὁ στόλος τῶν σωληνο|κεντῶν τὸν ἴδιον εὐ|εργέτην διὰ πάντων

137. Mylasa, *I. Mylasa* 212, II–I BC. Lease document issued ἐπὶ στεφανηφόρου Ἀριστέου τοῦ Μέλανος τοῦ Ἀπολλωνίου ἱερέως Διὸς ὑψίστου καὶ Τύχης Ἀγαθῆς

138. Mylasa, *I. Mylasa* 310, imperial. -]ΕΔ[– | Διὶ | ὑψίστῳ

139. Rhodian Peraea (Pisye), *I. Rhod. Per.* 756, imperial. Ἀρίστων καὶτὰ χρησμὸν ἀ|νατίθι Δὶ ὑψ||στῳ [ε]ὐχα|ριστήριον

140. Stratonicaea, *I. Strat.* 330, AD 138–61. [Διὶ] ὑψίστῳ | καὶ Ἑκάτῃ Σω[τίρῃ | κ]αι Διὶ Καπε[τωλίῳ | κ]αὶ Τύχῃ τοῦ μ[εγίστου | Αὐτ]οκράτορος Κα[ίσαρος] | Τίτου Αἰλίου Ἀδριανοῦ [Ἀντω|νίνου] Σεβαστοῦ [Εὐσεβοῦς]

141. Stratonicaea (gymnasium), *I. Strat.* 1306, imperial. Small altar with representation of two ears. Διὶ ὑψίστῳ καὶ | τῷ θίῳ | εὐχαρι|στήρι[ον]

142. Stratonicaea (gymnasium), *I. Strat.* 1307, imperial. Διὶ ὑψίστῳ | καὶ θείῳ ἀνγέλῳ οὐρανίῳ Βόληθος καὶ Μένιπ|πος ὑπὲρ τῆς | ὑγίας πανοικίου χαριστή|ριον

143. Stratonicaea, L. Robert, *Anadolu,* 3 (1958), 115, II–III AD. Διὶ ὑψίστῳ καὶ θείῳ Φρόνιμος καὶ Πειθὼ ὑπὲρ τῶν ἰδίων χαριστήριον

144. Stratonicaea, *I. Strat.*, 1110, II–III AD. [Δ]ιὶ ὑψίστ[ῳ] καὶ θείῳ Εὐτυχὴς καὶ Σ[υν]φιλοῦσα, Ἀνδρέας, Ἀντίοχος ὑπὲρ ἑαυτῶν καὶ τῶν ἰδίων χαριστήριον

145. Stratonicaea, *I. Strat.* 1111, II–III AD. [Δι]ὶ [ὑψίστῳ καὶ | θ]είῳ μεγάλ[ῳ] | Κάρπος Ἀρ|τεμήους μ[ε|τ]ὰ τῶν τεκν[ώ]|ἰν καὶ τῶν ἰδίων πάντων | [χαρ]ι[στήριον]

146. Stratonicaea, *I. Strat.* 1112, imperial. Διὶ ὑψίστῳ | καὶ θείῳ εὐ|χαριστήριον

147. Stratonicaea, *I. Strat.* 1113, imperial. θεῷ ὑψίστῳ | [κ]αὶ τῷ θίῳ | Ἑκατᾶς ευχαριστῖ ὑπὲ[ρ] | ἑαυτοῦ καὶ | τῶ(ν) ἰδίων π|άντων καὶ | τῶν γιτόν[ων]

148. Stratonicaea, *I. Strat.* 1114, imperial. [Δ]ιεὶ ὑψί[σ]τῳ καὶ θ[εί]ῳ ἀγαθῷ | [Ἰ]σοκράτη[ς]

149. Stratonicaea, *I. Strat.* 1115, imperial. Διὶ ὑψίστῳ | καὶ θίῳ βα|σιλικῷ Φλ. | Φαῖδρος | ὑπὲρ αὐτοῦ καὶ τῶν ἰδίων | χαριστή|ριον

150. Stratonicaea, *I. Strat.* 1117, II–III AD. Διὶ ὑψίστῳ καὶ θείῳ ἀγγέλῳ Νέ(ω)ν καὶ Εὐφροσύνη ὑπὲρ τῶν ἰδίων

151. Stratonicaea, *I. Strat.* 1118, imperial. Διὶ ὑψίστῳ καὶ | ἀγαθῷ ἀνγέλῳ | Κλαύδιος Ἀχιλλεὺς καὶ Γαλατ[ί]|α ὑπὲρ σωτηρί[ας] | μετὰ τῶν ἰδίων | πάντων χαριστ[ή]|ριον

152. Stratonicaea, *I. Strat.* 1166, imperial. Διεὶ ὑψίστῳ καὶ θίῳ βασιλικῷ ε[ὐ]|χ[α]ριστή|ριον Λεον|τίσκος, Ἰ[α]τ|ροκλῆς, Ἀ|ντίοχος

153. Stratonicaea (gymnasium), *I. Strat.* 1308, II AD? [θε]ῷ ὑψ[ίστ]ῳ καὶ τ[ῷ | θ]είῳ ἀνγέλῳ | Φλα. Διοκλῆς | καὶ Μάμαλον | ὑπὲρ αὐτῶν | [κ]αὶ τῶν παιδί|ων καὶ τῶν ἰδίων | πάντων χαρισ|[τήριον]

154. Stratonicaea (gymnasium), *I. Strat.* 1309, II AD? θείῳ | βασιλῖ καὶ Ὑψίστῳ Αἴ. | Ἐκατό|μνων ὑπὲρ | αὐτοῦ καὶ | τέκνων, γυ|ναικός, φίλων, | ἀνανκαίων, | ἰδίων ἀν|θρώπων καὶ | τῆς πόλεως

155. Stratonicaea (gymnasium), *I. Strat.* 1310, imperial. Δειὶ ὑψίστῳ | καὶ θείῳ Θρέ|[πτ]ὸς ὑπὲρ αὐτο̨[υ–] | –

156. Stratonicaea (gymnasium), *SEG* 38 (1988), 1091, imperial. [Δι]ξὶ ὑ[ψί|σ]τῳ καὶ θίλῳ Τρυφῶ|σα ὑπὲρ | τῶν ἰδίων εὐχαρι|στήριον

157. Lagina, *I. Strat.* 519, II–III AD. Διὶ ὑψίσ[τῳ] καὶ θείῳ τ[ῷ βα]σιλικῷ Σ[τ]εφανίων ὑπὲρ ἑαυτοῦ καὶ τῶν ἰδίων πάντων εὐχαριστήριον

158. Tralles, *I. Tralles* 14, imperial. Relief of eagle. θεῷ ὑψίστῳ | κατ᾿ ὄναρ

Ionia

159. Ephesus?, R. Merkelbach, *EA* 20 (1992), 55 (*SEG* 42 (1992), 1680), III AD. Bronze votive plaque depicting eyes. θεῷ ἐπηκόῳ ὑψίσ|τῳ Αὐρηλία Ἀρτ[ε]|μισία Ἐφεσία εὐ[ξα]|μένη καὶ ἐλ[εη]|θῖσα ἀνέθη[κεν]

160. Ephesus, *I. Eph.* 1234, imperial. θεῷ ὑψίστῳ | Ἀλέξανδρος | Ἀττάλου | εὐξ[άμενος | ἀνέθηκεν]

161. Ephesus, *I. Eph.* 1235. θεῷ ὑψίσ[τῳ] | εὐχαριστ[ήσ]ας | εὐχήν· Τιβ. Κλαύδιο[ς] | Εὐτυχιαν[ὸς] | ἐπὶ ἱερέως Νεικ[–] | καὶ τῆς γλυκυτάτης | –
See G. H. R. Horsley, *Novum Testamentum,* 34 (1992), 121–7 on Jews at Ephesus and the Theos Hypsistos inscriptions.

162. Smyrna, *I. Smyrna* 764, imperial. Σέργις θεῷ | ὑψείστῳ ΣΩ | – – ΛΟΥΝΟΥ ἀνέ|[θηκεν]

Lydia

A. T. Kraabel, *GRBS* 10 (1969), 81–93 with *Bull. ép.* 1970, 153 for Theos Hypsistos in Lydia.

163. Bagis, *TAM* 5. 1. 220, AD 165/6. θεῷ ὑψίστῳ Ἀ|γαθόπους καὶ | Τελέσειρα εὐ|χήν. ἔτους σν΄ | μη. Δαισίου κ΄

164. Bagis (Aktaş), *TAM* 5. 1. 7, II–III AD. Τυρανὶς Ἀφφ[ι]|άδος ὑψ[ίστῳ] | εὐχήν

165. Maeonia, *TAM* 5. 1. 461a, II–III AD. Ἀρτεμᾶς θε|ῷ ὑψίστῳ εὐ|χὴν ἀπέδωκα

166. Maeonia (Kula), *TAM* 5. 1. 266, II–III AD. Ἀπολλωνίσκος | ὑπὲρ τοῦ υἱοῦ Ἑρ|μογένου θεῷ | ὑψίστῳ εὐχήν

167. Gölde (Kula), *TAM* 5. 1. 359, II–III AD. θεᾷ ὑψίστῃ Γλύκων | εὐχήν

168. Hierocaesarea, *TAM* 5. 2. 1258, imperial. Λούκιος θε|ῷ ὑψίστῳ εὐ|χήν

169. Hierocaesarea (Sarıçam), *TAM* 5. 2. 1400, I–II AD? Τειμόθεος Διαγόρου | Λαβραντίδης καὶ Μόσχιον | Τειμοθέου ἡ γυνὴ αὐτοῦ | θεῶι ὑψίστωι εὐχὴν τὸν | βωμόν. | Διαγόρας, Τειμόθεος, Πύθεος, | οἱ Τιμοθέου τοῦ Διαγόρου υἱοὶ | Λαβραντίδαι τὰς λυχναψίας | Ὑψίστωι ἀνέθηκαν

170. Hierocaesarea (Teyenli), *SEG* 41 (1991), 1014, III AD. [*A*]ὐρ. Βασιλικὸς |
[*Ἀ*]σκληπιακοῦ | ὑπὲρ Αὐρ. Κτησιᾶ | [–]*ΥΔΙΟΥ* θεῷ ὑψίστῳ εὐχὴν |
[ἀ]νέστησα

171. Philadelphia, Keil and von Premerstein, *Erste Reise*, D. Ak.
Wien 53 (1908), 27 no. 39, W. H. Buckler, *JHS* 37 (1917), 93 no. 6, II–III AD. θεῷ ὑψίστῳ καὶ
μεγάλῳ θε[ίῳ] | [Δ]ιόφαντος Ἀκιάμου ἱερεὺς | [ε]ὐχήν

172. Saittai (Borlu), *TAM* 5. 1. 186, III AD. Stele with relief of the goddess
Larmene. θεῷ ὑψίστῳ καὶ μεγ[ά]λῳ θείῳ ἐπιφανεῖ Δημὼ θυγάτηρ Τυράννου
θεὰν Λαρμηνὴν ἀνέστησεν

173. Silandus, *TAM* 5. 1. 52, II–III AD. θεῷ ὑψίστῳ εὐχὴν ἀνέθηκε Ἑλένη ὑπὲρ
Θρασυβούλου τοῦ υἱοῦ Θρασυβούλου

174. Silandus, *SEG* 33 (1983), 1027, II–III AD. [θε]ῷ ὑψίστῳ εὐ|[χ]ὴν Απφιον
Νέωνος | [ὑ]πὲρ αὐτῆς καὶ | [τ]ῶν τέκ[ν]ω[ν]

175. Thyaera (lower Caystrus valley), *I. Eph.* 7. 1. 3303, AD 172. θεῷ ὑψίστῳ |
Νεικηφόρος Ἑρ|μοκράτου ἱερε|[ὺ]ς σὺν καὶ Ἑρμοί[κρ]άτει τῷ ἀδ[ελἰφῷ] τὸν
βωμὸ[ν | ἀνέσ]τησαν | [ἔτ]ους σκ´

176. Thyateira, *TAM* 5. 2. 897, II–III AD. Inscribed below relief of an eagle.
Μοσχιανὸς Βασσιαν[οῦ] | θεῷ ὑψίστῳ εὐχήν

177. Thyateira, *TAM* 5. 2. 898, II–III AD. Τρυφῶσα | [θ]εῷ ὑψίστῳ | εὐχήν

178. Thyateira, *TAM* 5. 2. 899, II–III AD. [θεῷ] ὑψίστῳ | [κ]αὶ ἐπηκόῳ |
[Ἀσ]κληπιακὸς | [εὐ]χὴν ἀνέθη|κεν

Troas

179. Alexandria Troas, G. E. Bean in J. M. Cook, *The Troad* (1973), 404 no. 26,
imperial. [ἐπηκ]όῳ θεῷ ὑψίστῳ | [χ]αριστήριον | [–]τυ[– –]

Mysia

180. Apollonia on the Rhyndacus, *LW* 1067, II AD. [Ἀγαθῇ] Τύχῃ | [–]ος
Οὔλπιος | [Παυσ]έρως | [Διὶ] ὑψίστῳ

181. Cyzicus, *JHS* 22 (1902), 267 no. 14, imperial. –]*ΩΓ*[– | Νεικάνδρ[ου] | Διὶ
ὑψίστῳ | εὐχήν

182. Cyzicus, Cook, *Zeus*, 2. 2. 881 with pl. xxxix, imperial. Διὶ ὑψίστῳ καὶ τῷ
χω(ρίῳ] Θάλλος Ἐπώνυμος τὸν τελαμῶνα ἀπέδωκα. A deity holding a phiale and
a sceptre, to be identified as Zeus, is shown in the main panel beside Artemis(?)
and Apollo.

183. Cyzicus, *CIG* 3669, I–II AD. Ἀγαθῆι Τύχηι | Γ. Πεσκέννιος Ὀνήσιμος | θεῷ
ὑψίστῳ σωθεὶς ἀν|έθηκα ἐκ μεγάλου κινδύ|νου μετὰ τῶν ἰδίων | νείκης
εὐχαριστήριον | ἀναθεῖναι

184. Hadriani, *SEG* 33 (1983), 1049, *I. Hadr.* 120, IV AD. Funerary epigram for
Neicatoris, who τειμὴν πλείστην ἐκτήσατο πᾶσι βροτοῖσιν [εἰν ἀγί]ῳ τε λαῷ
Θεοῦ ὑ[ψίσ]του ποίμνεια τέρπ[εν καὶ] ψ]αλμοῖς τε ἀγείοις κ[ἀνα]γνώσμασιν
πάντας ἔθε[λγεν ἐν ἀγείῳ τε τόπῳ εὔ[δει νῦν] Χρείστου ἄχραντο[ς]

185. Miletupolis (Karacabey), *I. Kyzikos* 2. 5, I AD. Stele depicts Zeus with

140 S. Mitchell

thunderbolt beside altar, a herm, and a female figure lying on the ground.
Τιβέριος Κλαύδιος | Σύντροφος Διὶ | ὑψίστῳ κατ᾽ ἐπιταγὴν ἐκ τῶ⟨ν⟩ ἰδίων
ἀνέθηκεν | βρονταίῳ
186. Pergamum, *I. Pergamon* 330, I AD. [Ἡλ]ίωι | θ[ε]ῶι | ὑψ[ί]στωι | Τάτιον |
εὐχήν
187. Pergamum, *I. Pergamon* 331, I–II AD. Γλύκινα | θεῷ ὑψίστῳ | εὐχὴν
ἀνέθηκα | ἐρωμένη μετὰ τὸν | –
188. Pergamum, G. Delling, 'Die Altarinschrift eines Gottesfürchtigen in
Pergamon', *Novum Testamentum*, 7 (1964/5), 73–80, II AD. θεὸς κύριος ὁ ὢν εἰς
ἀεί. | Ζώπυρος τῷ κυρίωι τὸν βωμὸν καὶ τὴν φω[ι]τοφόρον μετὰ τοῦ φλογούχου

Bithynia

189. Prusa?, *I. Prusa* 2. 1013, I BC–I AD ? [ἡ κ]ώμη ἀνέθηκεν Διὶ ὑψίστῳ | [τὴν]
εὐχήν, ἐπιμελητοῦ | Διοφάνου. | Πατερίων ἐχαρίσατο χώραν | τῇ κώμῃ
μεδίμνων δέκα
190. Nicomedia, *TAM* 4. 1. 62, decorated with eagle, imperial. Ἀγαθῇ Τύ[χῃ] |
Διὶ ὑψίστῳ Στράτων Μουκάζου | κατὰ ὄναρ ἀνέσ|στησα
191. Nicomedia, *TAM* 4. 1. 80, decorated with eagle, imperial. [Ἀ]γαθῇ Τύχῃ |
Λούκις Ἄφ|φου θεῷ | ὑψίσστῳ εὐ|χαριστήρι|ον
192. Nicomedia, *TAM* 4. 1. 81, imperial. θεῷ ὑψίστῳ | ἐπηκόῳ | Στάτιος |
Ῥουφῆνος | ἑκατόνταρ|χος τὸν | βωμόν

Pontus

193. Sebastopolis, *SEG* 41 (1991), 1115, late II–III AD. θεῷ ὐ|ψίστῳ | εὐχῆς | χάριν
Πον|τία Οὐαλε|ρία
194. Trapezus, unpublished (*Studia Pontica* 417b), cf. Timothy Mitford, *ZPE* 87
(1991), 190 no. 4

Paphlagonia

195. Amastris, Marek, *Stadt und Ära*, 157 Am. 1b, *c.* AD 45. Rock-cut inscription
carved on base supporting a column topped by an eagle. The text is inscribed
alongside an inscription set up on behalf of the imperial peace and in honour of
the emperor Claudius by the *praefectus fabrum* C. Iulius Aquila. θεῶι ὑψίστωι |
ἐπηκό[ω]ι Ἡλ[ιος?] | εὐ[ξάμενος?] | – –
196. Amastris, *SEG* 35 (1985) 1322, Marek, *Stadt und Ära*, 167 Am. 32, III AD? θεῷ
ὑ[ψ]|ίστῳ Αὐρ. | Βασιλεὺς | ὑπὲρ τε ἑ|αυτοῦ καὶ | τῶν ἰδίων | εὐχῆς | χάριν
197. Hadrianopolis, Marek, *Stadt und Ära*, 194 H. 24, III AD. [Ἀγαθῇ Τύχῃ |
[θεῷ] ὑψίστῳ | Αὐρ. Ἐπιθυμη|τὸς κὲ Βασιλι[κ]ὴ σὺν τοῖς πα|[ιδί]οις ἡμῶν
εὐ|χαριστοῦμεν | θεῷ ἀθανάτῳ
198. Sinope, D. M. Robinson, *AJA* 9 (1905), 306 no. 29; L. Robert, *Études
anatoliennes* (1937), 286, II–III AD. θεῷ ὑψίστῳ Αἴλιος Θρεπτίων Ποντιανός,
Σεουῆρος, Μάκερ, οἱ ἀδελφοὶ εὐξάμενοι
199. Sinope, G. Mendel, *BCH* 27 (1903), 333 no. 49; D. M. Robinson, *AJA* 9

(1905), 304 no. 26, imperial. θεῷ μεγάλῳ ὑψίστῳ εὐχῆ[ς] χά[ριν ἀνέ]θηκε [–]ος μετὰ [τῆς γυ]ναι[κ]ὸς Ῥου[φ]εί[νης]

200. Sinope, D. H. French, EA 23 (1994), 104–5 no. 2, I–II AD. Ἀγαθῆ Τύχῃ Ι θεῷ ὑψίστῳ Ι Ὀνησίτειμος Ι καὶ ὁ υἱὸς αὐτοῦ Ι Ἀγαθήμερος Ι εὐχήν

201. Tieum, L. Robert, Études anatoliennes (1937), 287 no. 12, imperial. Ἀγαθῆ Τύχῃ. θεῷ ὑψίστῳ Ὀκλατιανὸς Δομιτιανός

Galatia

202. Ancyra (Kalecik), SEG 31 (1981), 1080, III AD? τῷ μεγάλῳ Ι θεῷ ὑψίστῳ καὶ Ι ἐπουρανίῳ καὶ Ι τοῖς ἁγίοις αὐτοῦ Ι ἀνγέλοις καὶ τῆ Ι προσκυνητῆ αὐ|τοῦ προσευχῆ τὰ Ι ὧδε ἔργα γείνεται

203. Germa (Holanta), RECAM 2. 141, cf. S. Mitchell, Anatolia 2. 36, IV AD? δύναμις Ὑψίστου

204. Tavium, RECAM 2. 418, II AD. Ἀγαθῆ Τύχῃ Ι θεῷ ὑψίστῳ Καρ|πὸς Ἀγκυρανὸς Ι ὁ καὶ Ταουιανὸς Ι μονοπώλης ἀνέ|θηκα εὐχῆς ἕνεκ[εν]

Phrygia

205. Acmonia (Çorum), SEG 26/27 (1976/7), 1356, III AD. Ἀγαθῆ Τύχ[ῃ] Ι Αὐρ. Τατις Ὀ|νησίμου χαλ|κέος σύνβιος Ι σὺν τῷ συμβίῳ Ὀνησίμῳ θε|ῷ ὑψίστῳ ἐκ τ|ῶν ἰδίων ἀνέ|[στ]ησαν

206. Acmonia (Yenice), SEG 26/27 (1976/7), 1355, II–III AD. Ἐβίκτητος Ι ἐπ[υνησεὶν θεῷ Ι ὑψίστῳ Ι εὐχήν

207. Acmonia (Yenice), CIJ no. 764; L. Robert, Hellenica 11/12. 407, III AD. Gravestone ending with the curse, [ἐὰν δέ τις ἕτερον σῶμα εἰσενέγκη ἔσ]ται αὐτῷ πρὸς τὸν θεὸν τὸν ὕψιστον καὶ τὸ ἀρᾶς δρέπανον εἰς τὸν οἶκον αὐτοῦ [εἰσέλθοιτο καὶ μηδέναν ἐνκαταλείψαιτο]

208. Aezani (Ağarı), MAMA 9. 59, II–III AD. – Ἀλεξάνδρου ΙΕΙΟΝΙΟΣ Ι ὑπὲρ ἑ[α]υτοῦ [θ]εῷ ὑψίστῳ εὐχήν

209. Aezani (Haci Kebir), Drew-Bear and Naour, ANRW 2. 18. 3, 2039 no. 33 (SEG 40 (1990), 1188), III AD. Αὐρ. Ἀσκληπιάδ[ης] Ι ἐληθεὶς ἀπ᾽ ὅλλων τῶν παθημάτ[ων] Ι εὐξάμενος θεῷ ὑ[ψ]|ίστῳ μετὰ Ι τῶν εἰδίων

210. Aezani (Kırgıl), MAMA 9. P68 (Körte, Inscr. Buresch. 27 no. 46), imperial. [– –] ὑπὲρ Ι τῶν τέκνων Ι θεῷ ὑψίστῳ Ι εὐχήν

211. Aezani (Kırgıl), Drew-Bear and Naour, ANRW 2. 18. 3, 2041 no. 34 (SEG 40 (1990), 1196), imperial. – – – Ι νου θεῷ ὑψίστῳ Ι εὐχήν

212. Aezani (Kırgıl), MAMA 9. P69 (LW 987), imperial. Ἀλεξάνδρου . . . υἱός . . . ὑψίστῳ εὐχήν

213. Aezani? (Tavşanlı), Drew-Bear and Naour, ANRW 2. 18. 3, 2036 no. 31, AD 257/8 (SEG 40 (1990), 1227). Altar decorated with a garland enclosing a triple sheaf of corn. Vine on reverse. ἔτους τμβ΄ Διοκλῆς Ι Ζήνωνος Ι μετὰ τῶν ἰδίων θεῷ ὑψίσ|τῳ εὐχήν

214. Apamea, SEG 6. 266, III AD. θεῷ Ι ὑψίστῳ Ι εὐχὴν Ι Αὐρ. Πα⟨ύ⟩λος Ι ὁ καὶ Ἐπ[ι]|θύμητ[ος] Ι ἰατρ[ός]

215. Cotiaeum/Aezani, Drew-Bear and Naour, *ANRW* 2. 18. 3, 2041–3 no. 6 (*SEG* 40 (1990) 1251), AD 308–9. ἔτους τϙγ´ | Αὐρ. Ἀλέξανδρος Τιμοlθέου καὶ ἡ | σύνβιος αὐlτοῦ Αὐρ. Ἄμμιlα εὐξάμενοι | θεῷ ὑψίστῳ | εὐχὴν σὺν | τοῖς τέκνοις | αὐτῶν Ἀττιlκὸς κὲ Ἀρτέμων | κὲ Τιμόθεος κὲ Ἀλέlξανδρος κὲ Πλάτων | ἀνέστησαν τοὺς κίονας σὺν τῷ προlπύλῳ

216. Dorylaeum (Kuyucak), *MAMA* 5. 186, III AD. Altar decorated with three ears of corn. Αὐρ. Ἀντίπατρlος β´ μετὰ τεκούlσας Ἀντωνίας | θεῷ ὑψίστῳ | εὐχήν

217. Laodicea, Ramsay, *Cities and Bishoprics of Phrygia*, 1. 78 no. 14, imperial. [– –]ς θεῷ ὑψέστῳ εὐχήν

218. Nacolea, *MAMA* 5. 211, III AD. Double altar, each decorated with an ear of corn. θεῷ ὑψίσlτῳ εὐlχὴν Αὐlρήλιος | Ἀσκλάπωlν ἦν ὁμολό⟨γ⟩ησεν ἐν Ῥώμῃ

219. Nacolea, *MAMA* 5. 212, II–III AD. Γάιος | Μανlου ὑπlὲρ βοώlν σωτηρlίας κὲ [τ]lῶν ἰδί[ων π]lάντων [ὑψ]lίστῳ εὐχ[ήν]

220. Nacolea, *SEG* 28 (1978), 1182, II–III AD. Δ [–] | ιος Λ[– –]l θέου ἀ[νέθηκα]lν ὑπὲρ ἑαυτ[ῶν] | καὶ τῶν εἰδίωlν πάντω⟨ν⟩ | θεῷ ὑψίστ[ῳ] | καὶ Ὁσίῳ καὶ Διὶ | εὐχήν. It is tempting to suppose that Δικαίῳ was meant at the end, although there is no space for the reading on the front of the stone.

221. Synaus (Ulaşlar), *MAMA* 10. 427, II–III AD. Ἀφίας μετὰ τοῦ | υἱοῦ Εἰρηνέου | θεῷ ὑψίστῳ εὐlχήν

222. Synaus (Aş. Yoncaağaç), *MAMA* 10. 435, AD 221/2. [ἔ]τους τς´ Αὐ[–l–]C θεῷ ὑψίσl[τῳ] εὐχήν

223. Synaus (Aş. Yoncaağaç), *MAMA* 10. 440, II–III AD. Ἀμμία Θάλενlτος θεῶι | εὐχήν

224. Synaus (Yuk Yoncaağaç), *MAMA* 10. 443, AD 211/12. [ἔτ]ους σπc´ θεῷ ὑψ[ί]στ[ῳ ἐπ]ηκ]όῳ Θερμηνοὶ εὐχήν

225. Tiberiopolis (Hasanlar), *MAMA* 10. 488, II–III AD. θ[ε]ῷ ἐπηκόῳ | Ἰουλι[– –] | σὺν τ[ῷ λύχν]ῳ (?) | καὶ τῷ πυράμῃ | ἀνέ[θ]ηκεν. Restorations uncertain.

226. Tiberiopolis (Hisarcık), *MAMA* 10. 504, AD 245/6. [ἔτ]ους τλ´ ΤΙΡΩ | . Διοδώρου κὲ [ἡ γυlνὴ] Ἀφφία ὑ[πὲρ – l – θε]ῷ ἐπηκό[ῳ ὑψlίστ]ῳ εὐχή[ν]

227. Upper Tembris valley (Arslanapa), Drew Bear and Naour, *ANRW* 2. 18. 3, 2038 no. 32 (*SEG* 40 (1990), 1235), *MAMA* 10. 261, AD 253/4. Altar with sheaf of corn within a garland. [ἐπὶ] Νικομ[ά]χου | [ἔτου]ς τλη´ Αὐρ. Ἰάσων θεῷ | ὑψίστῳ εὐχήν

Pisidia

228. Andeda, G. Bean, *AS* 10 (1960), 65 no. 115, II–III AD. Κόιντος Νουμέρlιος ἱερεὺς | Μηνὸς Ο[ὐ]lρανίου καlτὰ χρημαlτισμὸν ἀνέlθηκε θεῷ | ὑψίστῳ

229. Sagalassus (Sala), *Mon. Ant.* 23 (1914), 262 no. 174, II–III AD. AMATAN– | καὶ MECA | θεῷ ὑψί[σ]lτῳ εὐχήν

230. Sibidunda, G. Bean, *AS* 10 (1960), 70 no. 122, II AD. θεῷ ὑψίστῳ καὶ | ἀγείᾳ καταφυγῇ | Ἀρτιμᾶς υἱὸς Ἀρlτίμου Μομμίου | καὶ [Μ]αρκίας ὁ αὐlτὸς κτίστης ἀlνέστησεν καὶ | τὸν θυμιατισlτήρ(ι)ον καὶ κέον(α) | ἐκ τῶν ἰδίων

231. Termessus, *TAM* 3. 1. 32, II AD. θεῷ ἐπηκόῳ ὑ|ψίστο Τύχ|ος ὁ καὶ Ἀτταλλιανός . . . | Σύρου . . κα|τὰ κέλευσιν | αὐτοῦ ἔστη|σεν | σὺν τῷ ἔπον[τι] | ἴχνει θεοῦ. This inscribed base originally supported a bronze statue of a left foot.

Lycia

232. Nisa, *TAM* 2. 3. 737, II AD. [– – Δι]ονύσιος Διο|[–] Διογένους Λυ|[–η]ς θεῷ ὑψίσι[τῳ καὶ Μητρ]ὶ Ὀρείᾳ κα(τὰ) κέλε|[υσιν] καὶ θεοῖς πᾶσι | [καὶ θεαῖς] πάσαις χαρισ|[τ]ήριον

233. Oenoanda., L. Robert, *CRAI* 1971, 597–619 (*SEG* 27 (1977), 933); see also A. S. Hall, *ZPE* 32 (1978), 263–7, for the archaeological context. III AD

[Α]ὐτοφυής, ἀδί|δακτος, ἀμήτωρ, | ἀστυφέλικτος, | οὔνομα μὴ χω|ρῶν, πολυώνυμος, | ἐν πυρὶ ναίων, | τοῦτο θεός· μεικρὰ | δὲ θεοῦ μερὶς ἄνγε||λλοι ἡμεῖς. τοῦτο πευ|θομένοισι θεοῦ πέ|ρι ὅστις ὑπάρχει, | Αἰ[θ]έ[ρ]α πανδερκ[ῆ | θε]ὸν ἔννεπεν, εἰς | ὃν ὁρῶντας εὔχεσθ' ἠώ|ους πρὸς ἀντολίην ἐσορῶ[ν]|τα[ς].

234. Oenoanda, A. S. Hall, *ZPE* 32 (1978), 265, II–III AD. Χρωματὶς θεῷ ὑψίστῳ τὸν λύχνον εὐχήν.

235. Patara, *TAM* 2. 1. 402, imperial. θεῷ | ὑψίστῳ | Δημοσθένης εὐχή

Lycaonia

236. Iconium, *MAMA* 8. 298, imperial. [.]ερατης Κ. Φιλο|λόγου μετὰ γυνα[ι]|κὸς καὶ τέκνων | θεῷ ὑψίστῳ εὐ|χήν

237. Iconium, Cronin, *JHS* 22 (1902), 124 no. 58, III AD. Γοῦρδος ἀνὴρ ἀγαθὸς | ἔνθ' εὕδει ὥστε πέλεια. | ἦεν ἐν ἀνθρώποις ἱερεὺς | θεοῦ ὑψίστου. | τῷ στήλην Τροκόνδας | ὁ διάδοχος καὶ ὀπάων | τεῦξ' ἕνεκα μνήμης | καὶ κοσμήσας ἐπὶ τύμβῳ

Cilicia

238. Seleucia on the Calycadnus, *MAMA* 3. 1, III AD. θεῷ | ὑψίστῳ | εὐχὴ|ν Ἀθή|ναιος

239. Seleucia on the Calycadnus, *MAMA* 3. 2, III AD. θεῷ ὑψίσ|τῳ Ἀμμί|α εὐχήν

240. Seleucia on the Calycadnus, *MAMA* 3. 3, III AD. θεῷ ὑ|ψίστῳ | Διογένης | [–]γου|ρίου εὐχ|ήν

241. Seleucia on the Calycadnus, *MAMA* 3. 4, III AD. Διὶ ὑ[ψίστῳ] | Νᾶς Μά|ρκου | [ε]ὐχήν

Cappadocia

242. Hanisa, L. Robert, *Noms indigènes*, 486, imperial. [θεῷ] |[ὑ]ψείστ[ῳ –] |.ιας κατ' ε[ὐ]χὴν ἀνέθηκεν καὶ ταύτας | (three more unintelligible lines)

Cyprus

On Theos Hypsistos in Cyprus, see T. B. Mitford, *ANRW* 2. 18. 3, 2207 (also *I. Kourion*, 305): ' a convenient meeting ground for Jew and judaiser, Christian and pagan.' He lists the relevant inscriptions at 2206 n. 163.

243. Amathus, P. Aupert, *BCH* 101 (1977), 810; Aupert and O. Masson, *BCH* 103 (1979), 378 no. 27 (SEG 27 (1977), 962), I–II AD. θεῷ ὑψίστῳ ǀ Κύπρης ὑπέρ ǀ παιδίου ǀ Κύπρητος ǀ εὐχήν

244. Amathus, *BCH* 3 (1879), 167 no. 12, I–II AD. θεῷ ὑψίστῳ ǀ Νεικόδημος ǀκατὰ χρηματισǀμόν

245. Citium, *SEG* 40 (1990), 1354 (LW 2740), III AD? [θε]ῷ ὑψίστωι Θέων οἰκόδομος εὐχήν

246. Curium (Sotira), *I.Kourion*, 304 no. 160, II–III AD. [θεῷ] ὑψίστῳ ǀ Ἀριστοκράτης ǀ εὐ⟨ξ⟩άμενος

247. Curium, *I. Kourion*, 305 no. 161, III AD. θεῷ ὑψίστῳ ǀ Τρύφων εὐξάǀμενος

248. Hagios Athanasios, *JHS* 66 (1946), 34 no. 11, I–II AD. θεῷ ὑψίστῳ ǀ Δίδυμος ǀ ὑπὲρ τέκνǀων εὐχήν

249. Hagios Athanasios, *SEG* 29 (1979), 1572, II–III AD. θεῷ ὑψίστο ǀ Διονύ[σιος ǀ κ[– –] ǀι εὐ[ξάμε]νο[ς]

250. Hagios Athanasios, *SEG* 30 (1980), 1607, ? II AD. θεῷ ὑψίστῳ ǀ [Μ]ελίτων ǀ Μελίǀ[τω]νος

251. Limassol, *SEG* 41 (1991), 1475, II–III AD. θεῷ ὑψίστῳ ǀ Σάμβων ǀ Σάμβωνος ǀ εὐχήν

252. Limassol, *RDAC* 1966, 63 no. 12 = *SEG* 25. 1089, II–III AD. θεῷ ὑψίσǀτῳ εὐξάǀμενος Δηǀμήτρις Ξεǀνοφίλου

253. Cyprus, unknown provenance perhaps from area of Limassol, *SEG* 40 (1990), 1377, imperial. θεῷ ὑψίστῳ ǀ Τιμόχαρις ǀ εὐχήν

254. Cyprus, unknown provenance perhaps from area of Limassol, *SEG* 40 (1990), 1377, imperial. Δημήτρις ǀ θεῷ ὑψίστῳ ǀ εὐχήν

255. Cyprus Museum, unknown provenance, *JHS* 66 (1946), 34 no. 12, III AD. θ(ε)ῷ ὑψίστῳ ǀ Τυχάρειν εὐξα[μέν]η

256. Cyprus Museum, unknown provenance, *JHS* 66 (1946), 35 no. 13, III AD. θεῷ ὑψίστῳ ἀσύλῳ ǀ Δημήτριος εὐχήν

257. Golgi, P. Perdrizet, *BCH* 20 (1896), 361 no. 1 (ex voto plaque with suspension hole, showing breasts), imperial. θεῷ ὑψίστῳ ἀνεθηǀκεν Προκτυος(?) εὐξαμέǀ[ν]η

258. Golgi, P. Perdrizet, *BCH* 20 (1896), 361 no. 2 (ex voto plaque with suspension hole, showing eyes), imperial. θεῷ ὑψίστῳ εὐξαμε[ν–]

259. Golgi, A. Dain, *Inscriptions grecques au Musée du Louvre*, 83 no. 71, (ex voto plaque with suspension hole, showing nose?), imperial. θεῷ ὑψ[ίστῳ] Ἀφροδείσις εἰξάμεǀνοςǀ ἀνέθηκεν

260. Mathikoloni, *SEG* 40 (1990), 1361, II AD? θεῷ ὑψίστῳ εὐχὴν ǀ Φίλα Πασικράτου

261. Paphus, *SEG* 40 (1990), 1368, *c*. AD 100? θεῶι ὑψίστωι ǀ Τρύφων ἱερεὺς ǀ εὐχήν

262. Paphus, *SEG* 40 (1990), 1370, I AD. θεῶι ὑψίσ|τωι Σώζουσα

263. Polemidhia, *SEG* 39 (1989), 1554, imperial. θεῷ ὑψίστῳ | τὸν ΕΔ.ΕΤΗ |
Βῶσον | Αὔξητος | ἀνέθηκεν

264. Polemidhia, *SEG* 39 (1989), 1555, imperial. θεῷ ὑψίστῳ | εὐχὴν | ΥΠΟΛΟC.

265. Spitali, *RDAC* 1973, 218 no. 7, I BC? θεῷ ὑψίστῳ | Ἀριστ[ο]κλῆς |
Κουκούμης | εὐχὴν ἐποίησεν

Phoenicia

266. Berytus, *BCH* 3 (1881), 265 no. 20; Cook, *Zeus* 2. 2. 886 (30), imperial?
Bronze votive hand with inscription [–] | εὐ|ξαμέν|η ὑπὲρ αὐτῆ[s] | καὶ
Θ[ε]οδώ|ρου ἀνδρὸ[s] | καὶ τέκνων | θεῷ ὑψίστῳ

267. Berytus, *BCH* 3 (1881), 265 no. 21. Bronze votive hand with inscription θεῷ
ὑψίστῳ Γηρlίων εὐξάl[μ]ενος ἀνέθη|[κ]εν

268. Byblus, *Rev. arch.* 28 (1896), 299, imperial. Διὶ ὑψίστῳ πεκουλάριος Μάρθας

269. Byblus, Διὶ οὐρανίῳ ὑψίστῳ Σααρναίῳ ἐπηκόῳ. Relief shows bust of
bearded Zeus with thunderbolt and sceptre.

Syria

270. South of Damascus, Dussaud, *Mission dans les régions désertiques de la Syrie*
(1903), 238, 2, imperial. Διὶ μεγίστῳ ὑψίστῳ

271. Palmyra, *SEG* 34 (1984), 1456, imperial. I.O.M.votum Amathallat f. Sabbiti
I[– –] opti eq. [– –]l Διὶ ὑψίστῳ [Αμαθα]λλαθ | Σαββ [ιτου – –]νος

272. On the road between Palmyra and Emesa, Lebas and Waddington 2627, AD
114. Three identical texts on altars with relief of thunderbolt. Διὶ ὑψίστῳ καὶ
ἐπηκόῳ ἡ πόλις εὐχήν, ἔτους εκυ΄ Δύστρου ακ΄. Further dating formula by civic
magistrates. Also Palmyrene text.

273. Palmyra, *OGIS* 634, AD 162/3. Διὶ ὑψίστῳ μεγίστῳ ἐπηκόῳ Βωλανὸς
Ζηνοβίου . . . τὸν βωμὸν εξ ἰδίων ἀνέθηκεν ἐν τῷ κφ΄ ἔτει μηνὸς Ὑπερβερεταίου
κ΄

274. Palmyra, *LW* 2572, AD 179. Διὶ ὑψίστῳ ἐπηκlόῳ τὸν βωμὸν ἀνέθη|κεν
Ἰούλιος Σ.υις ἀπελεύθερος Γαίου Ἰουλίου Βάσσου ὑπὲρ σωlτηρίας Ἴλειβας
υἱοῦ | αὐτοῦ ἔτους Ϟυ΄ μηlνὸς Ξανδίκου

275. Palmyra, *LW* 2571b, AD 233. Διὶ ὑψίστῳ καὶ [ἐ]lπηκόῳ Ἰου. Αὐρ.
Ἀlντίπατρος ὁ καὶ | Ἀλαφωνᾶς Ἀειλλαμος τοῦ Ζηνοβίου τοῦ Ἀκοπάου |
εὐξάμενος ἀνέlθηκεν ἔτους δμβ΄ Αὐδναίου κδ΄ Also Palmyrene text.

276. Palmyra, *LW* 2573, III AD. Διὶ ὑψίστῳ Α[ὑρ.] Διογένης Σωσιβίου ἅμα |
Δομνῇ εὐξάμενοι καὶ ἐπακουσθέντες

277. Palmyra, *LW* 2574, I–II AD. Διὶ ὑψίστῳ | καὶ ἐπηκόῳ | εὐξάμενος | ἀνέθηκεν
| Α . . . ευρος καὶ | Σώπατρος καὶ | θεῷ μεγάλῳ | CΛΛΛΟΥΝΤΩ |
ΕΝΕΟΥΑΒΕΙ

278. Palmyra, *LW* 2575, imperial. Διὶ ὑψίστῳ καὶ ἐπηlκόῳ τὸν βωμὸν
ἀνl[έθηκεν] εὐχαριστ[–] | – – Palmyrene text.

279. Sahin, between Arados and Baetocaece, *IGLS* 7. 4027, AD 260/1. θεῷ ὑψίστῳ

146 S. Mitchell

οὐρανίῳ ΥΤ[–Ι–]ΘΡΑ ὁ βωμὸς ἔκτισθ[η – Ι –ὀ]ρθῶς ἐν τῷ κφ΄ ἔτε[ι–Ι ὑπέρ]
σωτηρίας ΘΕΟΠΑΡΩ [–Ι–] ἐπὶ ἀρχῆς Σολυμανο[υ]

Palaestina

280. Negev, Haluza, Y. Ustinova and J. Naveh, *Atiqot*, 22 (1993), 91–6, II–III AD.
θεῷ ὑψ|ίστῳ Ι (Palmyrene/Aramaic text meaning 'remember')
281. Negev, Wadi Haggag, *SEG* 26/7 (1976/7) 1697, IV AD. Decorated with a
menorah or seven leaf palm branch and a nine-leaf palm branch. εἷς Θεὸς
ὕ(ψιστος ?) Θ(εὸς ?) Ι ὁ βοηθῶν Ι Οὐαλέριος ἈντιΙγούνου στραΙτηγός. γ΄
ἰνδικτι(ῶνος). The readings and interpretation are uncertain, see *SEG* 39 (1989),
1635, Horsley, *New Docs*. 2. 206–9.

Arabia

282. Petra, *SEG* 36 (1986), 1386, imperial. [Διὸ]ς ὑψ[ίστου] Ι [– –]ια

Egypt

For *Hypsistos* applied to deities in Egypt see G. Ronchi, *Lexicon theonomycum
rerumque sacrarum et divinarum ad Aegyptum pertinentium* (1977), 1120–2
283. Alexandria, G. H. R. Horsley, *New Docs*. 3. 121, II BC. [– θε]ῶι ὑψίστωι Ι
[– τ]ὸν ἱερὸν Ι [περίβολον καὶ] τὴν προσΙ[ευχὴν καὶ τὰ συγ]κυροῦντα
284. Alexandria, A. D. Nock, *Essays on Religion and the Ancient World*, 1 (1972),
422–7, reprinting *HTR* 29 (1936), 61–9, θεῷ ὑψίστῳ καὶ πάντων ἐπόπτῃ καὶ
Ἡλίῳ καὶ Νεμέσει αἴρει Ἀρσεινόη ἄωρος τὰς χεῖρας· ἤ τις αὐτῇ φάρμακος
ἐποίησε ἢ καὶ ἐπέχαρέ τις αὐτῆς τῷ θανάτῳ ἢ ἐπιχαρεῖ, μετέλθετε αὐτούς
285. Athribis, Horsley, *New Docs*. 4 (1987), 101, 181–45 BC. ὑπὲρ βασιλέως
Πτολεμαίου Ι καὶ βασιλίσσης Κλεοπάτρας Ι Πτολεμαῖος Ἐπικύδου Ι ὁ ἐπιστάτης
τῶν φυλακιτῶν Ι καὶ οἱ ἐν Ἀθρίβει Ἰουδαῖοι Ι τὴν προσευχὴν Ι θεῷ ὑψίστῳ
286. Fayum, *CIJ* 2. 1532, 29 BC. θεῶι μεγάλῳ Ι μεγάλῳ ὑψίστῳ Ι ὑπὲρ Ἐπιτυχίας
τῆς καὶ Διονυσίας Ι [κ]αὶ ὑπὲρ τοῦ ἀνδρὸς Ι [Ἀ]σποχρᾶτος καὶ τῶν τέκνων Ι
κατ᾽ εὐχήν. (ἔτους) β΄ Καισάρου Ι Φαῶφ. ς΄.
287. Fayum?, Horsley, *New Docs*. 1 (1976), 28–9, c.69–57 BC. Ἀγαθῆι Τύχηι Ι
νόμος ὃν ἔθεντο [κα]τὰ κοινὸν οἱ ἐκ τῆς τοῦ Διὸς ὑψίστου συνόδου τοῦτον εἶναι
κύριον, κτλ. ('The guild of Zeus Hypsistos')
288. Leontopolis, *SEG* 33 (1983), 1326, I–II AD? [– τὴν] προσε[υχὴν –] Ι [–
θε]ῶι ὑψίσ[τωι –]

Unprovenanced

289. From Asia Minor?, *SEG* 30 (1980), 1790, II–III AD. Inscribed on chest and
left shoulder of a headless bronze female torso, Μοσχεὶν εὐχὴν Ι θεῷ ὑψί⟨σ⟩τῳ
290. From Asia Minor?, *SEG* 30 (1980), 1791, II–III AD. Bronze plaque with
tabula ansata, ΘεόδωΙρος θεῷ ὑΙψίστῳ εὐΙχαρισΙτήριον
291. From Asia Minor?, *SEG* 30 (1980), 1792, II–III AD. Bronze plaque with
tabula ansata, [Τρό]φιμος θεῷ ὑψίΙ[στῳ] εὐχαριστῶν Ι [ἀ]νέθηκα

292. From Asia Minor?, Horsley, *New Docs.* 5 (1989) front cover, II AD? Bronze plaque, tabula ansata. θεῷ | ὑψίστῳ εὐ|ξάμενος Φλεγεθιανὸς | ἀπέδωκα

293. From the Asia Minor coast, perhaps Bithynia, J. H. Mordtmann, *AEMÖ* 8 (1884), 198 no. 18, cf. Cook, *Zeus*, 2. 2. 883 (24), I–II AD. ἀγαθῇ τύχηι | θεῷ ὑψίστῳ | Ἀσκληπιόδο|τος Σωσιπά|τρου κατ' ὄ|ναρ

SELECT BIBLIOGRAPHY

1. Oracles
LANE FOX, R., *Pagans and Christians* (London, 1985), 168–261.
ROBERT, L., 'Trois oracles de la Théosophie et un prophète d'Apollon', *Comptes rendus de l'Académie des inscriptions et belles lettres* 1969, 568–99.
—— 'Un oracle gravé à Oinoanda', *Comptes rendus de l'Académie des inscriptions et belles lettres* (1971), 597–619.

2. Hypsistarians
SCHÜRER, E., 'Die Juden im bosporanischen Reich und die Genossenschaft der σεβόμενοι θεὸν ὕψιστον ebendaselbst', *Sitzungsberichte der preussischen Akademie zu Berlin* (1897), 200–25.

3. The Cult of Theos Hypsistos
COOK, A. B., *Zeus: A Study in Ancient Religion*, II. 2 (Cambridge, 1925), 873–90.
CUMONT, F., 'Hypsistos', *RE* IX.1 (1916), 444–50.
MAREK, C., 'Der höchste, beste, größte, allmächtige Gott. Inschriften aus Nordkleinasien', *Epigraphica Anatolica* 32 (2000), 129–46.
RICL, M., 'Hosios kai Dikaios. Première partie: Catalogue des inscriptions', *Epigraphica Anatolica*, 18 (1991), 1–70; 'Seconde partie: Analyse', *Epigraphica Anatolica*, 19 (1992), 71–103.
SCHWABL, H., 'Zeus', *RE Suppl.* XII (1974), 1477–80.
USTINOVA, Y., *The Supreme Gods of the Bosporus: The Celestial Goddess and the Most High God* (forthcoming).

4. Chronological Method
MACMULLEN, R., 'The Epigraphic Habit', *American Journal of Philology*, 103 (1982), 233–46.

5. Theos Hypsistos and the Jews
AMELING, W., 'Die jüdischen Gemeinden im antiken Kleinasien', in R. Jütte and Abraham P. Kustermann (eds.), *Jüdische Gemeinden und Organisationsformen von der Antike bis zur Gegenwart* (1996), 29–55.
SCHÜRER, E., *A History of the Jewish People in the time of Jesus Christ.* New English edition edited by F. Millar and G. Vermes, III. 1 (1986), 150–76.

SIMON, M., 'Theos Hypsistos', *Ex Orbe Religionum. Studia Geo. Widengren* (1972), 372–85.

TREBILCO, P., *Jewish Communities in Asia Minor* (1991).

6. *God-fearers*
FELDMAN, L. H., *Jew and Gentile in the Ancient World* (1993), 342–82.
MITCHELL, S., 'Wer waren die Gottesfürchtigen?', *Chiron*, 28 (1998).
REYNOLDS, J. M., and Tannenbaum, R., *Jews and Godfearers at Aphrodisias.*
Cambridge Philological Society, supplementary volume 12 (1987).

7. *Christians*
MITCHELL, S., *Anatolia: Land, Men, and Gods in Asia Minor*, ii (1993), 37–51, 96–108.

5

The Chaldaean Oracles: Theology and Theurgy

POLYMNIA ATHANASSIADI

1. TYPOLOGY AND ORIGIN

The Chaldaean Oracles are a divine revelation in Greek hexameter verse of a cosmological and soteriological system and of a set of moral and ritual rules and instructions.[1] In this, as in many other respects, the poem is not unlike the Koran. A persistent tradition, first detectable in Iamblichus, echoed by the emperor Julian and repeated by Proclus, attributes its authorship to a certain Julian the Theurgist; this claim is corroborated by the tenth-century Suda Lexicon, where, in two separate entries, Julian the Theurgist is described as the author of oracles in hexameters who lived at the time of Marcus Aurelius, and Julian the Chaldaean as his father and a philosopher.[2] Additional information on the two Julians is provided by the eleventh-century polymath Michael Psellus, who displayed what might be thought too lively an interest in the

The following abbreviations have been used throughout this chapter:

CP A, B, C, D, E	Proclus' *Chaldaean Philosophy* in *Oracula chaldaica*, ed. and trans. E. des Places (Paris, 1971), 206–12.
Lewy	H. Lewy, *Chaldaean Oracles and Theurgy*, ed. M. Tardieu, 2nd edn. (Paris, 1978).
Marinus VP	Marinus, *Vita di Proclo*, ed. and trans. P. Masullo (Naples, 1985).
Parm.	Damascius, *In Parmenidem*, ed. C. A. Ruelle (Paris, 1889).
PH	Damascius, *The Philosophical History*, ed. and trans. P. Athanassiadi, (Athens, 1999).
PP	Damascius, *De primis principiis*, i–iii, ed. L. G. Westerink, trans. J. Combès (Paris, 1986–91).
PT	Proclus, *Theologia Platonica*, i–vi, ed. and trans. H. D. Saffrey and L. G. Westerink (Paris 1968–97).

[1] Proclus, *In Tim.* i, 408, 12, characterizes them as θεοπαράδοτος θεολογία. The passages in Neoplatonic literature which refer to the λόγια as direct divine revelation have been collected by W. Theiler, *Die chaldäischen Orakel und die Hymnen des Synesios* (Halle, 1942), 2.

[2] Suda ii, 642, 1, s.v. Ἰουλιανός 434: λόγια δι' ἐπῶν (λόγια being the technical Neoplatonic term for the Chaldaean Oracles), ii, 641, 32, s.v. Ἰουλιανός 433.

Oracles for a Christian dignitary: the father Julian, reports Psellus, obtained for his son an archangelic soul, which he then put into contact with that of Plato.[3] All this is well known, yet the reason for restating these oft-quoted pieces of evidence is that the veracity of the sources has recently been questioned in connection with the authorship, and consequently the date, of the Chaldaean Oracles.[4] Since I see no virtue in doubt for doubt's sake, and since a strong and continuous Neoplatonic tradition advocates the attribution of the oracular verses to Julian the Theurgist, I have chosen to accept the evidence on which late antique spiritual orthodoxy was built,[5] and in what follows I shall attempt to explore the circumstances of the birth and codification of the Chaldaean Oracles by looking at the information available against a broader chronological and geographical background.

A first concern is Psellus' source. By his own confession, Psellus had read Proclus and found him at the pinnacle of all science and wisdom,[6] and a study of the method followed by him as he compiled his own Collection of the Chaldaean Oracles suggests that he had before his eyes the whole of Proclus' now lost Commentary on the Oracles. Extracting from the Proclean text those oracular lines which particularly appealed to him, Psellus appended to them first Proclus' own commentary and then a commentary on a commentary—his own highly interesting exegesis.[7] He also used Proclus' Commentary as the basis for several

---

[3] Psellus, Περὶ τῆς χρυσῆς ἀλύσεως τῆς παρ' Ὁμήρῳ, REG 1875, 217 and cf. Lewy, 224.

[4] The recent bibliography, inconclusively contesting the veracity of the sources, is assembled and discussed by S. Iles Johnston, *Hekate Soteira* (Atlanta, 1990), 2–3; cp. D. Porter, *JRS* 81 (1991), 225–6, claiming a 3rd-cent. date for the Oracles.

[5] Cp. Julian (*ep.* 12) and Proclus, *In Tim.* III, 63, 24: ὁ Θεουργός (. . .) ᾧ μὴ θέμις ἀπιστεῖν, where the word θεουργός should be understood as a personal name referring to Julian the Theurgist.

[6] Cp. *Chronogr.* 6. 38: προβαίνων εἰς τὸν θαυμασιώτατον Πρόκλον ὡς ἐπὶ λιμένα μέγιστον κατασχών, πᾶσαν ἐκεῖθεν ἐπιστήμην τε καὶ νοήσεων ἀκρίβειαν ἔσπασα.

[7] Psellus has transmitted forty fragments, which cover the entire thematic spectrum of the Oracles though the emphasis is definitely on ritual and eschatology (most recent edition by D. O'Meara, *Philosophica Minora* II (Leipzig, 1989), *opusc.* 38). It has been convincingly argued that he depends entirely on Proclus, cf. E. des Places, *Les Oracles Chaldaïques* (Paris, 1971), pp. 154, and esp. 203 with refs. L. G. Westerink's thesis, according to which Psellus had at his disposal only Proclus' refutation by Procopius of Gaza ('Proclus, Procopius, Psellus', *Mnemosyne* 10 (1940), 275–80) has been further undermined by the attribution to the Chaldaean Oracles of a doubtful Heraclitean hexameter deriving from Arethas (M. L. West, 'A Pseudo-Fragment of Heraclitus', *CR* NS 18 (1968), 257–8), which provides evidence for the availability of the Proclean Commentary beyond the Byzantine 'dark age'. Besides, a careful reading of Psellus' own Commentary suggests that he had read Proclus with a sympathetic eye, in the original rather than in the refutation of

summaries on the theology of the Oracles, and for the compilation of an anthology.[8] No other text on the Chaldaean Oracles seems to have been available to Psellus, so that one may safely assume that both the archangelic texture of the Theurgist's soul and its interviews with Plato belong to a Neoplatonic tradition which reached Psellus through Proclus.[9]

If we view this information in the light of what we know about the tradition of inspired theological poetry in the Near East, we are provided with several clues which may help us towards a reconstruction of the circumstances attending the emergence of the Chaldaean Oracles. After years of spiritual training, an individual born with the gift of prophecy may become 'transparent to God' and, falling into a state of trance, utter verse in the language of the cultural tradition to which he or she belongs. The 'revelation' that will thus ensue may comprise one or many lines, and is bound to recur in a matter of hours, days, months or years, so long as the 'vehicle of the divine' continues to be committed to other-worldly concerns. Once the link with the supernatural becomes established, those around 'the prophet' begin to anticipate the utterances and are ready to take them down. Such was the practice in Babylonian temples, as now emerges from the publication of their archives;[10] it was also the case with Muhammad,[11] and, nearer to home, with Ismail Emre (1900–70), an illiterate Turkish welder from Adana, to whom we owe more than two thousand songs of a distinctly theological content.[12]

Procopius, and made his own philological and theological comments with a view to the Christian audience that he was addressing. It must also be pointed out that despite his criticisms, a conscious effort towards a reconciliation of the Christian with the 'Chaldaean' theology alongside an uncommon involvement with the eschatology and the magical aspect of the Oracles are to be detected throughout.

[8] The five extracts from Proclus' *Chaldaean Philosophy* have been edited and translated by des Places (pp. 206–12); the three abstracts on Chaldaean theology are to be found in O'Meara's edition of Psellus, *opsc.* 39, 40, 41.

[9] Proclus himself was informed by means of a dream that he belonged to the 'Hermetic chain' and that he had the soul of Nichomachus of Gerasa: Marinus *VP* 28.

[10] 'Enthusiastic divination' (as opposed to 'rational' or 'technical' divination) was traditional in Mesopotamia: cp. J.-M. Durand, 'Les Textes prophétiques', *Archives épistolaires de Mari* 1/1 (1988), 375–452. For the continuing awareness of the nature and role of individuals possessed by the god, cf. Proclus, *In Remp.* II, 246, 24: οἱ τῶν θεῶν ἱεροὶ καὶ οἱ κλήτορες καὶ οἱ δοχεῖς, where δοχεύς is distinguished from the other categories.

[11] For Muhammad, about the conditions of whose revelation we have detailed information, see the penetrating study of M. Rodinson, *Mahomet* (Paris, 1961), 95–124.

[12] On Ismail Emre, see my Introduction to the translation into Greek of a collection of his poetry in Ἰσμαὴλ Ἐμρέ, *Πνοές* (Athens, 1991), 9–43; cf. A. Schimmel, *Mystical Dimensions of Islam* (Chapel Hill, 1975), 337, describing as an eyewitness the circumstances attending his trance during the 'birth' of a mystical song.

If we rethink what Psellus says about the two Julians in the light of this continuous tradition, we may formulate the following hypothesis: in the time of Marcus Aurelius there lived somewhere in the eastern part of the Roman empire a father and a son who belonged to a sacred caste. The latter used in a state of possession to utter hexameters on metaphysical, moral and scientific issues which his father, and possibly other members of the priestly caste to which the two men belonged, wrote down as they emerged.[13] The revelations must have occurred over a period of years, possibly decades, and as they were taken down by several hands they would have given rise from the very beginning to slightly differing versions which needed editing, doubtless with the help of the Theurgist himself. Whether the codification of the revealed wisdom was the work of Julian himself alone or the result of the intervention of several 'keepers of the holy word' we cannot know.[14] What seems certain however is that by the late third century, if not before, the Chaldaean Oracles had reached their canonical status, and were recognized as a sacred text at least within the boundaries of a charmed religious circle with international connections.[15]

The very first people known to us who sought to understand, explain,

---

[13] The co-operation of the father and the son in this connection formed part of Neoplatonic orthodoxy: cp. Proclus, *In Crat.* 72, 10–11 for the expression τοῖς ἐπὶ Μάρκου γενομένοις θεουργοῖς.

[14] That the Oracles did not form a continuous poem, but were a collection of revelations given on different occasions, was already perceived by Lewy (36). Following Geffcken, P. Hadot advances the view that the Chaldaean Oracles 'comme les écrits hermétiques, les *Oracles Sybillins* et les textes magiques, ont été un livre de révélation toujours en devenir, auquel de nouveaux textes sont venus sans cesse s'ajouter' (Lewy, 706). I would suggest instead that the codification of the text occurred early in its development, possibly even under the Julians themselves, and this is why so much exegesis was needed, as in the parallel case of the Koran. What I describe here was definitely the case of Ismail Emre who, after recovering from his trance, used to have read to him the sometimes conflicting versions that had been taken down by the different people present, and pronounce on the correct word or phrase.

[15] The Chaldaean Oracles have been aptly called 'The Bible of the Neoplatonists'; for this now standard expression, which was probably first used by Cumont, see M. P. Nilsson, *Geschichte der griechischen Religion*, ii, 2nd edn. (1961), 479. The first testified commentator on the Oracles is Porphyry, cf. Marinus *VP* 26, 622–3: τοῖς Πορφυρίου καὶ Ἰαμβλίχου μυρίοις ὅσοις εἰς τὰ λόγια καὶ τὰ σύστοιχα τῶν Χαλδαίων συγγράμματα, a claim confirmed by John Lydus *Mens.* IV, 53, and by the Suda IV, 178, 22, *s.v.* Πορφύριος 2098. D. Potter, *JRS* 81 (1991), 225–6, sees a Manichaean influence on the Oracles and accordingly proposes a third century date for their composition. 'Manichaean' vocabulary was part of the theological *koine* of the period and, though I find it possible that in their definitive form the Oracles belong to the third century, I would place their 'emergence' in the second century, while pointing out that their status as a canonical text was not recognized before Iamblichus penned his massive commentary on them (cf. Julian, *ep.* 12 and Damascius, *PP* II, 1 for the length).

and propagate this occult wisdom were Porphyry, Amelius, and finally Iamblichus,[16] who established the Chaldaean Oracles as the holy book of paganism. The extant fragments point to a global revelation, and, given both their character and mode of transmission, it is only natural that the Oracles should always have appeared to the analytical scholarly mind as inconsequential or even illogical. Indeed it is an indication of how obscure and incoherent this automatic poetry must have sounded even in its complete form that from Iamblichus to Damascius a commentary on the Oracles in oral or written guise was considered the crowning achievement of an exegetical career. Equally, for a student to be admitted to a course on the Chaldaean Oracles amounted to an acknowledgement that he was part of the golden chain and on a potential short-list for the Platonic Succession.[17]

The Apamean Connection

A much-discussed issue is the connection of the philosophical system expounded in the Oracles with that of Numenius of Apamea. As formulated by Dodds, in cautious but perceptive terms, 'some sort of bridge must have linked the two systems; but I find it hard to be quite sure which way the traffic ran. It could even have been a two-way traffic, since (. . .) Numenius and Julianus may well have been contemporaries'.[18] Leaving aside for the moment this unprovable proposition, we may begin to explore the hypothesis of a connection between the Chaldaean Oracles and Apamea by looking closely at the town's religious and philosophical tradition.

Both recent archaeological surveys and late antique literary sources suggest that the as yet unexcavated oracular temple of Bel dominated the market place of Apamea, conveying by its sheer size and splendour the omnipotence of the cosmic god who dwelt in it, something that it is not difficult for us to visualize if we think of the Bel complex of another Syrian city—Palmyra. 'Bel', meaning 'Lord', is an epithet of the Babylonian storm god Adad,[19] whom Proclus identifies with the Twice-

---

[16] A random reference in Plotinus (1. 9) on the subject of suicide does not constitute evidence that Plotinus knew the Oracles, and may even be due to the editorial intervention of Porphyry. For the view that Plotinus was vaguely aware of the existence of the Oracles but made no conscious use of them, J. Dillon, 'Plotinus and the Chaldaean Oracles', in S. Gersch and Ch. Kannengiesser (eds.), *Platonism in Late Antiquity* (Notre Dame, Ind., 1992), 131–40.

[17] Marinus, *VP* 26 for Proclus and Domninus, Damascius, *PH* 145B for Hegias, and *JHS* 113 (1993), 4–5 for the Platonic chain.

[18] 'New Light on the "Chaldaean Oracles"', *HThR* 54 (1961), 271.

[19] Adad is the East Semitic or Babylonian form of the name of the storm god (as distinct

Beyond, the creative principle of the Chaldaean Oracles and a central divinity of the system in both theological and philosophical terms.[20]

As regards the Chaldaean roots of Bel recent research has made a strong case not only for the early spread of Babylonian religious culture to Syria, but also for its continuing influence throughout antiquity,[21] indeed an influence that was reinvigorated in Hellenistic times, when 'Chaldaean' as a technical term travelled westwards acquiring wide notoriety.[22] Leaving aside the wandering diviners identified in legal and everyday language as Chaldaeans, we should focus on the huge monuments to Bel in the contiguous territories of Palmyra and Apamea and advance the reasonable hypothesis that they perpetuated a venerable tradition firmly rooted in pre-Seleucid Babylon. It is within this context that the inscription KLDY from Roman Palmyra should be read as 'Chaldaeans', as was originally suggested, and be assumed to refer to a local priestly caste involved with the cult of Bel.[23]

Whatever the title of the Apamean priests of Bel (though the inscriptional evidence from Palmyra encourages one to think that 'Chaldaean' would be a plausible name), their involvement with the intellectual life of a town which had produced Posidonius is epigraphically attested. A second-century AD inscription, on a reused column of the great colonnade, identifies a priest of Bel as the head of the local Epicurean

from its West Semitic or Phoenician cognate 'Hadad'). Qualified as 'Bel', that is 'Lord' (and again distinguished on the same grounds from his western counterpart whose epithet was Beel/Baal), Adad had a great centre of worship in Aleppo among other places, as testify the festivals of the god held there in the second millennium BC: H. Klengel, *Geschichte Syriens im 2. Jahrtausend v.u.Z.*, II *Mitte- und Südsyria* (Berlin, 1969), 64 (Tablet V Bo T 89). Stephanie Dalley points out that 'the epithet Bel could be applied to various national gods or patron deities of major cities, but only to deities whose ancestry was Mesopotamian': 'Bel at Palmyra and Elsewhere in the Parthian Period', *ARAM* 7 (1995) [1998], 145 and by way of further clarification mentions 'Bel' as the epithet of the moon god Sin at Harran from at least as early as the Assyrian Empire.

[20] The gods of the Oracles speak in Syriac identifying the One with Ad and the intelligible creator of the world with Adad: Proclus, *In Parm.* VII (Klibansky–Labowsky), pp. 58, 30 ff.

[21] See Klengel, (n. 19) *passim*; for Niya (the predecessor of Apamea) as an important centre c.1500–1200 BC, ibid. 58–74. For the location of Niya, M. C. Astour, 'The Partition of the Confederacy of Mukis-Nuhasse-Nii by Suppiluliuma', *Orientalia*, 38 (1969), 386–7.

[22] See Diodorus 2. 29–31, Strabo 16. 1. 6. In 139 BC the *praetor peregrinus* banished the 'Chaldaeans' from Rome and Italy: 'edicto Chaldaeos citra decimum diem abire ex Urbe atque Italia iussit, levibus et ineptis ingeniis fallaci siderum interpretatione quaestuosam mendaciis suis caliginem inicientes' (Valerius Maximus 1. 3. 2).

[23] For the view that KLDY represents the local tribe 'Claudias', as suggested by T. Milik, *Dédicaces faites par des dieux* (Paris, 1972), 259–61, see Y. Hajjar, *ANRW* II 18, 4 (1990), 2255. In a private communication (16.9.00), for which I am most grateful, J.-B. Yon reviews the available epigraphic evidence from Palmyra to date and shows that KLDY can only be read as 'Chaldaean'.

School.[24] And while the exact nature of Numenius' connection with the temple remains unclear, one can see how philosophy and religion, tradition and innovation mingled with and fertilized each other in the sanctuary of Bel. Integrated then in the intellectual life of Apamea and at the same time respecting its immemorial cultic tradition, a caste of hereditary priests may have continued the Palaeo-Babylonian tradition of enthusiastic divination,[25] through which the oracles of the Apamean Bel enjoyed such high credence in the Roman empire,[26] until one priest by the name of Julian seems to have produced a revelation in the theological idiom of the region and of the times and yet firmly rooted in the millennial Babylonian tradition. The heritage of Posidonius and especially that of Numenius are discernible in the theology of the fragments that we possess, so that the hypothesis that the two Julians may have moved in Numenius' circle in Apamea, at a time when religious consciousness was shifting from pantheism to transcendentalism, appears highly attractive.[27]

The crucial piece of evidence linking the Apamean Bel with the Chaldaean Oracles may be lurking behind the lines of a Greek inscription on an altar dedicated to the god by a certain Sextus in far away Vaison-la-Romaine (Vasio): 'To the ruler of fortune Belus, Sextus dedicated an altar in remembrance of the Apamean oracles' (τῶν ἐν Ἀπαμείᾳ μνησάμενος λογίων).[28] Whether the dedicator of the inscription is Sextus Varius Marcellus of Apamea, the father of Elagabal, or some obscure soldier,[29] it is extremely likely that the phrase 'the λόγια at Apamea' refers to a collection of oracles which was to become universally known as 'the Chaldaean Oracles'.[30]

---

[24] J.-P. Rey-Coquais, 'Inscriptions grecques d'Apamée', *Annales Archéologiques Arabes Syriennes*, 23 (1973), 66–8. For the date, cp. pl. v 2, p. 84.

[25] In this connection cf. Iamblichus' programmatic statement, *Myst.* I, 2. Lewy (427–8) understood the duality of the term 'Chaldaean' in this context as referring both to the homeland of the Babylonian theologians and to their membership of a priestly caste.

[26] According to Cassius Dio (78. 8. 5–6) Septimius Severus consulted the oracle on his imperial fortunes (twice, in 180 and 201/2), and so did Macrinus in 218 (78. 40. 3).

[27] The Stoic concept of πῦρ νεορόν is ubiquitous in the Oracles. For an assessment of Posidonius' role in shaping Syrian solar theology, see the classic treatment in K. Reinhardt, *Kosmos und Sympathie: neue Untersuchungen über Posidonios* (Munich, 1926), 308–85. Two characteristic examples are Posidonius fr. 101 (Edelstein–Kidd) for a definition of the first principle, and Numenius fr. 2 for the way of grasping it.   [28] IG XIV 2482.

[29] For a discussion on the identity of Sextus, see J. Balty, 'L'oracle d'Apamée' *Ant. Class.* 50 (1981), 9. Rey-Coquais nevertheless seems to favour the identification with Sextus Varius Marcellus ('Inscriptions grecques d'Apamée', 68).

[30] It is worth pointing out that the term 'Chaldaean' is not to be found anywhere in the surviving fragments, making it appear as the definition of an outsider, presumably a commentator.

It is against this background that the settling in Apamea in the latter part of the third century of two leading Platonists turns into a quasi-certainty the assumption that the sacred verses were preserved in tha‸ part of the world, indeed in the archives of the temple of Bel. Disappointed for whatever reason with the circle of Plotinus, the westerner Amelius chose Apamea as his permanent home around 270 and, whether or not he was attracted there by a possible archive of 'Chaldaean Oracles', he seems to have espoused their theology and interpreted Plato along its lines.[31] Likewise, after years of travelling, the Syrian Iamblichus based himself in Apamea as an exegete of the mysteries of the Beyond, gathering around him students from all over the Mediterranean world;[32] and it was precisely through the action of this 'chorus of philosophers'[33] that by the fourth century both the canonical text and Iamblichus' voluminous commentary on it had travelled westwards, revitalizing philosophy in the Roman empire, creating new intellectual centres, and endowing old ones with a lease of originality.

Meanwhile in Apamea the increasing sanctity of its temple was seen by the Christian establishment as a major scandal which called for an appropriate treatment. The detailed account by Theodoret of the destruction of the temple—admittedly composed half a century after the event—suggests that an edict specifically aimed at the Apamean temple, regarded as a particularly important pagan symbol, was promulgated in the 380s. Leading a force of two thousand men, the Praetorian Prefect of the East Cynegius, an ardent Christian, arrived at Apamea and set his forces to work against the temple, but in vain. The gigantic edifice resisted; its eventual destruction by the combination of human cunning and divine intervention was brought about a little later thanks to Bishop Marcellus in the first act of violence by a bishop against a religious monument in the Roman empire.[34]

---

[31] The connection between the Oracles and Amelius is brought out by H. D. Saffrey, whose critical reading of Proclus, *In Tim.* I, 361, 26–362, 2 makes Amelius' link with the theology of the Chaldaean Oracles a near certainty: Saffrey, 'Les Néoplatoniciens et les Oracles Chaldaïques', *REAug* 27 (1981), 224–5.

[32] For an attempted reconstruction of Iamblichus' travels, see Athanassiadi, 'The Oecumenism of Iamblichus: Latent Knowledge and its Awakening', *JRS* 85 (1995), 245–6.

[33] For the expression ὁ τῶν φιλοσόφων ἐξ Ἀπαμείας χορός referring to Iamblichus' pupils in connection with the Emperor Julian, see Libanius, *or.* 52. 21.

[34] For the circumstances of the destruction of the temple, see Theodoret, *HE* 5. 21. 5–14; cf. Libanius' shocked comment to Theodosius in an oration composed shortly after the event (*or.* 30, 43).

2. METHODOLOGICAL CONCERNS

The Present Collection

Any attempt at a description and analysis of the Chaldaean Oracles should begin with the fundamental question of their transmission. The fragments that we possess—some 350 lines divided into 190 fragments of uneven length—have entered the Collection primarily through two channels: Proclus and Damascius.[35] The Proclean fragments, which represent a little less than four-fifths of the whole, come either directly from his extant works—especially the short commentary on the *Cratylus* and the *Platonic Theology*—or through the intermediary of Michael Psellus. The Damascius fragments on the other hand, amounting to a little more than one fifth of the Collection, are direct quotations, the overwhelming majority of which derives from two works: *On the First Principles* and the Commentary *On the Parmenides*. Fourteen quotations by Proclus and Damascius overlap in part or *in toto*. As regards other authors, if we except John Lydus (who is represented in the Collection by nine short fragments, but whose exclusive source again seems to be Proclus), the contributions of Julian, Didymus, Synesius, Boethius, Hierocles, Hermeias, Simplicius, and Olympiodorus amount to a total of a few lines. It is clear therefore that any attempt towards building a Collection should rest on a meticulous study of the respective readings of the Chaldaean Oracles by Proclus and Damascius, two authors whose substantial disagreement in their understanding of the Platonic heritage[36] also pervades their differing approaches to the Oracles.

Yet dealing with the *membra disiecta* of the Oracles according to provenance was not the way that appeared to their first modern editor as the most obvious methodological course. The reason for this may be that W. Kroll was not interested in producing a straightforward edition, but in extricating from the fragments a philosophical and theosophical system for the purposes of a post-doctoral thesis, which was indeed defended on 19 April 1894 at the University of Breslau.[37] Accordingly he gleaned through later Greek literature, plucked the Chaldaean hexa-

---

[35] As suggested by Saffrey (*REAug* 210), a more methodical reading of the sources is necessary both in view of the discovery of new oracles and for the fuller understanding of the ones that we have already. One should add that several phrases and sentences which have been transmitted periphrastically in a non-poetic form should also be included in the collection, as e.g. the reference to the visions of the theurgists in Proclus, *In Remp.* II, 155, 5 ff., cp. in line 7 the phrase ὥς φασιν οἱ θεουργοί.

[36] Cp. *JRS* 85 (1995), 247–8 with refs.

[37] *De Oraculis chaldaicis*, submitted *ad veniam docendi* (Breslau, 1894).

meters wherever they cropped up and arranged them in an order which starts with the theoretical and descends to the practical.[38] The emphasis however is on theory, something for which Kroll was criticized—to my mind unjustifiably—by subsequent researchers, especially as he was well aware of the fact that the poem related to mysteries, and was therefore more relevant to religion than to philosophy.[39]

Seventy-five years later Kroll's systematic—and arbitrary—codification was unquestioningly adopted by des Places who, in the Budé edition of 1971, simply inserted a few new fragments identified as Chaldaean by Bidez and others.[40] Finally, Kroll's order of the Chaldaean Oracles became a sacrosanct fossil for the wider world, when in 1989 Ruth Majercik appended to des Places's text an English translation and commentary.[41]

A Return to the Sources

Given that the original order of the metaphysically transmitted utterances can never be recaptured, it is not merely legitimate, but may be most appropriate methodologically to reorganize the Collection according to the provenance of the fragments, while searching for clues and guidance to this obscure text in the reaction of its ancient readers rather than in the commentaries of Psellus, as has been the case so far. For indeed, from Hans Lewy, whose *Chaldaean Oracles and Theurgy* was completed in 1945, to Joseph Combès, the most recent editor of Damascius, the tendency has been to take Psellus' summaries as a basis for the construction of Chaldaean theology and then try to fit the ancient authors round it. What ensues in most cases is utter confusion, since what seems not to have been realized so far is that what we have in the preserved commentaries of Proclus and Damascius is not complementary interpretations of a theological system, but two conflicting understandings of it, which cannot possibly be reconciled. For this

---

[38] Kroll's bipartition of the Chaldaean Oracles into a Platonic-philosophical and a magico-theurgical section has been a decisive influence on subsequent scholarship; Lewy further rigidified it, while recently it suggested to Saffrey (*REAug* 127, 220) the following bold, if unprovable theory: 'Les Oracles Chaldaïques sont donc une collection composite réunissant d'une part de vieux oracles chaldaïques [assumed to be of a magical character], peut-être rassemblés par Julien-père, et de nouveaux oracles chaldaïques proférés par Julien-fils. Ces nouveaux oracles sont les oracles platoniciens.' Even the appellation 'Theurgist' of the younger Julian contradicts this theory.

[39] 'mysteria non e philosophia sed e religione oriuntur' *De Oraculis chaldaicis*, 68.

[40] For the new fragments, see M. Tardieu in Lewy 520–2, and H. D. Saffrey 'Nouveaux oracles chaldaïques dans les scholies du *Paris. gr.* 1853', *RPh* 43 (1969), 59–70.

[41] See R. Majercik, *The Chaldean Oracles: Text, Translation and Commentary* (Leiden, 1989), together with D. Potter's review in *JRS* 81 (1991), 225–7.

reason I propose to forget Psellus and turn instead to Proclus and Damascius individually.

3. PROCLUS

Proclus was a born teacher, a compulsive writer, and a gifted commentator.[42] Confident in his unequivocal understanding of whatever text he read, he invariably knew how to explain those points which he felt to be in need of clarification in a lucid if prolix manner. As a reader of the Oracles Proclus concentrates on astronomy, metaphysics, ethics, ritual, and magic; in short on all the subjects touched on by the Chaldaean revelation. His interests are thus far wider than Damascius', even if we allow for the fact that the works of Damascius which have come down to us are primarily metaphysical. What is important, however, for our purposes is not so much the breadth of the themes covered by Proclus (though this is significant too), as the manner of approach and presentation of each one of them. As a preliminary remark one may comment on Proclus' strongly hieratic and hierarchical perception of cosmic space, which defines both his metaphysical and soteriological vision and his understanding of astronomy.

The basic Platonic antithesis between a paradigmatic and a created world becomes a trichotomy in the Chaldaean system:

> For it is in three that the Intellect of the Father said that all things should
> be divided
> And before he had even nodded his will everything was divided. (fr. 22)

These lines have been preserved both by Proclus and by Damascius. Commenting on them Proclus lays emphasis on the triadic nature of all things in all the worlds.[43] Conversely Damascius stresses the united character of the trinity—τὸ ἀληθῶς ἡνωμένον—and is further concerned to prove that God is one, despite the triadic hypostasis reflected in the adjective τριγλώχις.[44] One is left with the sense of an ineluctable

---

[42] As Marinus realized, the hallmark of Proclus' existence was 'full happiness' (εὐδαιμονία), the alternative title of the *Life of Proclus* being Περὶ εὐδαιμονίας. As the leitmotiv of the book, the theme of εὐμοιρία is discussed in *VP* 2 and 34; cf. also ibid. 33, 809 for the divine gift *par excellence* of εὐμοιρία, also bestowed by the gods on Isidore, *PH* fr. 33C. On Proclus' ease as a universal exegete and on his superhuman daily routine of ritual, lecturing, and writing tasks, *VP* 22, 549–55; after his seventieth year, when Proclus was struck by senility, he attempted to keep up his customary programme, though πάντα (. . .) ἐπὶ τὸ ἀσθενέστερον πράττων: *VP* 26, 642–4.

[43] *Parm.* 1091: τὸ τριαδικὸν ἄνωθεν πρόεισι μέχρι τῶν ἐσχάτων; for another comment on the same fragment by Proclus, *In Tim.* III, 243.

[44] *PP* III 58; cf. III, 136: ὅτι τὰ πολλὰ τὸ ἀπειροδύναμόν ἐστι τοῦ ἑνός—it is the potentiality rather than the reality of creation that interests Damascius.

ambiguity, intentionally created by Damascius, who does not seem to believe that things can be schematically represented if one wants to remain faithful to the fundamental intuition that the world of sensible experience is illusory through and through. While in theory agreeing with this proposition, Proclus is compelled to follow his strong analytical and didactic streak and to present metaphysics in terms of a neat spatiality which is extended to the function as well as the location of the first principles.[45]

Divided into the empyrian, the aetherial, and the material world, which correspond to the *νοῦς*, the soul, and the body in man,[46] the cosmos is seen by Proclus in its tripartite division as the realm of Ouranos, Cronos, and Zeus, whom he conceives respectively as the cohesive, the partitive, and the creative principle.[47] All three of these worlds are enveloped in metaphysical light, an often 'singing light' whose behaviour varies according to the place that it occupies in the universe.[48] Unlike the light of the sun, this is not a derivative of fire, but a transubstantial entity which proceeds from the Father and weaves all things together before entrusting them for all eternity to the binding principle of love.[49] Indeed if one were asked to define the monotheistic element in the Chaldaean system according to Proclus' understanding, one would certainly name light, as the most spiritual and at the same time most ungraspable and ubiquitous principle in that system.

Proclus' pedagogic sense however leads him to apply to his metaphysical analysis categories borrowed from the disciplines of physics and ethics; thus he describes 'this-worldly fire' as something *contra naturam* (*παρὰ φύσιν*).[50] This literal approach, which obviously constitutes a much more successful teaching device than does Damascius' poetic ambiguity, also allows Proclus to talk about time as a multi-tiered reality and the arena within which salvation is achieved, in a way that would have shocked Plato but which is in tune with theurgic practice.[51]

[45] See e.g. *In Tim.* II, 106; *PT* IV, 111. Cf. *CP* A, dominated by a didactic anthropomorphism. Another example illustrating this point is provided by the classificatory attempt of *PT* IV, 103–15.

[46] *In Tim.* II, 57–8 and fr. 5; cf. also *PT* IV, 111 and fr. 85 for the role of each teletarch in his respective sphere.

[47] *In Crat.* 63–4 and fr. 8 (though see *In Remp.* II, 220–1 for a contradiction).

[48] See *In Remp.* II, 201 and fr. 49, commenting on which (*In Tim.* III, 14) Proclus speaks of the duality of unifying light (*ἑνοποιὸν φῶς*) which involves at once eternal movement and absolute rest.

[49] *In Tim.* II, 9 and fr. 60; *In Tim.* II, 54 and fr. 39 together with *In Parm.* 769 and fr. 42.

[50] *In Tim.* III, 130, 7.

[51] *In Tim.* III, 43, an extremely important passage, which in connection with *In Tim.* III, 20 sets the theoretical bases for the theurgic ascent.

At the same time the astronomical and more generally mathematical dimension of the Oracles exerts too lively a fascination on Proclus to be put down to the mere accidents of transmission. In this connection he finds that Plato's 'level' understanding of astronomy cannot compare with the 'spherical' conception of the Oracles,[52] and, though he concedes that on certain points Plato held the same theories as the divinely inspired Chaldaeans (*In Tim.* III, 124), occasionally even uttering the odd Chaldaean Oracle, in spirit at least if not literally,[53] both in science and in metaphysics Plato's understanding remained all too human.[54]

The most important aspect of the Oracles for Proclus is the soteriological, which he understands and presents in the light of his own rigid asceticism and ritualism.[55] Indeed these two features, which on the evidence of Proclus alone have been assumed to be paramount in the Oracles, may well have played a less prominent role within the framework of the original teaching. Often the language of Proclean asceticism is far more strident than the oracle that it purports to explicate; thus, commenting on fr. 116, which says that divine matters are not for those who think in a 'bodily' way, Proclus declares that to live in a body is 'unnatural', whereas to be in Hades without a body is 'natural'.[56] 'The root of evil is the body just as that of good is the intellect', he intones elsewhere.[57] In tune with his moral radicalism, Proclus chose to remain a virgin,[58] regarding sexual abstinence as an asset towards salvation. Another prerequisite was cultic correctness.[59] Accordingly he set out to explain the hidden rules which govern universal sympathy, and to reveal the ways in which they can be put into practical use.[60] He himself used these paths often enough in his life to help others as well as himself, and

---

[52] *In Tim.* III, 60–61.

[53] *PT* v, 130.

[54] Note the critical remark (*In Remp.* II, 143; καὶ οὐκέτι ταῦτα Πλάτωνος οὐδὲ Τιμαίου λόγοι τινός, ἀλλὰ θεουργῶν καὶ θεῶν ἄγνωστα γραφόντων) on the superiority of the Chaldaean revelation over Plato as regards the magical sign X which marks the substance of the souls.

[55] On Proclus' excessive asceticism, *VP* 12 (Plutarch found the young man's diet so frugal that he feared for his life); ibid. 19. For his extreme ritualism, *inter alia, VP* 18, 19. *In Remp.* II, 99 describes a hierarchy of ascent and deliverance from the cycle of birth according to the soul's behaviour.

[56] *In Crat.* 87, 25–8.

[57] *CP* C (p. 108).

[58] *VP* 17, 412–15, 20, 512–13; Damascius *PH* fr. 56.

[59] Cp. *In Tim.* I, 212, 15 ff: so that God dispenses grace, the faithful must ἀδιαλείπτως ἔχεσθαι τῆς περὶ τὸ θεῖον θρησκείας.

[60] See *CP* A (pp. 206–7); *In Crat.* 31 (which advocates a magical view of salvation); *In Remp.* II, 154–5; *In Remp.* I, 110, 28; *In Crat.* 95 (on the importance of βάρβαρα ὀνόματα/ συνθήματα) etc.

had numerous encounters with the divine, whether on his own initiative or on that of the gods themselves.[61]

Several chapters of the *Life of Proclus* are dedicated to the miracles that he performed on behalf of individuals and the community, and the 'Chaldaean' basis of both his prophetic and magic art is explicitly stated by his biographer. Of particular significance in this connection is the rain miracle which delivered Attica from a drought.[62] Produced by the movement of an iynx, this thaumaturgy related to a θεουργικὴ ἀγωγή which had been used a hundred years earlier for similar purposes by the hierophant Nestorius. Nestorius transmitted it to his grandson, the diadochus Plutarch, who in turn handed it down to his daughter Asclepigeneia, Proclus' instructor in magical lore.[63] One is forcefully reminded of the original rain miracle of AD 172 performed in accordance with 'Chaldaean' methodology by Julian the Theurgist who thus saved the Roman army from thirst and assured its victory over the Quadi.[64]

Proclus' personal involvement with the divine—his interviews with specific gods, which he publicized in a now lost treatise, and his playing around with the cosmic powers—[65] inevitably tinged his overall vision. Yet, if his anthropomorphic way of conceiving and expressing divinity should be seen as the natural expression of his literal, untormented understanding in metaphysics and of his formalism in the sphere of

---

[61] Cp. Marinus, *VP* 7, 28, 31, 32. Simplicius (*CAG* IX, 795) reports that Proclus demonstrated that divided time was a god since he could be called to produce an epiphany (cp. Proclus *In Tim.* III, 20). When Athena's statue is removed from the Parthenon, the goddess informs Proclus that she would like to come and cohabit with him: *VP* 30, 736–42.

[62] *VP* 28, 686–8.

[63] For Nestorius' deliverance of Attica from the earthquake of 375, which destroyed much of Greece, see Zosimus 4. 18. 2–4; he performed it θεοειδέσιν ἐννοίαις παιδαγω γούμενος: ibid. 3 (cp. Proclus, *In Remp.* II, 64 and 324–5, for his theurgic proficiency). The miracle was celebrated by Syrianus in a hymn in honour of Achilles (Zosimus ibid. 4 and F. Paschoud n. *ad loc.* in Zosime, *Histoire Nouvelle* II/2 (1979), 368–9). For the line of transmission of the *Theurgic Conduct*, *VP* 28, 677–83. It is likely that Nestorius himself transmitted his occult wisdom to a daughter who then passed it on to Plutarch. That would be in tune with the well-known practice of transmitting certain aspects of magical lore only by a cross-sexual route. Alternatively Plutarch may have been Nestorius' son, as argued on the evidence of *PH* fr. 64.

[64] This standard piece of Neoplatonist hagiography, which tallies so well both with Nestorius' and Proclus' acts, has also been contested recently: for the relevant bibliography, Iles Johnston, *Hekate Soteira*, 3 n. 6. A combined miracle, reminiscent of that of AD 172 and anticipating that of Nestorius, was performed in Constantinople by the Emperor Julian (who in all probability had been initiated in the Eleusinian Mysteries by Nestorius himself): Libanius, *or.* 15. 71.

[65] Cp. *VP* 28, 677–9: ταῖς γὰρ τῶν Χαλδαίων συστάσεσι καὶ ἐντυχίαις καὶ τοῖς θείοις καὶ ἀφθέγκτοις στροφάλοις ἐκέχρητο. 685–6: φάσμασι μὲν Ἑκατικοῖς φωτοειδέσιν αὐτοπτουμένοις ὡμίλησεν, ὡς καὶ αὐτός που μέμνηται ἐν ἰδίῳ συγγράμματι.

morals, in strictly pedagogic terms it provided those who strove to conceptualize the unseen with a tangible progressive approach.

Constant solicitude for salvation, sought as much through practical and magical as through intellectual means, presupposes an eschatological view of the world, which indeed Proclus finds in the Oracles (frs. 164, 165, 157–162) and on which he duly expands, sometimes lending it apocalyptic overtones (fr. 170). He never tires of repeating that in this harmonious cosmos, which is punctuated all along with mementoes of the divine presence, the only enemy of man is 'the turbulence of matter' (*In Tim.* III, 325) 'by which many are pulled down into twisted streams' (fr. 172). And though he concedes that 'we are images of the intellectual entities, and effigies of the unknown symbols',[66] he also insists on the element of forgetfulness of our true status, which makes us vulnerable to attack—that of the passions engaging their battle from within and of the demons from without. Yet this picture of the human adventure is only painted in such dark colours so that the message of salvation may stand out in relief; for in his struggle towards recollection and recognition of the signs which are to set him free from the servitude of matter, man is not alone. The Father has sown among us 'the race of theurgists who in their freedom from envy aspire to equal God's goodness instead of being drawn down to the conflicts and strifes of men'.[67] This hero of wisdom and love that is the theurgist represents for Proclus—as he also did for the Emperor Julian—the constant manifestation of the divine in the field of historical relativity, the element and guarantee of permanent, uninterrupted grace for all generations of men.

4. PROCLUS AND DAMASCIUS: DEBTS AND LEGACIES

In approaching the Chaldaean Oracles Proclus and Damascius seem to have had widely diverging aims, the former being drawn by the systematic classification of an emanational structure and its practical adaptations for salvational and magical purposes, the latter choosing to comment on those passages which delineate a fundamentally negative theology. The particular concerns of Proclus and Damascius *vis-à-vis* the Oracles should however be envisaged in wider context, and an inquiry about both the debts and the legacies of the two men in this connection may prove particularly enlightening. Such an inquiry would reveal

---

[66] *CP* E (p. 211).
[67] *CP* C (pp. 208-9); what the theurgist has in common with Plato's God is the divine characteristic *par excellence*, that of τὸ ἄφθονον.

Damascius as a straightforward case: as in other matters, here too he followed in the footsteps of Iamblichus, while showing a fair degree of independence, and left no progeny whatever.[68] Unknown to Psellus and Pletho,[69] his treatment of the Oracles caused Kroll to raise an eyebrow,[70] while it seems to have perplexed des Places to the point that in his Introductory Notice to the Chaldaean Oracles he omitted him altogether from a list of readers of the Oracles which includes even authors who have not preserved a single line!

By contrast the approach of Proclus, whose now lost commentary on the Oracles was eagerly studied and on several occasions summarized by Psellus, appealed to contemporaries and posterity alike. In his fascination with the ritual and systematic aspects of the Oracles, Proclus too can be seen to depend on Iamblichus, though equally unilaterally; abetted by Psellus, these two concerns of the Athenian diadochus—the practical and the scholastic—have determined how the Chaldaean Oracles were perceived by scholars from Lewy to Dodds and Majercik, and have served as guidelines in our retrospective appreciation of Iamblichus. Thus a meticulously hierarchical theology and a ritualistic—almost mechanical—method of ascent towards the First Principles have become synonymous with the Chaldaean Oracles and, by extension, with their original exegete, Iamblichus. Yet this simplistic vision of the Oracles, for which Psellus even more than Proclus is responsible, vanishes if one is prepared to consider the Damascian view.

5. THE ALTERNATIVE CHALDAEAN ORACLES

Damascius' Peculiar Way

Like his predecessors, Damascius intended to devote an independent commentary to the Chaldaean Oracles,[71] a project which may have never

---

[68] Combès (*PP* ii, 215 n. 3) advances the plausible hypothesis that many elements of Iamblichus' *Chaldaean Theology* were integrated by Damascius in his treatise *On the First Principles*. Indeed he describes the entire first volume as 'une justification critique de la doctrine selon laquelle l'inéffable est transcendant, à l'un, et l'un transcendant à la triade qui suit', which on his evidence was Iamblichus' interpretation, not accepted by Proclus, and not apparent from the *De Mysteriis*. As regards Damascius' posterity, even his own pupil and companion Simplicius admits that he finds him too difficult, indeed incomprehensible (*CAG* ix, 625, 2 and 775, 32).

[69] See the new edition of Pletho's *Chaldaean Oracles* by B. Tambrun-Krasker (Athens, 1995).

[70] G. Kroll (*De oraculis chaldaicis*, p. 10 n. 2) complains of Damascius' lack of originality in rather strong terms when he refers to his *ingenii sterilitas*. He is even ruder about Damascius' editor, Ruelle (*nihil fere intellexit*: p. 8 n. 2), whose edition came out in 1889.

[71] A planned course of lectures on the Chaldaean Oracles is several times referred to by Damascius; cp. *Parm.* 9, 21–2; 11, 11–15; 132, 9–10.

come to fruition. Nevertheless the pages consecrated to this subject in his systematic work *On the First Principles* (III, 108–59) come close to constituting a treatise *per se* (despite Damascius' modest statement in III, 159), and, if one adds the discussion contained in his *In Parmenidem* and the random remarks of the *In Phaedonem*, something like a monograph on the theology of the Chaldaean Oracles begins to emerge. More importantly, many oracles are given there in full, or in a different context from that of Proclus, while several others lie unrecognized, concealed in paraphrase in the text.[72] In short there is enough in Damascius for a meaningful—and fresh—reconstruction of the Chaldaean system, which can then be compared with the one that we owe to Psellus as commentator and interpreter of Proclus.

Before approaching Damascius however it is worth remembering that, if all history is contemporary history, all theology is autobiographical. To these truisms one should add the no less obvious statement that any holy book addresses itself to many levels of understanding and piety, and the Bible of the Neoplatonists with its poetic diction and metaphorical language does not constitute an exception to this rule. With these caveats in mind one may turn to Damascius' doubly revealing and highly ambiguous text.

It is easy to see straight away why Damascius remained without a posterity. Much more than any accident of history, it was his own attitude towards the human mind and its possibilities which must be held responsible for his lack of spiritual descendants. For Damascius is a ferocious detractor of any classificatory attempt in the realm of metaphysics—a jester with a philosopher's mask. With great care and meticulousness he constructs superb intellectual edifices, which he then proceeds to contemplate from several angles by cleverly turning them inside out and upside down. In doing this he displays his own thoroughness, subtlety and ingenuity, while at the same time exposing the extreme relativity of these structures, with which our divided intelligence is forever condemned to play as a result of the dislocated state to which the Titanic War has reduced it (*PP* I, 66; III, 92). Tortured by his inability to achieve real synthesis,[73] in his rage Damascius suddenly administers a blow to the edifice which he has so carefully constructed

---

[72] Cp. *PH* fr. 3A for a possible oracle which I reconstruct as follows: ⟨Ἰσίν τε⟩ ἀενάου ζωῆς ὀχετοῖς ἀμετρήτοις.

[73] See *PP* I, 66: εἰ δὲ ἡ συναίρεσις ἡμᾶς ὑπερβαίνει τοὺς ἐν τῷ τιτανικῷ πολέμῳ διεσπασμένους, τί τὸ θαυμαστόν; The word always used by Damascius in this connection is συναίρεσις, which, *pace* Combès and Galpérine, has the meaning of synthesis: cp. I, 56.

and cherished, and demolishes it. Then, having recourse to a poet's imagery, he derides his attempt, though not without some shedding of tears:

And yet, if, when we attempt to sound and explore in all its senses the intelligible depths, we fall short of that truth and deviate as we do towards what is low and divided, through being dragged and pulled down towards them by the compulsion of our miserable nothingness, we should nevertheless resign ourselves to this deviation and this fall. For it is not possible in our present state to grasp these things otherwise and we must be content if we can touch them from afar as it were, with great difficulty, very faintly, or indeed if we can gain the trace of a hint which will suddenly flash before our eyes, even though the spark comes from the self, rising out of the soul; a small gleam, not really bright, yet still an indication by analogy of that huge all-shining light. As regards this discourse too, this is the thing for which it should be praised: that it despises itself and confesses itself blinded by that united, intelligible light and unable to stare at it. (*PP* III, 141).

Primarily a poet, with a superb feel for the language which he moulds round his considerable needs, Damascius is an exceptionally ambitious thinker. At the same time he is poignantly aware of the limitations of both human understanding and expression, but quite unwilling to restrict himself to the orbit of his given abilities.[74] A lucid and tenacious fighter in the metaphysical field—as in real life—he appears in our eyes as an intellectual acrobat who is forced to create new terms in response to his emotional and metaphysical leaps.[75] This is indeed what happens when he attempts to grasp and describe the sternly apophatic region of the Beyond.

The Beyond

Far beyond the transcendent One (*PP* I, 84; cf. fr. 16) lies the hypercosmic abyss (*PP* III, 144; fr. 18 and *Parm.* 16. 6) or sanctuary of silence (*PP* I, 84),[76] the secret world which summarizes in itself all worlds (*PP* III,

---

74 There is a tragic helplessness in expressions like the following: ἀλλ' ὅμως (. . .) ἀνερεθιστέον τὰς ἐν ἡμῖν ἀρρήτους ὠδῖνας εἰς τὴν ἄρρητον (οὐκ οἶδα ὅπως εἴπω) συναίσθησιν τῆς ὑπερηφάνου ταύτης ἀληθείας. Note the usage of the ambivalent word ὑπερήφανος. On the relativity of language, *PP* II, 59 ff., *PP* III, 96 etc.

75 Next to a considerable number of neologisms (παντοῦχος, ὑπεράγνοια etc.), Damascius often gives his own peculiar meaning to already existing words (ἐγκεντρίζω in *Parm.*).

76 Other expressions denoting the unclassifiable ἀκοσμία, which is more harmonious than any κόσμος (*Parm.* 86), are 'undefined depths' (*PP* III, 92), 'impossible beginning' (*PP* I, 84), 'the infinite' (*Parm.* 65, 14) which is both ἀπρόοδον and ἀνάριθμον (*Parm.* 87).

77 Conversely for Proclus the One is beyond all this: *Parm.* 1171, 4: εἴτε γὰρ γαλήνη τίς ἐστιν ὑμνουμένη νοερὰ παρὰ τοῖς σοφοῖς, εἴτε ὅρμος μυστικός, εἴτε σιγὴ δῆλον ὡς

91).⁷⁷ Damascius describes it as an as yet unmanifested birth-pang for the cosmic Form, a pre-suffering for the coming into being of all the partial intelligible births. It is the realm of non-being (*PP* II, 91)—also equated with the Orphic Night—that we in our touching ignorance attempt to classify and adorn (*PP* III, 144). Below this ἀπρόοδον καὶ ἀνάριθμον ἄπειρον (*Parm.* 86, 87)—the infinite which is not subject to procession and number—the Oracles place the unorganized, undisciplined (ἀσύντακτος) cause of being, itself beyond essence and intellection (*PP* II, 2); being beyond even the One, it too is an entity beyond knowledge and ignorance, an object of *hyperignorance*.

Reminiscent of the Gnostic *agnosia*, Damascius' neologism is crucial to our understanding of the subtleties of his negative theology: hyper-ignorance is our natural state of mind when it comes to anything of importance; it governs us as we move on to the next metaphysical stage and attempt to grasp the One: our perception of it is overshadowed by ὑπεράγνοια (*PP* I, 84)—metaphysical ignorance. Yet we know about it through non-intellectual means, for our experience of the ineffable is a travail which fails to result in child-birth (*PP* I, 86). The metaphor of labour with a view to a spiritual birth is repeatedly used by Plato, but always with a positive hue, pointing to the final delivery and deliverance from pain.⁷⁸ Damascius strips this image of any exhilarating connotations and turns it into a symbol of sterile pain before raising it into the nightmarish leitmotiv which haunts both the *De Principiis* and the *In Parmenidem*. Through 'knowledge in labour' we attempt in our pathetic, divided Titanic condition to reach the most indivisible of things.⁷⁹

This, of course, is a polemical passage directed against Proclus, whose grand systematic edifices Damascius takes pleasure in deconstructing, mainly by attacking the quiet self-confidence which lies behind them. The Oracles, insists Damascius, urge us to forget all our philosophical notions, to discard and reject all definition, and to concentrate solely on this unending pang—the ὠδίς, which is also the ὁδός, a recurrent pun—(*PP* I, 87–8; II, 105; *In Parm.* 28, 31–2), for it is not possible to grasp what is indescribable and unqualifiable (*PP* I, 87) even by 'the flower of the intellect', as Iamblichus had realized (*PP* II, 100). What is needed is a complete emptying of the mind, a state of utter passivity, of annihilation of the self so that 'the gods bestow the view' (*PP* II, 106).

ἁπάντων τῶν τοιούτων ἐξῄρηται τὸ ἕν, ἐπέκεινα ὂν καὶ ἐνεργείας καὶ σιγῆς καὶ ἡσυχίας καὶ πάντων ὁμοῦ τῶν ἐν τοῖς οὖσιν ἀνυμνουμένων στασίμων συνθημάτων.

⁷⁸ Cp. *Symp.* 206d; *Phaedr.* 251e; *Rep.* 490b.

⁷⁹ *PP* I, 87: τοῦτο τιτανικὸν πάσχομεν καὶ ὅμως τοῦτο τὸ πάθος ἐπὶ τὸ πάντων ἁγιώτατον καὶ παντὸς ὅλου ἀμερέστατον ἀνάγειν ἐπιχειροῦμεν.

It is not with vehemence that you should attempt to conceive that Intelligible
But by the subtle flame of a subtle mind, (a flame) which measures all things
Except that Intelligible. You must not perceive it
Intently but, while keeping the pure eye of your soul averted,
You should lend the Intelligible an empty mind
So that you may comprehend it. For it exists outside the mind. (fr. 1)[80]

This passivity in God is described by Damascius in connection with
another Chaldaean fragment as 'more perfect than all power of self-
movement, as being a supernatural movement from without',[81] an illumination which may or may not come despite human effort. Typically,
when commenting on the same passage, Proclus' emphasis is on action
rather than passivity, on human initiative rather than divine grace which
is granted anyway; thus for Proclus the particle of the divine fire
bestowed by the Father on the descended soul has to be activated by a
series of operations both ritual and moral before the specific personality
may move out of the orbit of fate.[82]

Does the all-encompassing 'vision' which follows the emptying of the
mind reach as far as the chaotic darkness of the Beyond? What does it
include? Is it a progressive experience from the divided to the One, as in
Plotinus or Proclus, or is it a sudden, unconscious and ineffable gift, as
in Numenius? The impossibility of answering these questions is reflected
in Damascius' refusal to endow us with clear-cut certainties at any level
of his description of the Oracles' theology. Confines are continuously
blurred and the triptych Abyss—Meta-being—One is as undivided as
the next—if the expression 'next' means anything in this context—stage
of the intelligible ennead.

Trinitarian Theology

Is it an ennead or a triad? In one place (*PP* iii, 116) Damascius declares it
to be neither, and in a series of passages of great poetic beauty and
poignancy he attempts to answer the question:

what is this intelligible ennead that we celebrate? It is merely a way of indicating
the total perfection of the triad above, and which we divide into three in our
inability to embrace with the mind its full perfection, its comprising the All, its
governing all plurality, its engendering all triads wherever and in whatever
manner they happen to be, its leading all procession to the ultimate degree, its
unbridled generating power . . .—all these concepts should be united into one

---

[80] See the verbose analysis of this oracle in Proclus, *CP* D (pp. 210–11).
[81] Cp. *In Phaed.* i, 169 and fr. 130.
[82] For the full context, see *In Tim.* iii, 266, 16 ff.

meta-concept, which would be a mere hint towards the understanding of the first triad. (*PP* iii, 132)

And in a further attempt to convey the nature of what is simple but appears as plurality, and is treated as triadic by us 'who see as in a mirror' (ὥσπερ ἐν κατόπτρῳ ὁρῶντες), Damascius evokes the illusory decomposition of the light of the sun into the colours of the rainbow (*PP* iii, 142).

At least one thing seems certain, that with what our mind understands as triads we have entered the sphere of Being—we have left transcendence. Before, even the One—'the cause of all essence, but not yet essence itself'—[83] was beyond (τὸ πάντων ἐπέκεινα). In one passage Damascius describes the ἕν and ὄν (the one and being) as ἀμφιπρόσωπον (ambi-faced), suggesting to the imagination a Janus figure guarding the door of transcendence. The ennead seems to be facing us and constitutes for Damascius a 'periphrastic' way of referring to the noetic or intelligible triad (*PP* iii, 141), which he views from various angles: in specific Chaldaean terms its three principles are the Father, the Power, and the Paternal Intellect (*PP* iii, 137; ii, 102), but also being, life and knowledge (*PP* ii, 173; iii, 127), or existence, power, and action (*PP* ii, 71). In its mythological aspect (which is no less Chaldaean) the primordial triad can be identified with Cronus (or some Oriental counterpart), Rhea, and Zeus, the demiurgic principle *par excellence*, who then proceeds to emanate unending series of beings in a twofold fashion, homonymously and heteronymously (*PP* iii, 31), giving rise in this way to the variety of creation, but at the same time preserving its essential unity in a cosmic order in which, as Damascius specifically states, 'it is not easy to distinguish the emanating principle from the emanation'—the vehicling from the vehicle (*PP* ii, 93; iii, 126). And of course the Pythagorean and Platonic notions of the monad, the dyad and the triad/united (*PP* iii, 115) or the limit, the limitless and the mixed (πέρας, ἀπειρία, and μικτὸν) (*PP* iii, 137) fit the Chaldaean triad perfectly.

Finally Damascius uses a simple geometric figure in order to convey the character of the triad and its function: 'we divide the intelligible triad into three' (*PP* iii, 153) and make its parts run horizontally and vertically; thus producing (*a*) a paternal triad, (*b*) a dynamic triad, and (*c*) an intellectual triad, each comprising in itself father, power, and intellect (*PP* iii, 145). An even more helpful model is that of 'an immaterial circle', with the One as its centre, the dyad as its radius, and the intellect as its circumference hurrying back to the One (*PP* iii, 135–6); indeed, this is a

---

[83] Αἴτιον μὲν πάσης οὐσίας, οὔπω δὲ οὐσία (*PP* iii, 153).

170 P. Athanassiadi

model which conveys as accurately as possible the monistic character of Chaldaean theology where, in Damascius' words, the second and the third principles are constantly swallowed by the peak of being (*PP* III, 147).

Dominated by the basic Neoplatonic scheme of manence—procession—return, Damascius tries to find ways of conveying it in Chaldaean terms; he thus states that 'the knowledge of the νοῦς returns to being through life' ((ἡ γνῶσις τοῦ νοῦ διὰ ζωῆς ἐπιστρέφεσθαι πέφυκε πρὸς οὐσίαν, *PP* II, 101), and repeats that the qualities of the second and the third principle of the Chaldaean triad are contained in the first, though not vice-versa (*PP* II, 88).

His insistence on what he sees as the Oracles' emphasis on the destruction of the triadic character of being rather than on its affirmation is for Damascius the surest means of bolstering Platonic monism, dislocated by the analysis of so many generations of interpreters.

For in all worlds shines the triad whose ruler is the monad. (fr. 27)

Emphasis on unity, concentration on 'the simply one' (ἁπλῶς ἕν), is the way in which one should grasp that which is 'unarithmetic, untriadic, un-oned' (ἀνάριθμον, ἀτρίαστον, ἀμονάδιστον). We should realize when discussing the Oracles that the principles 'are neither one nor three nor even three in one'. It is only we who, in our human way of comprehending 'the realities which lie beyond all intellect, life and essence, use these names' (*PP* III, 140). Does this sentence contain an attack on Christian trinitarian theology and, by the way, a criticism of the literal way in which Proclus understands the Oracles by someone who thought that classification was just a convention and not a metaphysical entity?[84] It is not possible to tell.

Damascius' main concern as commentator of the Oracles is to preach rather than prove that even in the material world the overpowering tendency is monistic (*Parm.* 87), or rather unitive. Whether this interpretation was prompted by his contact with late Zoroastrianism, with which Damascius clearly became acquainted as a guest of Khusrau Anushirwan in Ctesiphon, is again impossible to tell.[85] But the

[84] See e.g. III, 92 (ἐτολμήσαμεν κατηγορῆσαι τοῦ νοητοῦ τὴν τριχῇ διαίρεσιν), a passage where Damascius declares our reasoning faculty to be a result of the fall. God's μονότης is inaccessible to the human intellect and can only be apprehended through the mystic experience: μὴ ἐπὶ δακτύλων ἀριθμῶμεν τὸ νοητόν, μηδὲ διωρισμέναις ἐννοίαις αὐτοῦ ἁπτώμεθα, ἀλλὰ πάντα συνελόντες ὁμοῦ νοήματα, καὶ μύσαντες, τὸ ἓν καὶ μέγιστον ὄμμα ἀνοίξαντες τῆς ψυχῆς, ᾧ καθορᾶται διακρινόμενον οὐδέν (. . .) ἐκεῖσε βλέποντες, εἰ καὶ πόρρωθεν καὶ οἷον ἀπὸ τῶν ἐσχάτων, ὅμως ὀψώμεθα τὸ νοητόν, ὅτι δή ἐστι πάντῃ ἀδιάκριτον. (*PP* III, 136).
[85] Khusrau was interested in philosophy (Agathias II, 28–31), and must have had many

passionate insistence with which he denies plurality even as a methodological device has a clear polemic intent and is probably aimed at targets closer at home: 'the idiom of numbers', he thunders on one occasion, 'is but a symbolic way of referring to realities which are unarithmetic and absolutely unqualifiable' (*PP* III, 135). Again, he bursts out on the subject of the Oracles probably against his students:

let us not attempt to count the intelligible on our fingers or grasp it by means of definitions, but, by seizing all concepts together and closing our eyes, let us open the one great eye of the soul which sees nothing as distinct (. . .) Seeing through this eye, even though from afar and as if from the very extremities, we will nevertheless perceive the intelligible and see that it is absolutely undifferentiated and unarithmetic. And yet, though this is how it is, it will also appear to us, if one may say so, as simplicity, plurality and totality, for the intelligible is one, many and all, to put in a triple way its single nature. (*PP* III, 136)

He could not have been more explicit.

Whether arithmetically, ontologically, existentially, mythologically, or schematically defined, the triad defies definition, and the very multiplicity of its manifestations is a sign of its ungraspability. It is within the confines of this metaphysical logic that we should try and place the various triadic entities of the Chaldaean system, for which Psellus, following Proclus, claimed a spatial allocation. Damascius by contrast claims as their territory a distorted, non-Euclidean space. And while doing this he warns us again that we define not according to truth (κατ' ἀλήθειαν, *PP* III, 123), but by analogy (κατ' ἀναλογίαν), since our organ of perception is 'something far dimmer than even the logical and human soul' (*PP* III, 121).[86]

Iynges, Connectors, Teletarchs

It is in a passage of rare polemical violence against Proclus (and Syrianus) that Damascius first defines the *origin* of the Chaldaean theoretical discussions with Damascius and his colleagues during the latter's stay at his court; as becomes apparent from a work addressed to him by Priscianus (surviving only in a Latin translation) under the revealing title *Answers to the questions asked by Chosroes, King of the Persians, CAG,* Suppl. 1 part 2 (I. Bywater) 1886, Khusrau held discussions with his guests on the nature of the soul, its relation to the body and fate after death, on dreams and visions, and on important subjects of geography and anthropology. On Khusrau's intellectual curiosity, see A. Christensen, *L'Iran sous les Sassanides* (Copenhagen, 1944), 2nd edn., 427–31, and more recently, N. Garsoian, 'Byzantium and the Sassanians', *Cambridge History of Iran,* 3 (1) (Cambridge, 1983), 577; J. Duchesne-Guillemin 'Zoroastrian Religion', ibid. 895. On Khusrau's more general interest in Greek philosophy, E. Zeller and R. Mondolfo, *La filosofia dei Greci nel suo sviluppo storico VI: Giamblico e la Scuola di Atene* (Florence, 1961), no. 111 (pp. 227–8).

[86] Cp. *PP* III, 57: πάντα εἰδητικὰ νοοῦμεν, ἴσως δὲ καὶ ψυχικά.

diacosmic triads, the iynges, the maintainers, and the teletarchs. These triadic powers, which operate throughout the worlds,[87] are produced by the Paternal Intellect in its undivided capacity as a henad (*PP* III, 110–11). And while each one is in itself divided into father, power, and intellect, they also enjoy their own peculiar nature as triads of the intermediary (intelligent) world: the iynges have a paternal character, the maintainers a potential or dynamic one and the teletarchs an intellectual nature (*PP* III, 145). Let us now consider these entities one by one.

The extreme ambiguity and elusiveness which is proper to the Chaldaean system naturally extends to the 'thoughts of the Father' or iynges.[88] Identified with the Platonic Ideas, and therefore seen as monads (*PP* III, 118), the iynges are also purveyors of unity in their character of magical instruments.[89] In its schematic representation, an iynx is a cone which begins in unity and becomes plurality through a vertiginous multiplication of itself. By producing a multitude of offspring and then seizing them all and swallowing them up in an act of true synthesis, the iynx suggests to Damascius the giddy movement of the soul's ascent towards the divine; 'this is why it is said that it snatches the souls upwards' (*Parm.* 95), a process which, as Damascius is at pains to remind us, owes nothing to magical means: for 'it is clear', he remarks in his *In Phaedonem*, 'that the man who follows the way of initiation in a foolish manner will not reap its fruits' (1, 168).

Μία γὰρ ἡ νοητὴ συνέχεια πάντων τῶν τοιούτων: 'the intelligible coherence of all these things is one' (*PP* II, 36, 13, cf. *Parm.* 60) is the sentence with which Damascius punctuates his discussion of the Oracles' theology. And it is within this logic of extendable unity between Man and the Beyond that we should contemplate the function of the maintainers (or connectors). As their name indicates, they are creators of cohesion (*Parm.* 44). They are also described as holopoioi (unifiers or synthesizers)[90] of the intellectual worlds and guardians of the unity of the cosmos;[91] they have, so to speak, a normalizing role in the cosmic economy and so do the teletarchs, or perfectors, who are envisaged by Damascius as initiators or even guides at all stages of the soul's striving towards spiritual union (fr. 85).

In their unending emanational capacity, the iynges, the maintainers,

---

[87] Cp. *Parm.* 59–60 with frs. 76, 80, 81, 82, 83.

[88] Fr. 76: the iynges are many; cf. *Parm.* 88. For Proclus' use of an iynx for magical purposes, see above, n. 62.

[89] Characterized in *Parm.* 98 as συναγωγοί.

[90] Fr. 83 and *Parm.* 43.

[91] *PP* III, 145; *Parm.* 125 and fr. 82.

and the teletarchs are understood by Damascius to be the totally benign powers present in all worlds—the empyrian, the aetherial, the material (*Parm.* 59, 87). Whether as rays of the visible sun (that is as material maintainers (fr. 80)) or as metaphysical paradigms (that is as intelligible iynges), they personify grace at all levels of existence. For grace, which is implicit in the act of emanation,[92] is a universal force for the Platonist, pre-eternally present in the world, working for salvation independently of any individual action or even existence. It is everybody's inalienable possession, which cannot be lost or snatched away, though it may lie unused by the individual who has fallen asleep.

The Dispensation of Grace

Mental sleep however—'the only Neoplatonist hell'[93]—is a very real danger, because unity is not the most obvious characteristic of the world when we contemplate it from the standpoint of sense-perception. The reason for this, as the oracle states, is that

an intellectual girdling membrane separates (fr.6)

the material world from the spheres above (*Parm.* 131). This is the so-called ὑπεζωκώς. Life on the other hand is a triadic unity, where, depending on individual circumstances, the intelligent, the logical, or the illogical factor may prevail (*Parm.* 157). The iynges, the maintainers, and the teletarchs cannot operate in favour of the individual who has fallen asleep and does not even suspect in his terrestrial hell that he is potentially one with an eternal, undifferentiated whole. Another benign power however—the triad of the inexorables—is there to help. Working either individually or collectively, the inexorables mend the severance caused by the ὑπεζωκώς—the girdling membrane—in the fabric of unity (*Parm.* 131–2). Like the three magical fathers, who oversee sensible creation (*Parm.* 204), the inexorables are 'mediators between the Father and matter' (*Parm.* 201), which is far from being described by Damascius as a positively evil power.

It is within the logic of mediation that this austerely monistic system—at least as Damascius understands it—finds a place for the main saviour-gods of later antiquity. Attis, Adonis, Sabazius, and Dionysus (all of them mortals who gained divinity through love and suffering, and achieved unity for having known fragmentation and even

---

[92] Cp. fr. 82 and *Parm.* 125.

[93] J. Trouillard, 'Procession néoplatonicienne et création judéo-chrétienne', *Les Cahiers de Fontenay*, March 1981 (Mélanges Trouillard), 13.

dismemberment) hold key positions in the theology of the Oracles, and their functions harmonize an astrological understanding of the cosmos with the requirements of a world-view solidly based on the workings of Providence (*Parm.* 44, 214).

Uninterested in the astrological dimension of the Oracles (at least if we are to judge by what survives of his work), uninterested even in the soteriological role of the theurgists, Damascius is the *philosophical* exegete of Chaldaean grace. More than any other theme, what governs his interpretation of the Oracles is a passionate insistence on the axiom of return. Indeed, whenever a reference to creation is made, his over-whelming emphasis is on the final absorption of the created by the emanating first principle. Thus Zeus, the creator *par excellence*, returns perpetually through Rhea to Cronos, who is the creator in an absolute sense

arranging matter not by action but with his mind[94]

within a cosmic order in which the real coincides with the potential, where the word or even the thought coincides with the deed.[95] In his purely Chaldaean hypostasis as Twice Beyond (Δὶς Ἐπέκεινα) or Adad, Zeus hastens back to the Once Beyond (Ἅπαξ Ἐπέκεινα) or Ad, through the ministrations of All-luminous Hekate (ἀμφιφαὴς Ἑκάτη).[96] Finally, as creative intellect, Zeus becomes absorbed by the pure intellect by means of the life-giving intellect, the ζωογόνος νοῦς (*PP* III, 118).

Thus it is by means of both a philosophical and a mythological language that Damascius explains the great mystery of return as preached by the Oracles: to be saved one must first be incarnated; then Rhea (identified with life) will provide the path of return. It is indeed Rhea in her manifestation as Nature[97] 'who sets before us as unity the dual life, the mundane and the supramundane' (*Parm.* 215). This elliptic sentence, which qualifies the Chaldaean axiom that differentiation begins at the level of life (*PP* III, 126, cf. 43), contains two separate propositions: first, that from the point of view of the living everything is simultaneously enacted on two levels—the mundane and the supra-mundane—corresponding to two ways of being—that of 'the individual

---

[94] *Parm.* 214 (cf. 133), surely a Chaldaean Oracle in extended prose form, repeated again in *Parm.* 284; note the resemblance with fr. 5.

[95] Two oracles (frs. 22 and 25) preserved by Proclus make this explicit. See also Proclus, *Parm.* 895, 6–7: from the point of view of the paternal intellect τὰ ὄντα νοήσεις εἰσὶ καὶ αἱ νοήσεις τὰ ὄντα.

[96] *Parm.* 152, cf. 154, 15 ff.

[97] *Parm.* 157: on Rhea: αὕτη δέ ἐστιν ἡ φύσις.

and perishable man' (ὁ ἄτομος καὶ φθαρτός), who is aware only of the divisible or Titanic world, and 'the archetypal and perennial man' (ὁ κοινὸς καὶ ἀίδιος ἄνθρωπος), who is the paradigm of the species and as such forms the goal of all existence (*Parm.* 203).[98] The second proposition is that Rhea-Nature is a guide and initiator who reveals the unity of the two worlds and makes it possible for man to cross the border which separates his Titanic from his divine condition. Unlike Proclus, who identifies Nature with Fate and urges us to avert our gaze from it,[99] Damascius takes a positive view of its role as a cosmic manifestation. Indeed, as a great traveller in search of the sacred, he can appreciate both its beauty and its moralizing power,[100] seeing Nature as a reminder of return rather than an instigator of perdition.

6. THE COMPARISON WITH PROCLUS

Even a superficial comparison between Proclus and Damascius as adepts and exegetes of Chaldaean mysticism reveals salient differences in the approach of the two men. Proclus comes across as a more literal reader of the Oracles, indeed as one who has a Euclidean conception of theological space; at the same time he also appears as one with a warmer, more psychic understanding of the Chaldaean methodology of ascent, which he presents in a practical—if forbidding[101]—way.

Unlike Damascius and his mentor Isidore, Proclus was a firm believer in religious practice, conceived as both a cultic routine and an ethical code.[102] He taught that for the committed adept there would at some point shine the trinity of Chaldaean virtues correspondingly emanating from the triple hypostasis of the noetic gods: faith from goodness, truth from wisdom, love from beauty.[103] The crucial—and highest—virtue is faith and it is on faith alone that any hope of salvation

---

[98] Again this dichotomy of man into an ephemeral and an eternal being, which sounds like a commentary on Plato *Tim.* 27d, surely comes from an oracle which cannot be reproduced in its poetic form.

[99] See fr. 102 with the Proclean commentary, *PT* v, 119. Even as a creation of the demiurge, Nature holds third rank, as προελθοῦσα μόνον, unlike higher types of creation which remain wholly or partly unmanifested: *In Tim.* I, 12.

[100] See *JHS* 113, 5–6; on the sanctity of Nature, see Damascius' *In Phaed.* I, 499.

[101] Those among his pupils who found his rules forbidding were many: cp. the horror of Isidore when he was ordered by Proclus to wear a coarse cloak (Damascius, *PH* fr. 59B). Others, like the Antiochene Hilarius, could not even begin to follow Proclus' injunctions: *PH* fr. 91AB.

[102] See e.g. *In Tim.* I, 212, 15 ff.; *In Tim.* II, 312; *In Remp.* II, 99; fr. 135 (*In Alc.* 40); *In Remp.* I, 110–11.

[103] For this and what follows, *PT* I, 100–13 and *In Alc.* 51–67.

should be founded. 'Superior to the cognitive faculty',[104] the Proclean faith, which takes its flight on the twin wings of truth and love, feeds on complete freedom from doubt and thus leads one to 'the secure haven' beyond. Surprisingly, for this Platonist the name of *unio mystica* is faith, not love. Another key is ritual observance: while salvation can be gained through the ardour of love or the rigours of philosophy, it is theurgy alone that provides the perfect way, surpassing as it does all human wisdom and science since it comprises in itself the benefits of divination and the purifying powers of initiation along with all the effects of divine possession.[105] It is only once one has embarked, under the action of blind faith, on the journey of ascent—a journey that Proclus conceives and describes in concrete objective, indeed magical, terms[106]—that 'wisdom begins to ache for the intelligible' and beauty emits 'a fore-radiance of the divine light' which is about to reveal itself (*PT* I, 108, 20 ff.). However, as the virtue corresponding to the good, Chaldaean faith (towards which the devotee must train himself by starving the demands of both the senses and the mind) is a cosmic entity and as such it can be sympathetically enhanced by the theurgist's concurring love.

It must be no coincidence that all the Chaldaean fragments on love, either as a benign universal principle or an asphyxiating human concern, have entered our collection through Proclus.[107] He warns us in his usual didactic style against the effects of wanton love,[108] but also provides a full analysis based on the Oracles' theology of the diverse nature and universal function of Eros as a transcendent, existential, and illuminating force[109] which binds together the elements whether in their physical or metaphysical aspect. It is within this cosmic logic of unity and union through love that Proclus proclaims his optimistic message that the theurgist's ascending practice brings salvation to humanity at large: at that moment 'imitating his own god by whom he is possessed, the divine lover breaks away and leads upwards the well-born, perfects the imper-

---

104 Τὸ γὰρ τοιοῦτον τῆς πίστεως γένος πρεσβύτερόν ἐστι τῆς γνωστικῆς ἐνεργείας: *PT* I, 110.

105 A close paraphrase of *PT* I, 25 (p. 113, 4 ff.)

106 *In Crat.* 31: the gods put their own secret symbols within what they produce; these symbols are ἄρρητα, ἄγνωστα καὶ τὸ δραστήριον αὐτῶν καὶ κινητικὸν ὑπεραίρει πᾶσαν νόησιν. Cp. *In Tim.* I, 211, 8–28; 212, 19–25; *In Remp.* II, 99 and esp. *In Parm.* 990, 27–911, 1 for trespassers.

107 It is safe to assume that fr. 44 which has been transmitted by Lydus owes its ultimate provenance to Proclus.

108 *In Remp.* I, 176 for the Chaldaean πνιγμὸν ἔρωτος ἀληθοῦς referring to human love; other expressions denoting sexual love are ψευδώνυμος and ὁ ἕτερος, to be found in *In Alc.* 50, 23 and 53, 12 respectively.

109 For the distinction, *In Alc.* 64–5 and *In Tim.* II, 54.

fect, and provides success to those in need of salvation' (*In Alc.* 53, 9–12). In other words in his sweeping ascent towards the realm of 'singing light' the theurgist bolsters the struggle of everyone who strives consciously or unconsciously towards union.

Damascius too has a trinity of virtues drawn from the Chaldaean Oracles, which is certainly sterner than Proclus' purifying and uplifting triad of faith, truth, and love, and at the same time indicative of his priorities: virtue, wisdom, and thought-engendering truth (ἀρετή, σοφία καὶ πολύφρων ἀτρέκεια, *Parm.* 45) replace in his understanding of Chaldaean soteriology the fervour of faith and love.

All along Damascius conveys a picture of Chaldaean theory and practice from the cosmic rather than the human point of view, the objective rather than the subjective, and this may be the reason why there is so little on any form of practice. There are no descriptions in his two treatises of the gradual extinction of the personality in its flight towards the One. The human perspective is absent even as a point of departure and what we have instead is a highly cerebral, impersonal account of noetic realities in didactic form. Thus the mystic union is described in terms of a negative gnosiology: ἡ γνῶσις ἀναχεῖται εἰς ἀγνωσίαν (*PP* 1, 84). This of course may be a true reflection of the style of the Oracles themselves, rather than a comment on Damascius, a consideration which ushers in a final crucial question: what is the relation of the Chaldaean Oracles with contemporary literature?

7. A THEOLOGICAL *KOINE*: THE LANGUAGE OF REVELATION

In the Chaldaean Oracles the gods speak directly, describing the structure of the universe, alluding to what lies beyond, and handing down to mankind a set of moral injunctions and ritual rules. The style is authoritative and the theological language apophatic, yet what lends the Chaldaean message such an austere tone and at the same time sets it apart from other holy books of later antiquity is the lack of a central myth. No allegorical interpretation based either on a charter myth or on a historical narrative is to be detected anywhere in the surviving fragments and this is what makes this collection appear so different from the Orphic hymns with which the Oracles were constantly compared and combined by their adepts.[110]

The Orphic hymns however were merely the compositions of the

---

[110] Characteristically the teacher of Proclus, Syrianus, had written a treatise in ten books on the Agreement of Orpheus, Pythagoras, and Plato with the Chaldaean Oracles: Suda s.v.

theologoi, that is the work of men; they were not the words of the *theoi* themselves. Indeed what the tone and content of the Chaldaean revelation brings to mind is the poem of Parmenides whose genesis may have been marked by the same circumstances as that of the Oracles if we are prepared to consider the bold suggestion of Martin West.[111] The only other contemporary literary products with which the Chaldaean Oracles can be compared are late antique oracles proper, indeed those oracles which A. D. Nock qualified as 'theological' in a brief but important article of 1928.[112] The metre, the language, the tone, the style, the ideas, and above all the negative theology are extraordinarily similar.

In the last decade or so epigraphists and historians have joined forces in researching one of the most intriguing phenomena of late antique intellectual history, that of the revival of oracles in the second and third centuries. A study of the surviving oracular literature from that period reveals two main concerns: the proclamation of an unambiguous monotheism and the reform of cult to match a more spiritual conception of the divine. What the oracles do in fact is to provide supernatural authority for the philosophical *koine* of the age and the cultic practices dictated by it.[113]

If monotheism was the universal religious idiom of the men of late antiquity, revelation was increasingly becoming the prominent methodology of communicating it.[114] As in the Hermetic treatises the truth is revealed by the gods; then it is incumbent on men to assemble the dispersed tokens of revealed wisdom into a corpus, study it, comment upon and propagate it. The Chaldaean Oracles were already a corpus, divinely assembled and communicated to humanity as a complete sacred text. Another such collection, heavily based on Didymean material, was produced, probably at the end of the third century, by Porphyry.[115] His *Philosophy from the Oracles* has its counterpart in the work of another contemporary Roman Platonist, Cornelius Labeo, who collected, and doubtless interpreted, revelations of the Clarian Apollo.[116] Until recently such collections were considered by scholars to be literary

[111] *Early Greek Philosophy and the Orient* (Oxford, 1971), 221–6.

[112] 'Oracles théologiques', *REA* 30 (1928), 280–90 [= *Essays* i. 160–8].

[113] See my articles 'The Fate of Oracles in Late Antiquity: Didyma and Delphi', *DChrAE* 15 (1989–90), 271–8 and 'Philosophers and Oracles: Shifts of Authority in Late Paganism', *Byzantion* 62 (1992), 45–62.

[114] Obviously commentary and interpretation remained the more common—if secondary—way of disclosing paganism's monotheistic core.

[115] For the late date, see *JRS* 71 (1981), 180.

[116] On the date of Cornelius Labeo, see *JRS* 71 (1981), 180.

forgeries, but, as more stones inscribed with oracles turn up in the cities of Greece and Asia Minor, this view is being amended and we can at last look at them in the way in which they were considered by their contemporaries. But the crucial difference between the Chaldaean and the Apollinian revelation to the men of late antiquity resided with the fact that the former had been (or was believed to be) handed down as a perfect corpus.

Volumes made up of authentic oracles and stressing the unity of the new transcendental theology clearly helped its propagation. It is even possible that, in producing their collections, men like Porphyry and Labeo did not act wholly spontaneously, but responded to invitations to conduct research in the archives of the oracles and to help proclaim that God is One by producing a publication which would both codify and spread the new theology. As their subsequent history and frequent quotation show, these collections enjoyed widespread circulation and were eagerly plundered by Christians to whom they suggested the ingenious idea that they could be used, with the necessary adjustments, to prove that the Greek gods had foretold the birth of Christ and the triumph of Christian trinitarian theology.

A case in point is provided by the *Tübingen Theosophy*, so-called from the codex which transmitted it, which formed under the title *Oracles of the Greek Gods* the eighth book of a larger composition called *Theosophia*.[117] The eleven books of the *Theosophia*, now largely lost, attempted to prove the superiority of Christianity over all other theologies, Greek and Oriental. Very akin in spirit to works like the *Ammonius* by Zacharias of Mytilene and the *Theophrastus* by Aeneas of Gaza, the *Theosophia* is known to have been composed during Zeno's reign, and comes across as a typical product of the intellectual climate of Alexandria in the 480s, mirroring the philosophical quarrels between pagans and Christians in Horapollo's school, so vividly portrayed in Zacharias of Mytilene's *Life of Severus* and in Damascius' *Philosophical History*, quarrels which resulted in the great pagan persecution of 488/9 and in Damascius' eventual flight from Alexandria.[118]

According to chapter 13 of the *Theosophia Tubingensis*, to the rather irreverent question of a certain Theophilus 'are *you*, or another, God?', Apollo at Claros answered as follows:

[117] The fragments are now re-edited by H. Erbse, *Theosophorum Graecorum Fragmenta*, 2nd edn. (Leipzig, 1995).

[118] For a fuller treatment, see *PH*, Appendix III. Erbse (*op. cit.* pp. xiii–xv) thinks that the author of the *Theosophia* was an educated Christian writing in Alexandria under Zeno and addressing monks and clerics on the utility of Greek literature.

> Born of himself, untaught, motherless, immovable,
> Not contained in a name, many-named, dwelling in fire
> This is God. We angels are but a particle of God.

Carved on an altar-shaped relief on a block of stone in the city wall of Oenoanda, between Lycia and Phrygia, this oracle has also come down to us in several versions through various literary channels, pagan and Christian.[119] But what interests us here is that in his *Chaldaean Oracles and Theurgy*, Hans Lewy identifies it along with another three *Theosophia* oracles (nos. 21, 27, 35) as Chaldaean.[120] As E. R. Dodds immediately pointed out, he was wrong in his identification,[121] but only as regards the letter, not the spirit of this literature. Indeed this is where the lasting achievement of Lewy's book lies: even if he did not formulate it in the right scholastic terms, he recognized the unity of late antique revelatory literature and understood the contemporary procedures which tended towards the formulation of a dogma based on the orthodox interpretation of a canon of sacred texts. The angels of whom the oracle speaks, and among whom Apollo counts himself, also belong to the theological *koine* of the period and it would be idle to attempt to identify them as of Jewish or Gnostic, Chaldaean or Platonic origin.[122] It is only worth pointing out that by this demotion of the old pantheon and its identification with mere angels, philosophic monotheism could accommodate tradition. We possess a number of oracles from this period by which cities and individual priests enquire about the hierarchical position of gods and the honours due to them. The answers are consistent with the new theology: a more spiritualized form of piety than the one associated with blood sacrifices is expected by the prophetic shrines. 'I do not want hecatombs and golden colossi, but sweet songs'[123] proclaims the Didymaean Apollo in the third century, repeating more or less the injunction of Ammon to a delegation from Cyzicus a hundred years earlier.[124]

Rather than in a 'Platonic Underworld', we are in a universal Platonic world, what I would label 'the late antique spiritual Commonwealth', which by the time of Damascius stretches from southern Arabia to the Black Sea coast and from Carthage to Harran. As has been recently

[119] For a list, Lane Fox, *Pagans and Christians*, 171. See the discussion by S. Mitchell in the present volume, pp. 86–92.

[120] Lewy, 8–65.

[121] *HThR* 54 (1961), 265–6.

[122] For such a discussion L. Robert, *CRAI* (1971), 613–14. Cf. *Theos. Tub.* 27–8.

[123] Rehm, *Didyma* II, 217.

[124] R. Merkelbach and E. Schwertheim, *Epigraphica Anatolica*, ii (1983), 147–54.

argued by G. Bowersock,[125] in its sweeping move towards unity and universality, Hellenism delivered the ethnic minorities of the Roman world from their parochialism—cultural, religious, and linguistic. Moreover, by integrating into one pyramidal monotheistic structure their local gods through the complementary processes of syncretism and hierarchization, Hellenism prepared the ground for the reception of another monotheism, Islam, and, I would add, not only in its external, but mainly in its mystical dimension.[126]

This spiritual globalization has its roots in Antonine times. The esoteric teaching of mystery religions, the Magical Papyri, the agonizing questions of men to their gods in private ceremonies or public shrines, and the writings of intellectuals alike make an increasing claim towards uniformity. There is a tendency in all this away from pluralism and relativism, a need for one answer to each question, which already points towards the Middle Ages. The formulation of an orthodoxy based on the correct interpretation of a canon of texts does not merely dominate Christianity; it dominates paganism too. And it is precisely in this connection that the Chaldaean Oracles should be seen as a landmark, both in their capacity as a revelation given in the late second century, and as an increasingly sacred text looming larger than all other revelations and finally obliterating them. In the late fifth century Proclus 'used to say that if it were in his power he would have preserved only the Chaldaean Oracles and the *Timaeus*, destroying all other books' as positively harmful to humanity.[127]

By the sixth century the understanding of the Oracles constituted the ultimate criterion of philosophical proficiency. Asclepiodotus of Alexandria and Aphrodisias, whose original mind still haunts the pages of Simplicius, is described by Damascius in the following terms:

Asclepiodotus' mind was not perfect, as most people thought. He was extremely sharp at raising questions, but not so acute in his understanding. His was an uneven intelligence, especially when it came to divine matters—the invisible and intelligible concept of Plato's lofty thought. Even more wanting was he in the field of higher wisdom—the Orphic and Chaldaean lore which transcends philosophical common sense (τὸν κοινὸν φιλοσοφίας νοῦν).[128]

---

[125] *Hellenism in Late Antiquity* (Ann Arbor, 1990), together with my review *JRS* 82 (1992), 286–7.
[126] See now in this respect, P. Kingsley, *Ancient Philosophy, Mystery, and Magic* (Oxford, 1995), *passim*, and esp. 371–91, 'From Empedocles to the Sufis: "The Pythagorean Leaven"'.
[127] Marinus, *VP* 38.
[128] *PH* fr. 85A.

The last thing to command respect in the religious world of late antiquity was 'philosophical common sense'. What was needed instead was a full awareness of the intuitive qualities with which God has endowed us: in the terms of a Chaldaean Oracle preserved by Proclus' spiritual grandson, John Lydus:

> Having mixed the spark of the soul with two concordant elements,
> Intellect and divine will, he added a third—pure love—
> As the bond of all things and holy guide.[129]

On its way to becoming the *Ancilla Theologiae*, Philosophy launched into the new world the crucial trinity: human understanding and divine grace bound together by love.

SELECT BIBLIOGRAPHY

Primary Sources

DAMASCIUS, *De primis principiis*, I–III, ed. L. G. Westerink, trans. J. Combès (Paris, 1986–91).

—— *De primis principiis*, trans. M.-C. Galpérine (Lagrasse, 1987).

—— *In Parmenidem*, ed. C. A. Ruelle (Paris, 1889) (all references to this edition).

—— *In Parmenidem*, I, II, ed. L. G. Westerink, trans. J. Combès (Paris, 1997).

—— *In Phaedonem*, I–II, ed. and trans. L. G. Westerink (Amsterdam, 1977).

—— *In Philebum*, ed. and trans. L. G. Westerink (Amsterdam, 1959).

—— *The Philosophical History*, ed. and trans. P. Athanassiadi (Athens, 1999).

MARINUS, *Vita di Proclo*, ed. R. Masullo (Naples, 1985).

ORACULA CHALDAICA, ed. and trans. E. des Places (Paris, 1971).

PLETHO, Μαγικὰ λόγια τῶν ἀπὸ Ζωροάστρου μάγων. Γεωργίου Γεμιστοῦ Πλήθωνος Ἐξήγησις εἰς τὰ αὐτὰ λόγια, ed. and trans. B. Tambrun-Krasker (Athens, 1995).

PROCLUS, *Hymni*, ed. E. Vogt (Wiesbaden, 1957).

—— *In Alcibiadem*, ed. L. G. Westerink (Amsterdam, 1954).

—— *In Cratylum*, ed. G. Pasquali (Leipzig, 1908).

—— *In Parmenidem*, ed. V. Cousin (Paris, 1864).

—— *In Rempublicam*, I–II, ed. W. Kroll (Leipzig, 1899–1901).

—— *In Timaeum*, I–III, ed. E. Diehl (Leipzig, 1903–6).

—— *Theologia Platonica*, I–VI ed. and trans. H. D. Saffrey and L. G. Westerink (Paris, 1968–97).

PSELLUS, *Philosophica Minora* II, ed. D. O'Meara (Leipzig, 1989).

---

[129] Fr. 44 preserved in *Mens.* III.

Secondary works

ATHANASSIADI, P., 'Persecution and Response in Late Paganism: The Evidence of Damascius', *JHS* 113 (1993), 1–29.

KROLL, W., *De oraculis chaldaicis* (Breslau, 1894).

LEWY, H., *Chaldaean Oracles and Theurgy* (ed. M. Tardieu), 2nd edn. (Paris, 1978).

MAJERCIK, R., *The Chaldean Oracles: Text, Translation and Commentary* (Leiden, 1989).

6

The Significance of the Speech of Praetextatus

WOLF LIEBESCHUETZ

It is agreed that the speech of Praetextatus in the *Saturnalia* of Macrobius, written about AD 430,[1] is one of the principal sources for the last stage of Roman paganism, more precisely for the interpretation of their traditional religion by the last generation of pagan senators. Modern interpretations differ in detail. But on essentials something like consensus has been reached: Praetextatus' speech shows that the paganism of the late fourth-century Roman senatorial aristocracy was approaching monotheism.[2] Praetextatus' view of the gods is much closer to Christianity than the classical paganism we know from the authors of the Latin golden age, in that it involved belief that the world was in fact ruled by a single deity and that the traditional gods were in reality aspects of the one god. Cumont pointed out that the theology of Praetextatus is very close to the pagan position summarized by the sophist Maximus of Madaura in AD 390 in a famous letter to St Augustine:

That the supreme God is one, without beginning, without offspring,[3] as it were the great and august father of nature, what person is there so mad and totally deprived of sense as to wish to deny. His powers (*virtutes*) diffused through the

---

[1] Alan Cameron has dated the work to AD 431, while Praetextatus died in AD 384 (*PLRE* 1. 722 s.v. Vettius Agorius Praetextatus 1). Cameron argues that Macrobius' book, though pagan, was written for a readership that was largely Christian, and that it was certainly not anti-Christian polemic. 'The Date and Identity of Macrobius', *JRS* 56 (1966), 25–38. On the last of these points see below, p. 201.

[2] Some specimens: F. Cumont, 'Praetextatus identifiziert in radicaler Syncrasie alle alten Götter mit der Sonne', *Orientalische Religionen im römischen Heidentum* (1928), 188. W. Fauth, *Helios Megistos, zur synkretistischen Theologie der Spätantike* (Leiden, 1995), 164: solarer Monotheismus mit pantheistischer Tendenz, nach stoischem Vorbild. A. Demandt, *Die Spätantike* (Munich, 1989), 471: 'wenn irgendeine unter den heidnischen Religionen dem Urchristentum nahe stand so war es der Sonnenglauben'.

[3] *Sine prole*: even though Maximus' letter is stressing the common ground, he is insisting, if only by implication, that the divine sonship of Jesus cannot be true in the literal sense.

world that is his work (*mundanum opus*) we invoke under various names, because we are obviously all ignorant of his real name. For the name god is common to all religions. The outcome is that while with our various prayers we each honour as it were his limbs separately, all together we are seen to be worshipping him in his entirety.[4]

That there is some kinship of thought between the letter of Maximus and Macrobius' speech of Praetextatus is evident. But in the context of a discussion on the development of monotheism in the ancient world more precision is needed. Praetextatus does not simply proclaim that all the polytheistic gods are fundamentally aspects of one supreme deity, he also argues that the supreme god, of whom all the others are aspects, is the sun, and he finally qualifies his argument by stating that it only applies to the gods below the heavens, that is to the encosmic gods;[5] indeed he expressly excludes the hypercosmic gods.

The qualification excluding hypercosmic gods is important. In Macrobius' view the earth at the centre of the world is surrounded by the seven spheres of respectively moon, sun, Mercury, Venus, Mars, Jupiter, and Saturn; beyond this the celestial sphere carries the fixed stars. The celestial sphere is the border of the universe of gods and men, beyond it is the realm of primeval unity, the First Cause, the Good, or as some would prefer the supreme God, and of his two successive emanations of Mind and Soul. In respect of their comprehensibility by the human mind the encosmic and hypercosmic zones are quite distinct. About the sub-celestial world, Macrobius tells us, philosophers employ myths and fables, but when they try to assign attributes to super-celestial deities

which not only pass the bounds of speech but that of human comprehension as well, they shun fabulous narratives, and resort to similes and analogies. That is why Plato, when he was moved to speak about the Good, did not dare tell what it was, knowing only that about it, that it was impossible for the human mind to grasp what it was. Of visible objects he found the sun most like it, and using this as an illustration opened a way for a discourse to approach what was otherwise incomprehensible.[6]

So in his speech Praetextatus expressly excludes the ultimate supreme being, and restricts himself to those emanations of the ultimate unity which are active in our universe. More precisely, the speech is about the gods who are worshipped, in terms of the tripartite classification of

---

[4] August. *Ep.* 16.

[5] 1. 17. 2 'dumtaxat qui sub caelo sunt'.

[6] Macrobius, *Commentarium in Somnium Scipionis*, 1. 2. 13–15; translation from W. H. Stahl's *Macrobius: Commentary on the Dream of Scipio* (New York, 1952), 85–6.

Varro the gods of politicians and of poets—and not about the god as visualized or understood by philosophers.[7] He argues that sub-celestial gods too can be shown to express a basic unity inasmuch as they all symbolize aspects of the government of the sub-celestial world by the sun.

Praetextatus does not attempt the obviously impossible task of showing that all gods worshipped in the Roman world represent aspects of the sun, but restricts himself to a selection. This includes some of the great gods of the Graeco-Roman pantheon: Apollo, Ares/Mars, Hermes/Mercury, Minerva/Athena, Aesculapius, Heracles/Hercules, Zeus/Jupiter. It includes eastern gods like the Egyptian Horus and the Jupiter of Baalbek, as well as gods of the Graeco-Roman mystery cults: Isis and Sarapis, and Attis. Of the great gods Poseidon/Neptune, Hera/Juno, Artemis/Diana are omitted,[8] but some minor deities, Pan, Nemesis, Echo, and each of the signs of the Zodiac are included. The list is long and varied, and the precise nature of the relationship of the different divinities to the sun varies too. The major gods might be said to represent different aspects of the sun's effect on the earth and its inhabitants.[9] Of others, like the signs of the Zodiac, Praetextatus argues only that they have something to do with the sun.

THE HISTORY OF SOLAR THEOLOGY

The ideas of Praetextatus' speech have a long history in Graeco-Roman thought. At the first meeting Martin West explained how from the very beginning of philosophy Greek thinkers tried to show that there was a single ruling principle of one kind or another behind the infinite variety of the world as we know it, and that this was thought to take the form of a divine substance somehow permeating all objects.[10] Subsequent Greek thinkers too tried to 'save' the gods by identifying them with conspicuous parts of the material world, e.g. the earth, the sea, the sky, the stars. The Stoics are probably the most famous group of thinkers to

[7] Augustine, *De Civ. Dei.* 6. 5–7.

[8] The sphere of responsibility of Poseidon/Neptune is the sea, of Diana/Artemis the moon. The stoics gave the air as the realm to Hera/Juno (Cicero, *De Nat. Deor.* 2. 66). None of the three could have been plausibly identified with the sun.

[9] The different gods represent different *effectus* or *virtutes* of the sun, as is explained: 'Sicut Maro, cum de una Iuno diceret *quo numine laeso*, ostendit unius dei effectus varios pro variis censendos esse numinibus, ita diversae virtutes solis nomina dis dederunt' (1. 17. 4). So also Maximus in the cited letter to Augustine (*Ep.* 16): 'huius nos *virtutes* per mundanum opus diffusas multis vocabulis invocamus.'

[10] See also G. S. Kirk and J. E. Raven, *The Presocratic Philosophers* (Cambridge, 1969), 178.

identify the various traditional gods with different components of a world which they thought was divine as a whole.[11]

No part of the visible world has a greater or more manifest influence on human life than the sun. In a very famous passage of the *Republic* Plato used the sun as an image of the Good.[12] Under the influence of Plato, it was widely agreed—the Epicureans being the principal dissenters—that the stars and the sun were divine.[13] Subsequently men's attention was drawn to the possible influence of the stars on human life, and astrology came to be widely accepted as what we would call a scientific technique for reading the future, and its experts were consulted by men and women of all classes.[14] But if the stars were divine beings, it was evident that the sun was a supreme divinity; for it was the sun that seemed to govern the motions of the other stars, as well as to have a fundamental and continuous influence on everything that happened on earth. It was therefore only logical to consider that the sun must be found a place among the leading gods—if indeed it was not the leading god itself.[15] This train of thought found another practical application in magic. Magical techniques of one kind or another were employed as widely in ancient society as astrology, and among the spirits invoked by the spells of learned magicians the sun god was considered pre-eminent in power and effectiveness.[16]

The view that the sun was a powerful if not the most powerful deity, supported as it was by philosophical theory and the practical 'sciences' of astrology and magic, was bound to have an impact on religion. There were numerous cults of the sun celebrated in different parts of the empire. Among them the most widespread, and the one which reflected

[11] e.g. Cic. *De Nat. Deor.* 2. 24–8 (62–72).

[12] *Rep.* 6. 508–9, 7. 516–17 (the allegory of the cave).

[13] A. Scott, *Origen and the Life of the Stars, a History of an Idea* (Oxford, 1991). Most recently, packed with references to texts, but also with the sentence structure of an encyclopedia article, W. Fauth, *Helios Megistos, zur synkretistischen Theologie der Spätantike* (Leiden, 1995). F. Cumont, 'Le Mysticisme astral dans l'antiquité', *Bull. Acad. Roy. de Belgique (Classe de lettres)* 5 (1919), 256 ff. A.-J. Festugière, *La Révélation d'Hermès Trismégiste*, ii. *Le Dieu cosmique* (Paris, 1949), esp. 196–218 on the *Epinomis*.

[14] A vast bibliography; *honoris causa*: A.-J. Festugière, *La Révélation d'Hermès Trismégiste*, ii. *L'Astrologie et les sciences occultes* (Paris, 1950).

[15] So Cicero, *Somn. Scip.* 4: 'Sol dux et princeps et moderator luminum reliquorum, mens mundi et temperatio.' Plin. *NH* 2. 6. 12: 'Sol . . . siderum ipsorum caelique rector; hunc esse mundi totius animam ac planius mentem, hunc principale naturae regimen ac numen credere decet.' The pioneer was F. Cumont, e.g. 'Théologie solaire du paganisme romain', *Mém. Acad. Inscr. et Bell. Lettrs.* 12. 2 (1909), 447 ff.

[16] Abundant evidence of sun god in magic: Fauth, *Helios Megistos*, 34–120. Social role of magic: J. B. Clerc, *Homines Magici, Étude sur la sorcellerie et la magie dans la société romaine impériale* (Bern, Berlin, and Frankfurt, 1995).

most closely the religious trends of the high empire, was the cult of Mithras. Mithras was not originally a sun god, but quite early in the history of the cult the god came to be identified with the sun, and to be known as Sol Invictus Mithras. In the same way Melul, Hellenized as Mandulis, the local god of the little town of Talmis in the extreme south of Egypt, appeared in a vision to a worshipper, and revealed himself as the sun.[17]

In the third century emperors began to put images of Sol on some of their coins. Aurelian established Sol among the gods of the Roman state cult. He built a temple and set up a college of priests, the *pontifices solis*, parallel to the old college of *pontifices*, henceforth known as *pontifices Vestae*. The sun-worship of Aurelian was probably a Romanized version of the cult of the sun-god of Emesa, to whose support Aurelian felt that he owed his victory over Palmyra.[18] Aurelian's promotion of Sol, the god who had given him victory, is comparable to Augustus' promotion of Apollo after Actium. As Augustus honoured Apollo so Aurelian honoured Sol as his own special protector. He certainly did not intend the cult of Sol to replace that of the other gods of the Roman state, nor was he proposing that Sol ought henceforth to be worshipped by all the inhabitants of the empire.[19] Moreover the state cult of Sol remained quite distinct from that of other sun-gods, for instance the ancient Roman cult of Sol Indiges or the private mystery cult of Mithras. In terms of ritual the Sol Invictus of Aurelian and Sol Invictus Mithras were quite separate, even though it was understood that both deities represented the sun, and though both had their festival on 25 December,[20] the day of the winter solstice—Christmas Day.[21]

In a religious atmosphere which inclined men to consider the sun as the most powerful of deities there can be little doubt that many thought that Christianity too was a solar cult, or at least that solar symbolism was not incompatible with it. After all Christ was proclaimed to have risen on

---

[17] A. D. Nock, 'A Vision of Mandulis Aion', *HTR* 27 (1934), 53–104 = *Essays on Religion and the Ancient world* (Oxford, 1972), 357–400. See also Introduction to this volume.

[18] R. Gross s.v. Aurelianus in *RAC* 1. 1006–10; Marbach s.v. Sol, *RE*² 3. 907–13. The *Life of Aurelian* in the *SHA*, certainly full of fiction, may nevertheless contain some fact. The problem is how to distinguish the latter. On Roman festivals of Sol see M. R. Salzmann, *On Roman Time, the Codex-Calendar of 354 and the Rhythms of Roman life in Late Antiquity* (Berkeley, 1990), 149–53.

[19] I know of no evidence at all to support K. Latte, *Römische Religionsgeschichte* (Munich, 1960), 350: 'Er wollte dem Reich an Stelle der alten Götter, die längst die Macht über die Menschen verloren hatten, eine einheitliche Religion geben.'

[20] Julian, *Or.* 4. 156c (*Natalis Invicti*), the *ludi solis* were held from 19 to 22 October.

[21] H. Usener, *Das Weihnachtsfest* (Bonn, 1911).

the day of the sun (Easter Sunday), and Christians attended worship every eight days on Sunday, i.e. the day of the sun, and while worshipping they faced east, that is towards sunrise. When Constantine became a worshipper of Christ, in circumstances not unlike those in which Aurelian had become a worshipper of Sol, and indeed Augustus of Apollo, he seems to have made a distinction between Sol Invictus and the other pagan gods. For while the others disappeared from imperial coinage after Constantine's conversion in 312, Sol remained. Constantine evidently considered that he could continue to use him as at least a symbol of the Supreme Deity, and/or with some ambiguity as a symbol of the role of the emperor in the world.[22] It was probably under his successor Constantius II that the Roman Church decided to celebrate the 25 December as the birthday of Christ.

In the paganism of Julian the Apostate the sun occupied an absolutely central role.[23] Julian was a follower of Neoplatonic philosophy. The Neoplatonists were concerned to show by what stages our infinitely divided material world could be shown to have been derived from a single, undivided, intelligible first principle. Strictly speaking this demonstration did not need the traditional gods at all, but these philosophers, as the Stoics before them, were also very much concerned to provide support for the gods of the traditional religion by including them, and giving them key positions in the succession of abstract and logical entities. They justified this by bestowing on the Chaldaean Oracles and the 'Orphic' poems the authority of divinely inspired books, with a philosophical message for those equipped to read it. The sun did not invariably occupy the place of absolute primacy in the Neoplatonic system.

It did not in the little treatise, 'The Gods and the World', written by one Sallustius.[24] The identity of Sallustius is debated. The two principal candidates were both high officials of Julian, Salutius Secundus, the more likely of the two, also a close friend of the emperor.[25] Gilbert

---

[22] W. Liebeschuetz, *Continuity and Change in Roman Religion* (Oxford, 1979), 282–5.

[23] J. Bidez, *La Vie de l'empereur Julien* (Paris, 1929); P. Athanassiadi, *Julian; an Intellectual Biography* (London, 1992); R. Smith, *Julian's Gods: Religion and Philosophy in the Thought and Action of Julian the Apostate* (London, 1995).

[24] G. Murray, *The Four Stages of Greek Religion* (New York, 1912), 157–84, translation of text: 187–214. A. D. Nock, *Sallustius: Concerning the Gods and the Universe*, ed. with prolegomena and translation (Cambridge, 1926).

[25] Most probably to be identified with Saturnius Secundus Salutius 3, *PLRE* 1. 814–17, PPO Orientis 361–5, 365–67, often, especially in Greek authors, referred to as Sal(l)ustius, to whom Julian dedicated *Or.* iv 'To King Helios'. But *PLRE* 1. 796 lists him as Sallustius 1, and tentatively identifies him with Flavius Sallustius 5, PPO Galliarum 361–3, cons. 363,

Murray described the pamphlet as an authoritative creed or catechism of late Hellenic religion, which could well be taken for an exposition of the philosophical principles behind Julian's religious policy.[26] Sallustius' doctrine is based on the concept of a first cause, eternal, timeless, and above all intelligible and non-material. Sallustius did not define the first cause as a hypercosmic sun, although he did incorporate Julian's version of the Attis myth.[27]

However in the version of Neoplatonism accepted by Julian, which he learnt from writings of the philosopher Iamblichus, the sun was the first cause and starting point of the universe and of everything in it. In Julian's *Hymn to King Helios* 'the sun' is the name of the first hypostasis, or Idea of the Good, then of the Good in the second hypostasis as what confers value on thought (existence, beauty, and the like), then of the Good in the second hypostasis considered as acts instead of objects of thought ('intellectual' instead of 'intelligible'), and finally of the sun in the sky which was 'a visible god'.[28] In private Julian was a worshipper of the sun too.[29] But his prayers and offerings were not dedicated to the 'First Hypostasis', or indeed to 'King Helios', but to two specific solar cults: the public cult of Sol, which had been established by Aurelian,[30] and the private mystery cult of Mithras. At the same time he clearly had the highest veneration for the other mystery cults, above all the cult of Cybele or Magna Mater for whom he wrote his 'Hymn to the Mother of the Gods'. Meanwhile his religious policy was directed to the revival of all the traditional cults.[31]

So the solar theology of Praetextatus' speech stands in a long tradition. Moreover the tradition did not end with it. We have three hymns, or

ibid. 397–8. While the latter's name fits better, there is no evidence that he was an intellectual, or close to Julian personally, as Secundus Salutius certainly was.

[26] The view also of Athanassiadi, *Julian: an Intellectual Biography*, 154–60. The relationship between 'Sallustius' and Julian might reward closer examination.

[27] Attis: Julian, *Or.* 5. *Hymn to Mother of Gods*, 166C–167D, Sallustius, *Concerning the Gods*, 4; discussed in Nock (ed.), li–liii. Perhaps Sallustius had read *Or.* 5, written for March festival of Cybile probably in 362 (Smith *Julian's Gods*, 137), but not *Or.* 4 written for festival of Sol on 25 December, probably of 362 (*Or.* 4. 131D).

[28] Cited from A. C. Lloyd's chapter, 'The Later Neoplatonists', *The Cambridge History of Later Greek and Early Medieval Philosophy* ed. A. H. Armstrong (Cambridge, 1967), 297.

[29] It is likely that Julian's allegiance to the sun goes back ultimately to an obscure Illyrian sun-god who was worshipped by his family—which was of course Constantine's family too (Himerius, *Eccl.* 12. 6, Julian *Or.* 4. 131). If we are to believe the author of *SHA Aurelian* 4, Aurelian's mother too was a priestess of an Illyrian sun-god.

[30] The *Hymn to King Helios* was written for Aurelian's god's festival: see *Or.* 4. 155.

[31] Athanassiadi, *Julian: An Intellectual Biography*, 141–54, 181–91; also 'A Contribution to Mithraic theology: Julian's Hymn to King Helios', *J. Th. S.* 28(1977), 360–71; and now Smith, *Julian's Gods* esp. 169 ff.

hym-like passages, all written in the fifth century in widely different places, which express basically the same ideas, though differing significantly in detail. These are: a 'Hymn to Helios', written by the Neoplatonist philosopher Proclus who lived AD 412–85;[32] a hymn-like passage addressed to Sol, included in the *Marriage of Mercury and Philology* of the North African Martianus Capella, writing perhaps around AD 470/80;[33] and finally an address in hymn form made by the god Dionysus to his divine colleague Heracles Astrochiton of Tyre in the *Dionysiaca* of Nonnus composed around the middle of the fifth century.[34] There is no reason to suppose that the five texts are dependent on each other. The doctrine was generally known.

PRAETEXTATUS' ARGUMENTS

To establish his point that all (or most) subcelestial gods relate to the sun, Praetextatus does not argue from any Neoplatonic or indeed other philosophical theory. His procedure is rather to examine in greater or lesser detail the nomenclature, iconography, ritual, and mythology of each deity, and to discover in them allusions to the sun. On this basis he goes on to argue that the detail of traditional cult and imagery, the etymology of the names by which the individual gods are known, and the myths told about them when interpreted allegorically, all reveal that worshippers have always been aware, whether consciously or unconsciously, of their deities' solar nature.

If the sections of the speech relating to different gods are examined one by one, it will be seen that some are built up of many more arguments than others. The cases are also of very unequal plausibility, in that the basically solar nature of some gods is argued from assumptions which had been more or less widely held for a considerable time, while for others the arguments seem to have been invented by the speaker *ad hoc*. So Praetextatus' case for the proposition that Apollo is a sun-god may well have seemed pretty conclusive. As originally worshipped Apollo of course had nothing to do with the sun, but individuals addressing Apollo as if he was the sun are already found in fifth-century

[32] *Hymni*, ed. E. Vogt (Wiesbaden, 1957).
[33] *Martianus Capella*, ed. J. Willis (Leipzig, 1983); Eng. tr. and introduction W. H. Stahl, R. Johnson, E. L. Burge, *Martianus Capella and the Seven Liberal Arts*, 2 vols. (New York, 1971 and 1977); D. Schanzer, *A Philosophical and Literary Commentary on Martianus Capella's De Nuptiis Philologiae et Mercurii, Book 1* (Berkeley, 1986).
[34] Nonnus, *Dionysiaca* 40. 369–410. Discussion of date: F. Vian (ed.), *Nonnos de Panopolis, Les Dionysiaques*, (Paris, 1976), p. ix.

BC drama.[35] Stoics seem to have favoured the identification,[36] and by the third century AD it was widely accepted.[37] The section dealing with Apollo is much longer than that of any other god. It fills sixty-five subsections of text. Macrobius was not short of evidence.

The second longest section is that arguing the solar nature of Liber/Dionysus. The core of this seems to be Orphic material.[38] In the Orphic cosmogony, dating from the Hellenistic age, Dionysus was identified with the sun, and the identification is assumed in the 'Orphic' hymns of the third century AD.[39] The 'Orphic' hymns make other identifications.[40] Not only is the sun identified with Apollo but also with Zeus (Hymn 15), and Heracles and Pan are each addressed as if they also wielded the powers of both Apollo and Zeus (Hymns 12 and 11). In late antiquity the 'Orphic' poems were credited with inspired status together with the Chaldaean oracles and the works of Homer; and the Orphic theology was built into their philosophic systems by Neoplatonists from Porphyry and Iamblichus onwards.[41] 'Orphic' poetry was closely linked with the mystery cult of Dionysus.[42] The mysteries of Dionysus had probably always been the most widely popular of the mystery cults, and were perhaps also the mystery cult that survived longest. In Italy it continued strongly into the fourth century, when it was attacked by Firmicus Maternus.[43] So it would seem that at least for worshippers of Dionysus/Liber and for many adherents of Neoplatonic philosophy the argument for the identity of Dionysus and the sun would have seemed incontrovertible.

The same is true for the proposed identity of the sun and Zeus/Jupiter. As we have just seen this was assumed in the Orphic hymns. In any case once it was accepted that the sun is the supreme ruler of this world, its identification with Zeus follows naturally. Praetextatus points out that

---

[35] P. Boyancé, 'L'Apollon Solaire', *Mélanges Carcopino* (Paris, 1966), 149–70, citing Aeschylus, *Septem*, 859; *Bassarae*, fr. 83 (Mette = Aeschylus, ed. H. W. Smyth and H. Lloyd Jones, LCL, London, 1971), 386). Euripides, *Phaeton*, fr. 781 Nauck².

[36] e.g. Cicero, *ND* 2.68 and the etymologies of Apollodorus 1046–63 (Jac.).

[37] *Sat.* 1. 17. 7–10. Nock, *Essays on Religion*, 397–8. The identification was accepted by Apollo himself through oracles at both Didyma and Claros (H. W. Parkes, *Oracles of Apollo in Asia Minor* (London, 1985), 98, 162; most recently R. Lane Fox at this seminar).

[38] 1. 18. 8, 12–13, 17–19, 22; ibid. 19–20 refer to an oracle of Claros.

[39] M. L. West, *The Orphic Poems* (Oxford, 1983), 206.

[40] According to West, *Orphic Poems*, 28 the eighty-seven Orphic hymns were composed in Asia Minor in the 3rd cent., probably by a single author.

[41] West, *Orphic Poems*, 227–9; Marinus, *Life of Proclus*, 27; Porphyry, *On Statues* fr. 3.

[42] West, *Orphic Poems*, 24–6; K. Ziegler, s.v. 'Orphische Dichtung', *RE* 18. 2. 1321–33.

[43] *De errore profanarum religionum*, 6. 1–6.

the identification of Zeus with the sun had already been made by
Cornificius, a writer interpreting Homer from a Stoic point of view,
probably in the first century BC, and also by an anonymous commentator on Plato's *Phaedrus* 246e.[44] At a less sophisticated level the Phrygian
villagers, who are the subject of the chapter by Stephen Mitchell, sym-
bolically linked their anonymous unique supreme god with both Zeus
and the sun. Macrobius further strengthens the identification of Zeus
with the sun by referring to the ritual and iconography of several eastern
supreme gods who, whatever their name, and whether as a result of a
Graeco-Roman misinterpretation or not,[45] were undoubtedly thought to
have solar characteristics.[46]

Of the gods included in Praetextatus' solar syncretism Horus, Isis and
Sarapis, Attis,[47] Venus/Aphrodite, and Adonis were all deities of mystery
cults. The mystery cults which flourished from the Hellenistic period
onwards did altogether a great deal to propagate syncretism. For they
regularly promoted the power and efficacy of their particular patron
deities by emphasizing their identity with one or more of the most
powerful traditional gods. So worshippers addressed Isis not only by her
own name, but also—if that was her wish—by the names of the other
principal female goddesses.[48] It would also seem that according to one
interpretation of the Isis myth put forward by her priests, Osiris the
husband of Isis, was an allegory of the sun.[49] Helios Sarapis occurs on a

---

[44] *Sat.* 1. 23. 1–4 (Stoic), 5–6 (Neoplatonic), 22 ('Orphic'), so also 1. 18. 18–19.

[45] H. Seyrig, 'Le Culte du Soleil en Syrie à l'époque romaine', *Syria*, 40 (1971), 337, cited
by F. Millar, *The Roman Near East 31 BC–337 AD* (Cambridge, Mass., 1993), 522; also ibid.
300–1, 304–8 on the god Elagabalus of Emesa, in whose name 'el' represents the Semitic
root 'god', and who came to be thought a sun-god, and as such was brought to Rome by
the emperor Elagabalus. According to *SHA Aur.* 25 the Sol Invictus of Aurelian too was the
god of Emesa, though K. Latte, *Römische Religionsgeschichte* (Munich, 1960), 350 prefers the
patron god of Palmyra (without evidence).

[46] *Sat.* 1.23. 10–16, Jupiter Heliopolitanus of Baalbec: the Greek name of the place proves
that at least Greeks made the identification; 23. 17–18, the 'Assyrian' Adad. Macrobius
claims that a comparable deity at Hierapolis in Mesopotamia was hellenized by his
worshippers as Apollo, and then gives a solar interpretation of the god's iconography
(1. 17. 66–70). The Baal of Tyre clearly had conspicuous fiery qualities. Even if they were
originally linked with the lightning of a sky-god rather than the sun, the identification of
the Phoenician Melquart with the sun had been made by Porphyry (Eus. *Praep. ev.* 3. 11. 25,
citing Porphyry, *Peri agalmat.* (Fauth, *Helios Megistos*, 164–83 on Nonnus, *Dionysiaca* 40.
369–410).

[47] *Sat.* 1. 21. 7: Magna Mater is the Earth.

[48] *Golden Ass* 11. 2–3, 5. Lucius offers to address her as Ceres, Venus, Artemis, and
Proserpina. The opening address 'queen of heaven' at least implies an identification with
Juno.

[49] *Sat.* 1. 21. 11–12. Firmicus Maternus, *De errore* 8. 2, the sun complains that it is said to

number of magic papyri.[50] Initiates of Magna Mater and Attis sometimes applied a solar interpretation to Attis, the lover of their goddess,[51] and followers of the cult of Aphrodite and Adonis, who were mainly found in the east, provided a solar explanation of the Adonis myth.[52] Yet another god of mysteries, Mithras, had the title Sol Invictus added to his name, even though the cult-myth told of an incident involving both Sol and Mithras, proving that the two gods were certainly originally distinct.[53] It is evident that allegorical interpretations of the myths of the mystery cults could have been the ultimate source of many of the arguments used by Macrobius to support his own more comprehensive divine merger.

But a number of Praetextatus' identifications seem contrived and arbitrary, though they are ingeniously argued. The most elaborately argued of these is the demonstration that Hermes/Mercury really represents the sun.[54] Macrobius puts forward fewer arguments for the solar nature of Ares/Mars[55] and Heracles/Hercules,[56] but they seem just as contrived. By 'arbitrary' I mean that in the case of these gods Macrobius does not claim that the identification has been proclaimed by any earlier philosopher or poet or oracle. Macrobius simply deduces the identification from attributes of the statues of the gods, using the same kind of logic as was employed by philosophers, and by Macrobius himself, to draw philosophical doctrines out of the text of Homer or Virgil, and by Christians to discover prophecies of Christ in the Old Testament.[57] Two examples—simplified for the sake of brevity—will

have undergone dismemberment as Osiris. The commonest 'physical' identification of Osiris was with the Nile or with corn, but at a deeper level his myth might be explained as referring to the god of creation and consolidation (Plutarch, *On Isis and Osiris*, 364e). In solar theology this would be the sun.

[50] *PMG* 31b. 1–10; 31c. 1–6; 73. 1–5; 74. 1–15; 5. 1–30 T114; cf. Fauth, *Helios Megistos*, 74–5.

[51] *Sat.* 1. 21. 7–11, cf. Firmicus Maternus, *De errore*, 8. 2; Martianus Capella 1. 18. 5.

[52] *Sat.* 1. 21. 1–6, cf. 'Orphic' Hymn 56 also calling him Eubouleus, i.e. Dionysus; Martianus Capella 1. 18. 5 an aspect of the sun; but Maternus, *De errore*, 9. 1 identifies Adonis with Mars. According to *Sat.* 1. 21. 1 the *physici* call the six signs of the Zodiac which the sun crosses in summer Venus.

[53] Mithras is not mentioned in Praetextatus' speech, although we know that he had many initiates among the Roman senatorial aristocracy in the late 4th cent. This is another example of the eastern bias of the material of Praetextatus' speech—or did Macrobius think it inappropriate and out of character that Praetextatus should talk about the mysteries of which he was *pater patrum*?

[54] 1. 19. 7–18.

[55] 1. 19. 1–6.

[56] 1. 20. 6–12.

[57] R. Lamberton, *Homer the Theologian* (Berkeley, 1986). That the allegorical interpretation of attributes and symbolism on statues of gods in treatises *Peri Agalmatōn*, notably

illustrate the method: the Egyptians give wings to their statues of the sun god, and snakes are symbols of different aspects of the sun. Hermes is winged, and his sacred staff, designed by Egyptians, bears a pair of snakes. It follows that Hermes is the sun.[58] Or again, Hermes has the epithet Argiphontes, that is 'the slayer of Argos'. Argos had been ordered by Hera to watch Io after she had been changed into a cow. But the cow is a metaphor for the earth, of which in the hieroglyphs of Egypt it is the symbol. So Argos is the sky and his many eyes the stars. Hermes' killing of Argos therefore is an allegory of the rising sun extinguishing the stars.[59] It may be that Macrobius was not actually the first to put forward these particular arguments, but as he presents them they certainly lack the authority of some of the other identifications.

In this connection it is worth while to examine Macrobius' account of how Praetextatus' speech was received by his fellow-diners:

As Praetextatus ended his discourse, the company regarded him in wide-eyed wonder and amazement. Then one of the guests began to praise his memory, another his learning, and all his knowledge of the observances of religion; for he alone, they declared, knew the secrets of the nature of the godhead, he alone had the intelligence to apprehend the divine and the ability to expound it.[60]

The dining senators had clearly witnessed a *tour de force*. One can safely deduce that what they had just heard was in some way new to them. But what precisely was new? Not presumably the idea that the sun was the supreme deity, nor the identification of quite a number of specific deities with the sun or with powers of the sun, nor indeed the underlying theory that all the gods of polytheism represented aspects of the one supreme god, and that this supreme god might be identified with the sun.[61] What they had not heard before, I would suggest, was that an individual should actually argue the case for every single god in turn—or at least for a sufficiently large number of gods to make the argument seem all-embracing. The hearers recognized an astonishing feat of learning and intelligence, and received it not unlike the way an academic

that of Porphyry, was an attempt to disarm Christian attacks on image worship, is argued by Schanzer, *A Philosophical and Literary Commentary on Martianus' Capella's De Nuptiis Philologiae et Mercurii* Book I, 133–7.

[58] 1. 19. 8–10.

[59] 1. 19. 12–13.

[60] 1. 24. 1.

[61] *Sat.* 1. 17. 1: Avienus who asks Praetextatus to speak assumes that 'we' worship the sun sometimes as Apollo, sometimes as Liber, sometimes under a number of other names. He is to explain *why* one name should cover such a variety of other names. Firmicus Maternus, *De errore* 7. 7, assumes that Liber/Dionysus, Attis, and Osiris are identified with the sun.

audience might receive a stimulating and original lecture on Roman religion today.[62] But the achievement lay in the learning and ingenuity and comprehensiveness of the argument, not in the doctrine of solar syncretism.

THE SOURCES OF PRAETEXTATUS' SPEECH

The question of Macrobius' sources is very much under debate. In his preface Macrobius implies that he compiled the *Saturnalia* from very wide reading. From this E. Syska has deduced that Macrobius has assembled the material for Praetextatus' speech himself. He lists the different types of argument found in *Sat.* i. 17. 1–70, and suggests the class of source from which each type might have been derived, e.g. commentaries on Homer, commentaries on Plato, treatises of Stoic allegorical etymologies, antiquarian writings,[63] one might add writings about mystery cults like Plutarch's *On Isis and Osiris*. This still leaves the question open how much of the synthesis was actually the work of Macrobius, and how much the work of predecessors. The question is probably unanswerable ultimately, but attempts to answer it do throw light on the character of the speech.

First most of the etymologies only work with the Greek names of the gods, and the bias in the selection of gods for discussion is not only Greek, but even oriental. It therefore looks as if much of the argument is ultimately derived from Greek treatises, even if Macrobius has here and there added Roman material.

The oldest treatise on solar theology to survive is the long prose 'Hymn to Helios' which Julian the Apostate wrote in December 362. Julian states that he based his hymn on some material by Iamblichus, which has not come down to our time.[64] According to Eunapius, Iamblichus (*c*.250–*c*.225) was a 'pupil' of Porphyry (*c*.233–302), but it is not clear in what sense, if at all, this is true.[65] A number of scholars,

---

[62] Or as his contemporaries in Roman priesthoods might have reacted to Cicero's *De Natura Deorum* or *De Divinatione*.

[63] E. Syska, *Studien zur Theologie des Macrobius* (Stuttgart, 1993), 214–18. His analysis of the types of argument and their likely ultimate sources convinces. But I find Syska's view of Macrobius' *Grundkonzeption* of the section of *Saturnalia* dealing with religion totally unconvincing.

[64] Julian, *Or.* 4. 157D.

[65] Eunapius, *V. Soph.* 5. 1. 2–3 and critical note in J. M. Dillon, *Iamblichi Chalcidensis in Platonis Dialogos Commentariorum Fragmenta* (Leiden, 1973), 10–11. See also Polymnia Athanassiadi, 'The Oecumenism of Iamblichus', a review of A. J. Blumenthal and E. G. Clark (eds.), *The Divine Iamblichus*, in *JRS* 85 (1995), 244–50.

following P. Courcelle,[66] have believed that they could trace the solar theology to Porphyry. But this raises a problem. Porphyry is famous as one of the founders of Neoplatonism. But the arguments Macrobius has put into the mouth of Praetextatus are not based on Neoplatonic cosmogony. In Neoplatonic systems the traditional gods represent agents or rather stages in the chain of emanation from the primeval intelligible One to the infinite diversity of the material world. The ultimate unity of the Neoplatonic gods lies in the fact that they all are emanations of the One, and thus can be shown to form the constituent parts of an essentially monotheistic scheme. This line of thought does not occur in Praetextatus' speech. It is however basic to Julian's *Hymn to King Helios*. For Julian defines the One, the source of the gods as of everything else, as the sun in its first hypostasis. The conclusion would seem to be that Macrobius followed neither Porphyry nor Julian,[67] even though his selection of gods is very similar to Julian's.[68]

In his monograph Flamant has argued that the speech does indeed go back to writings of Porphyry, but to writings of Porphyry's supposed 'philological' period. He proposes that the lost treatise *Peri Agalmatōn*[69] supplied Macrobius with his portfolio of divine attributes, the lost *Peri Theiōn Onomatōn*[70] with the etymologies of divine names, and the lost *Peri Heliou*[71] with solar syncretism.[72] But more recent scholarship has made it extremely doubtful that Porphyry ever passed through a 'philological' period. Bidez's chronology of the writings of Porphyry is no longer accepted, and it is no longer thought that apparent inconsisten-

---

[66] P. Courcelle, *Les Lettres grecques en occident de Macrobe à Cassiodore* (Paris, 1943), 3–36.

[67] Even where Macrobius uses the same material (see table of gods identified with the sun by Julian in the Appendix below), or the same kind of argument as Julian had done, he does so with variations which make it unlikely that Julian was his source, e.g. at 1. 18. 18 Macrobius quotes 'One Zeus, one Hades, one Sun, one Dionysus (or Iao?) from Orpheus', Julian, *Hymn to Helios* 136 refers to Zeus, Hades, Helios, and Sarapis and gives Apollo as source.

[68] See Appendix below.

[69] The fragments are assembled as an appendix to J. Bidez, *Vie de Porphyre* (Gent, 1913), 1*–23*. They certainly give allegorical interpretations of the emblems of statues of gods, e.g. Zeus, but they do not seem to be concerned with demonstrating solar characteristics.

[70] Nothing but the title, cited in the *Suda*, is known about this work.

[71] The existence of Porphyry's *Peri Heliou* is witnessed only by Servius, *In Buc.* 5. 66: 'constat secundum Porphyri librum quem solem appellavit triplicem esse Apollinis potestatem . . . Sol apud superos . . . Liberum patrem in terris . . . Apollinem apud inferos . . .' which is related to, but not identical with *Sat.* 1. 18. 8. 8: 'ut sol cum . . . in diurno hemisphaerio est, Apollo vocitetur, cum in . . . nocturno, Dionysus.'

[72] J. Flamant, *Macrobe et le néoplatonisme latin à la fin du IVᵉ siècle*, EPRO 58 (Leiden, 1977), 667–8 (summary).

cies in the oeuvre of Porphyry are to be explained in terms of the evolution of his thought.[73]

In any case there is no need to suppose that Macrobius had to 'follow' any single principal source. He surely was a very well-read man. As we have seen the view that the sun was in some way or other the supreme governor of the world was widely accepted. So the outline of the speech can well be Macrobius' own. He would however have needed some reference works with etymologies of divine names and descriptions and interpretations of unusual images of gods in remote sanctuaries. I think that we can be fairly certain that such reference works as he used were Greek, and that they were particularly slanted towards Egypt and Syria. The suggested works of Porphyry satisfy these conditions but they are not likely to have been the only ones available to Macrobius.[74]

A further possibility might be mentioned. Macrobius could conceivably have used writings of Praetextatus himself. It is true that none of these writings has survived. But Praetextatus was very learned in both Greek and Latin. He produced improved editions of Greek and Latin texts, both poetry and prose, especially it would seem of philosophy ('the wise to whom the gate of heaven lies open').[75] The only known title is a translation of Themistius' commentary on the *Analytics* of Aristotle.[76] Praetextatus was a priest of Aurelian's sun-god, and both he and his wife were initiated into several mystery cults.[77] He was also evidently

---

[73] 'Two Images of Pythagoras: Iamblichus and Porphyry', in H. J. Blumenthal and E. G. Clark (eds.), *The Divine Iamblichus; Philosopher and Man of the Gods* (Bristol, 1993), 159–72, esp. 163–5. J. J. O'Meara, *Porphyry's Philosophy from Oracles in Augustine* (Paris, 1959). Against the view that Porphyry's views changed radically: A. Smith, 'Porphyrian Studies since 1913', *ANRW* 36. 2 (Berlin, 1987), 719–90, esp. 719–33.

[74] Porphyry was of course a Greek and he was familiar with the mysteries of Egypt and the Near East, see Bidez, *Vie de Porphyre*, 9–10, and he was read in the West. But the internal evidence for Macrobius' use of Porphyry is actually very slight. Porphyry is only once mentioned in Praetextatus' speech, that is in connection with 1. 17. 70: 'Minervam esse virtutem solis.' Flamant argues that Porphyry is mentioned there because that passage is taken from a different book of Porphyry's than the rest, but that is far from conclusive. Macrobius' method of arguing from divine names, images, and ritual is close to the symbolic theology of the Egyptians defended by Iamblichus against Porphyry in *De Mysteriis* 7. 1–3.

[75] *ILS* 1259; the verses which are normally taken to refer to editing of texts, though *PLRE* 1. 723 interprets them as referring only to translations, are:
Tu namque quidque lingua utraque est proditum
cura soforum porta quis caeli patet,
vel quae periti condidere carmina,
vel quae solutis vocibus sont edita,
meliora reddis quam legendo sumpseras.

[76] Boethius, *De interpretatione sec. edit.* 1. 289.

[77] *CIL* 6. 1778, 1779 = *ILS* 1259, *CIL* 6. 1780 = *ILS* 1260.

interested in the gods collectively, since he restored the porticus of the
dei consentes, and replaced the images of the twelve gods whose shrine
this was. So it would perhaps have been in character if he had edited, and
perhaps translated, Greek texts on the religious topics close to his heart.
This could in fact be the reason why Macrobius gave him a speech which
stands out in the *Saturnalia* by its lack of a specifically Roman character.
But this is of course sheer speculation.[78]

THE PURPOSE OF THE SPEECH OF PRAETEXTATUS

The *Saturnalia* is an encyclopaedia of Roman antiquities, above all
literary antiquities, in the genre of literary dialogue. Macrobius wrote
another encyclopaedic work in the form of a commentary on Cicero's
Somnium Scipionis.[79] This time the subject matter concerned three
branches of philosophy: moral behaviour, the structure of the universe,
and the descent and return of the soul.[80] To some extent the two books
are complementary: Macrobius would seem to have avoided treating the
same topic twice. This is probably one reason why Macrobius did not let
Praetextatus argue his case in terms of Neoplatonic philosophy.

Modern scholarship has picked on Praetextatus' speech as the key to
the understanding of the *Saturnalia*.[81] In fact it only occupies a very small
part of this long work, which is devoted to Roman antiquities as a whole.
Certainly the fact that Macrobius honours and values the Roman past in
its entirety means that he honours and values Roman religious
antiquities, but this is not the same as to call on his contemporaries to
return to the traditional worship. Since the Renaissance many generations of European academics have honoured and valued Graeco-Roman

---

[78] If Macrobius tried to recall the actual religious concerns of Praetextatus it is remarkable that he has omitted Mithras in whose mysteries Praetextatus was *pater patrum*
and who was popular among the last generation of pagan senators; see H. Bloch, 'The
Pagan Revival in the West at the End of the Fourth Century', in A. Momigliano (ed.),
The Conflict between Paganism and Christianity in the Fourth Century (Oxford, 1963),
193–218. Macrobius, whose dates of birth and death are unknown (*PLRE* 2. 1102–3, s.v.
Macrobius Ambrosius Theodosius 20) can scarcely have known Praetextatus, who died in
384, personally though he must have known men who did.

[79] W. H. Stahl, *Macrobius: Commentary on the Dream of Scipio*, tr. with introd. and
notes (New York, 1952).

[80] Macrobius' summary of the book: Stahl, *Commentary* 2. 15.

[81] Flamant, *Macrobe et le néoplatonisme latin*, 183 ff., 217 ff. makes the point that banquet
conversations are by genre entertaining and urbane, even when dealing with an important
topic, as already in Plato's *Symposium*. In contrast, almost all contemporary Christian
writing is entirely without humour.

antiquities, including religious antiquities, without urging their pupils to abandon Christianity.

In the *Saturnalia* there is no trace of anti-Christian polemic.[82] The fact that Jesus is not included in Praetextatus' syncretism is not to be taken as an expression of hostility.[83] At this time we would not have expected any references in high literature to something as unclassical as the Bible. There is actually an allusion to Herod's slaughter of the innocents, which is unusual enough, but it is only there because the incident is supposed to have occasioned a celebrated joke on the part of the emperor Augustus.[84] The pagan material expounded by Praetextatus was part of the Roman cultural tradition and as such still tolerated by all but the most fanatical Christians. Serena, wife of Stilicho and niece of the emperor Theodosius I was a strongly committed Christian. Yet she supervised her daughter's reading not only of Sappho and of Homer, but even of the poems of Orpheus, which as we have seen were used as an important source of divinely inspired information about the gods by late pagans like Macrobius and Proclus.[85]

The fact that Praetextatus' speech avoids Neoplatonic metaphysics helps to keep it uncontroversial. It means that Macrobius' account could be restricted to the visible world, and that he would not have to introduce the Good, the Primal Unity, the First Hypostasis, or whatever term might be used to define the ultimate divine idea beyond the cosmos and time. It means that he could avoid the problem of the creation, and of the eternity or otherwise of the world. In other words by omitting Neoplatonic cosmogony Macrobius avoided a clash with Genesis and Christian theology.[86]

It is however not the case that Macrobius was afraid to show himself

---

[82] I am convinced by the argument of Alan Cameron, *JRS* 56 (1966), 35–6.

[83] Flamant, *Macrobe et le néoplatonisme latin*, 668 argues that the omission of Jesus from the syncretism proves that Macrobius' 'hostilité envers les chrétiens est totale'. Surely not. Though even at the time of writing, *c.* AD 430, one would not expect any explicit reference to Christian beliefs in a work of high literature, it would be completely out of place in what purports to be the record of a conversation of pagan senators fifty or so years earlier. That the speech has an anti-Christian point is suggested more moderately by J. Vogt, *Decline of Rome*, tr. J. Sondheimer (London, 1967), 146; and P. Chuvin, *A Chronicle of the Last Pagans*, tr. B. A. Archer (London, 1990), 127.

[84] *Sat.* 2. 3. 11: 'Cum audisset inter pueros, quos in Syria Herodes rex Iudaeorum intra bimatum iussit interfici, filium quoque eius occidi (not in Matt. 2: 16), ait mallem Herodis porcus esse quam filius.' Macrobius has applied to the Gospel incident what was probably Augustus' comment on Herod's execution of members of his own family.

[85] Claudian, *Nupt. Hon.* 234–5.

[86] That he refrained from using either Julian or the Chaldaean Oracles would serve the same purpose of sparing Christian susceptibilities.

a Neoplatonist. In his *Commentary on the Dream of Scipio* Macrobius' account of the origin of the soul, in successive emanations from the First Cause, Mind, and Soul in the hypercosmic world, is manifestly seen in terms of Neoplatonic cosmogony (esp. 1. 14). But in neither of his treatises does Macrobius offer a philosophic description of the creation of the world.[87] The origin of the souls was less problematic. There is no account of it in the Bible, and some Christian writers had employed Neoplatonic concepts to be able to explain it in terms of a view of the world which was both Christian and philosophical.[88] In both books Macrobius was concerned to show that the ancestral cultural heritage remained valuable, and at the same time to avoid conflict with the now dominant Christian religion.

So the purpose of Praetextatus' speech is neither pagan propaganda nor anti-Christian polemic. For the Christians the Roman gods were of course by far the most objectionable part of the Roman heritage. Praetextatus' proposition that the whole of ancestral religion was fundamentally monotheistic suggests that the incompatibility of the old religion and the new was less complete than people might think. This thought would not of course have been accepted by many of the Christian authors whose writings have come down to us, certainly not by Augustine who did not respond to Maximus' plea that we all worship the same being under different names.[89] Nor did Ambrose respond positively in AD 384, in the affair of the Altar of Victory, to Symmachus' plea that each nation has its own gods and its own rites and that so great a mystery cannot be approached by one avenue alone.[90] The Christians held that their name and their approach were correct, and all the others were wrong. But the thought that their ancestral worship was after all in the last resort monotheistic might have made it easier for Macrobius' senatorial contemporaries to reconcile veneration of the pagan past with their fairly recently acquired Christian religion.

[87] In the *Commentary* 2. 10. 9 Macrobius seems to accept the teachings of philosophy that the world has always existed, that it was indeed created by God, but before time. This formulation would have been acceptable to Christians. It corresponds to Augustine's interpretation (*Conf.* 12. 9) of the verse 'in the beginning God created the heavens and earth' (*Genesis* 1: 1). But taken as a whole the 2. 10. 5–16 reads like an uneasy compromise between the two views, that the world has always existed, and that it was created. There is nothing Neoplatonic but a definite resemblance to Lucretius 5. 306–50.
[88] I. P. Sheldon-Williams, 'The Greek Christian Platonist Tradition from the Cappadocians to Maximus and Eriugena', *Cambridge History of Later Greek and Early Medieval Philosophy*, 425–533, esp. 447–56 on Gregory of Nyssa.
[89] Augustine's reply, *Ep.* 17.
[90] Symmachus, *Relatio* 3. 10; Ambrose, *Ep.* 18.

THE SOLAR THEOLOGY AND PRACTICAL RELIGION

Praetextatus argues that the gods of polytheism ultimately relate to a single deity. But how far can he be said to be advocating monotheistic religion? As far as his speech has a practical application it offers a justification for continuing to worship the whole crowd of ancestral gods.[91] Nowhere is worship of the sun proposed as a substitute for existing polytheistic cult. Solar syncretism provided an underpinning for polytheism in the fourth century, just as the Stoic interpretation of the gods as natural forces had done during the late republic and early empire.

This was the position of the Neoplatonic tradition from beginning to end. As we have seen Julian tried to revitalize the whole of traditional cult. His friend and perhaps spokesman Sallustius[92] significantly has nothing to say about actual worship. He assumes from beginning to end that his readers and fellow 'Hellenes' will continue to worship the traditional gods. The Neoplatonic doctrine is in no sense a substitute, or even a supplement to the traditional cults. Its function is rather to provide rational justification for the belief in the reality of supernatural non-material divinities by demonstrating that immaterial Mind has created, or rather is ever creating, the universe.[93]

What we know about the practical religion of the real Praetextatus—as against Macrobius' literary portrait—shows that it was just as polytheistic as that of Julian under whom Praetextatus had governed Achaia, and as that of Sallustius. Praetextatus was *pontifex solis*, and he was initiated into the mysteries of Liber (Dionysus), Cybele,[94] and Mithras.[95] At the same time he was a member of the traditional Roman priestly colleges of the augurs and the decemviri. A number of Praetextatus' contemporaries in the Senate also held a range of priesthoods, and were

[91] Explicit in *In somnium Scipionis* 1. 2. 20: 'divinities have always preferred to be worshipped in the fashion which antiquity for the sake of the general public figuratively assigned to them (qualiter in vulgus antiquitas fabulata est), antiquity which made images of beings which in fact have no physical form, and represented them as of different ages, though they are subject to neither growth nor decay, and gave them clothes and ornaments though they have no bodies' (tr. Stahl).

[92] On Sallustius see Athanassiadi, *Julian: An Intellectual Biography*, 154; Nock, *Essays on Religion*, pp. ci–civ; also above, no. 25.

[93] Augustine describes how the Neoplatonic books taught him precisely this, *Conf.* 7. 9. His response in practical religion was to become a Christian.

[94] The *taurobolium* was at this late stage associated with Cybele.

[95] *CIL* 6. 1779 = *Dessau* 1259; cf *PLRE* 1. 722–3, s.v. Vettius Agorius Praetextatus 1.

initiated into several mystery cults.[96] Thus it might be said that they practised a kind of personal syncretism, but one which recognized the strict separateness of the numerous cults of the traditional religion which must continue to be performed exactly as they had always been.[97] This is the attitude which Cicero had long ago ascribed to Cotta the *pontifex* in the dialogue *De Natura Deorum*: 'from you as a philosopher I must accept a rational reckoning of religion, but I must believe our ancestors even without such a reckoning.'[98]

APPENDIX

The Priesthoods and Initiations of Praetextatus and his Wife

Praetextatus (*PLRE* 1. 723 s.v. Vettius Agorius Praetextatus 1): augur, pontifex solis, quindecemvir, curialis Herculis, pontifex Vestae = pontifex, sacratus Libero et Eleusinis, hierophanta, neocorus, tauroboliatus, pater patrum (or sacrorum).
Paulina (*PLRE* 1. 675, s.v. Fabia Aconia Paulina): sacrata apud Eleusinam deo Iaccho, Cereri et Corae; sacrata apud Laernam deo Libero et Cereri et Corae; sacrata apud Eginam Hecatae; tauroboliata, Isiaca, hierophantria deae Hecatae, Graecosacranea deae Cereris, priestess of Didymenes and Attis.

Solar Syncretism of Macrobius, Julian, Orphic Hymns, Nonnus, and Martianus Capella

1. Gods identified with the sun by *Macrobius*: Apollo, Liber/Dionysus, Mars/Ares, Mercury/Hermes, Aesculapius, Hercules, Sarapis, Adonis, Attis, Osiris, Horus, 12 signs of the Zodiac, Nemesis, Pan, Echo, Saturn, Hestia, Zeus/Jupiter, Adad, Athena/Minerva.

2. *Julian*: Closely linked with Helios: Zeus, Apollo, Hades, Sarapis, Dionysus, Ares, Athena, the signs of the Zodiac etc. 36 in all, Aphrodite, Hestia, Aesclepius, Mithras, Attis. Assistants to Helios: Aphrodite, Ares, Hermes, and above all

---

[96] H. Bloch, 'A New Document of the Last Pagan Revival in the West, 393–4', *Harv. Theol. Rev.* 38 (1945), 199–244.
[97] In the *City of God* Augustine shows himself fully aware of monotheistic, and especially pantheistic, views of the ultimate nature of the divine held by pagans, but he also is clear that practical religion remains polytheistic; and the weight of his attack is directed against the innumerable traditional gods, e.g. 4. 11–12, 6. 8, and 8. 12: the Platonists like Plotinus, Porphyry, Iamblichus, and Apuleius have a doctrine of one God who made heaven and earth, nevertheless 'diis plurimis esse sacra facienda putaverunt'.
[98] *ND* 3. 1. 6: 'A te enim philosopho rationem accipere debeo religionis, maioribus nostris etiam nulla ratione reddita credere.'

Magna Mater. Of course for Julian everything is ultimately derived from Helios in his capacity of first cause.

3. *Orphic Hymns*: Identified with the sun: Apollo, Dionysus, Zeus, Pan, Adonis, Cronus.

4. *Nonnus*: Identified with the sun: Heracles, Belus on the Euphrates, Ammon in Libya, Apis by the Nile, Cronos in Arabia, Zeus in Assyria, Cronus, Phaeton, Mithras, the Sun at Babylon, Paean/Apollo, Uranus/Caelum.

5. *Martianus Capella*: Jupiter, Apollo, Sarapis, Osiris, Mithras, Dis/Hades, Horus, Typhon, Attis, Memnon, Adonis.

SELECT BIBLIOGRAPHY

AMBROSII THEODOSII MACROBII, *Saturnalia*, ed. J. Willis (2nd edn.; Leipzig: Teubner, 1970).

MACROBIUS, *The Saturnalia*, tr. with introd. and notes by P. V. Davies (New York and London: Columbia University Press, 1969).

CAMERON, A., 'The Date and Identity of Macrobius', *JRS* 56 (1966), 25–38.

FAUTH, W., *Helios Megistos, zur synkretistischen Theologie der Spätantike* (Leiden: Brill, 1995).

FLAMANT, J., *Macrobe et le néoplatonisme latin à la fin du IVe siècle*, EPRO 58 (Leiden, 1977).

KASTER, R. A., 'Macrobius and Servius: *Verecundia* and the Grammarian's Function', *HSCP* 84 (1980), 219–62.

NOCK, A. D., *Sallustius: Concerning the Gods and the Universe*, ed. with prolegomena and trans. (Cambridge, 1926; repr. Hildesheim: G. Olms, 1966).

SMITH, R., *Julian's Gods: Religion and Philosophy in the Thought and Action of Julian the Apostate* (London: Routledge, 1995).

STAHL, W. H., *Macrobius: Commentary on the Dream of Scipio*, tr. with introd. and notes (New York: Columbia University Press, 1952).

SYSKA, E., *Studien zur Theologie des Macrobius* (Stuttgart: Teubner, 1993).

Index